Savoring Salt

Savoring

the Salt

The Legacy of
Toni Cade Bambara

Edited by

Linda Janet Holmes and
Cheryl A. Wall

TEMPLE UNIVERSITY PRESS
Philadelphia

Linda Janet Holmes is a writer, independent scholar, curator, and women's health activist. She is co-author (with Margaret Charles Smith) of *Listen To Me Good: The Life Story of an Alabama Midwife*. Her short story, "The True Story of Chicken Licken," appeared in Toni Cade Bambara's *Tales and Stories for Black Folks*.

Cheryl A. Wall is Professor of English at Rutgers University, and author of *Worrying the Line: Black Women Writers, Lineage, and Literary Tradition*, and *Women of the Harlem Renaissance*. She is editor of *The Writings of Zora Neale Hurston* (2 volumes) and *Changing Our Own Words: Essays on Criticism, Theory, and Writing by Black Women*.

TEMPLE UNIVERSITY PRESS
1601 North Broad Street
Philadelphia PA 19122
www.temple.edu/tempress

⊗ The paper used in this publication meets the requirements of the American National Standard for Information Sciences—Permanence of Paper for Printed Library Materials, ANSI Z39.48-1992

Design by Kate Nichols

Library of Congress Cataloging-in-Publication Data
    Savoring the salt : the legacy of Toni Cade Bambara / edited by Linda Janet Holmes and Cheryl A. Wall.
        p.   cm.
    Includes index.
    ISBN 13: 978-1-59213-624-7   ISBN 10: 1-59213-624-9 (cloth : alk. paper)
    ISBN 13: 978-1-59213-625-4   ISBN 10: 1-59213-625-7 (pbk. : alk. paper)
    1. Bambara, Toni Cade–Criticism and interpretation.   2. African Americans in literature.   I. Holmes, Linda Janet   II. Wall, Cheryl A.
PS3552.A473Z85   2007
813'.54–dc22   2007008836

2 4 6 8 9 7 5 3 1

For our daughters

GHANA AND CAMARA

Contents

VI. "Have to be whole to see whole"

Photographs follow page 150

Acknowledgments

In the process of bringing *Savoring the Salt* to print, we have incurred more debts than we can properly acknowledge. But we must express our deep gratitude to three special women:

- Karma Bene Bambara, who provided indispensable support and shared precious memories and photographs of her mother

- Toni Morrison, who in the beginning affirmed our belief that a book on Bambara's legacy should be published

- Marie Dutton Brown, who counseled us to hold fast to our vision of this book, one that in the tradition of *The Black Woman*, would weave together a tapestry of voices that speak to a diversity of readers

Our one regret is that we could not include all of those who wanted to contribute to *Savoring the Salt*.

Conjuring by Any Other Name

Foreword by PEARL CLEAGE

When she was a small child, so the story goes, Toni Cade Bambara was sitting in the middle of her mother's kitchen floor, writing. Since I was also a child who wrote at a very young age, when I encountered this autobiographical anecdote, I was able to fully imagine the specifics of the scene. She was probably still writing in pencil. She was probably using one of those small spiral notebooks, tiny enough to fit in your grandmother's Sunday pocketbook so she could hand it to you with the nub of a yellow number two pencil and expect you to amuse yourself during the rest of the service. In my mind, the notebook is green and Toni is sitting cross-legged, leaning over to use the kitchen linoleum as her writing surface, oblivious to her mother coming up behind her with the even, rhythmic strokes of a woman who has mopped this floor more times than she could count. What would be the point?

The point today was that her small daughter was right in the middle of the mopping. There were only two choices: she could tap the child on the shoulder and tell her to take her green notebook and stubby number two pencil and find somewhere else to dream. Or, she could recognize the fragile nature of the creative process and cede the space to the mystery that is great art in the making. That Toni's mother made the second and best choice is the gift she gave to all of us who later came to love her daughter's writing.

The problem with thinking deeply about Toni Cade Bambara for those of us who knew and loved her and still miss her each and every day the Goddess sends, is that thinking too hard about Toni is perilously close to trying to conjure her up, and we've already tried that whenever there is a full moon, or it's her birthday, or we read something she wrote and want to talk to her about it. Of course, sometimes the magic works and sometimes it doesn't, but that's how much we miss her. *Each and every day.*

When I think about Toni, I always think about the stories. The amazing ones she wrote and the equally amazing ones she lived. I met the written ones before I ever had the great good fortune to encounter the woman whose words absolutely enchanted me. I know that sounds corny, but how else to describe the feeling that swept over me when I opened *Gorilla, My Love,* and read the very first line of the very first story, "My Man Bovanne": "Blind people got a hummin jones if you notice."

It was so simple and funny and off-hand and real and loving and truthful. It made me smile. *No.* It made me grin. The kind of grin you have on your face your first day of college when you see your best friend from home coming toward you across the campus with her new freshman beanie sitting on top of her head like a crown. The whole story was like that—familiar, *but better*—and I surrendered to it without even putting up a struggle.

At the end of those few pages, I just sat there for a few minutes, smiling to myself, savoring what she had done as a writer. Her characters were so real, so complex, so free of condescension and cliches. *This,* I thought, *is the best short story I have ever read.* That's when I got a little nervous. This was only the first ten pages. How could she possibly meet the standard she had just set? Was it going to be all downhill from here? Keeping my finger in the pages to mark my place, I turned the book over to look at the author, whose picture I had only glanced at briefly before I started reading. There she was, on the back cover of her masterpiece, smiling at me with such absolute beauty, humor, confidence, and all-around-New-York-City, perfect-afroed *cool,* that I figured *what the hell? This sister looks like she knows what she's doing. Why not read the rest of her stories and then worry about whether or not she can equal or top herself? She wrote that one, didn't she?* I scolded myself gently and opened the book again, full of hope and anticipation.

By the time I read the closing lines of "The Johnson Girls" (a story everybody I knew claimed to be in, although Toni always protested with a big laugh that she was writing "straight-up fiction"), I was fully under her spell. That's where the enchanted part comes in, because Toni Cade Bambara's wonderful writing is so clearly in that magical realm all its own. It pleases your senses even as it challenges your assumptions about yourself, about people, about politics, about the power of love, and the necessity for hard work. She remains the writer I most admire for the graceful way she always gets to the heart of the matter. Her short stories, her novels, her screenplays, and her passionate prose are all infused with her absolute determination to tell us the truth of ourselves, not because we needed it, or wanted it, or even *deserved* it, but because she didn't know any other way to tell the story straight.

When I met her in Atlanta in the mid-seventies, we were both caught up in the excitement of those first few years when black folks assumed political power in the city and race became a different kind of discussion unlike any we'd had before. Introduced by a mutual friend, Jan Douglass, each of us recognized in the other a kindred spirit and we started talking as if we were picking up on an ongoing dialog from another lifetime. We talked about writing and politics and our daughters and our mothers and our friends and our freedom. And that was just the first twenty minutes! If I had been a fan before, now I was delighted to be a friend.

These conversations continued for the rest of her life. Some were conducted face to face. More often, they were part of a regular exchange of post cards, notes, messages from the road, communiqués from the front lines of whatever war we were fighting. When my book of essays, *Deals With the Devil and Other Reasons to Riot,* was published in 1993, I got a card from Toni the day before I was due to set out on a grueling three week book tour. She had read the advance copy I sent her and wanted to let me know how she felt about it.

> Dear Pearl[the card read,] I can't tell you how grateful I am for this book. It's so healthy and lucid and passionate and on time and useful and necessary. Thanks so much. I go around quoting it! You know what else is big fun? Walking past the book stores in umpteen different cities and either seeing it in the window as I approach, in which case I smile, or seeing it in the window after I stick in my head and say (not very loudly, mind you) "you're the only bookstore in town that doesn't have Pearl Cleage's *Deals With the Devil* in the window!" And sure as shit someone pipes up with "Yeah, yeah!" This is great! It's got legs, Sistuh! Love you! Toni

I taped that card to the back of my inside book cover and went out into the world, *fearless!*

When Toni died, it was almost impossible to believe such a life force had moved on so quickly. She had so many more words to craft into unforgettable stories. So many more dinners around my kitchen table with Zeke making his world-famous spaghetti and Toni telling tall tales and me, drinking wine and laughing, trying to get a word in edgewise. She deserved so much more time with her daughter Karma. So many more birthday parties full of her friends, like the one we had to celebrate her fiftieth at Atlanta's Hammonds House where we all had a chance to publicly confess just how much she meant to us and to her adopted hometown. So many more days with all of us who need her insight, her compassion, her friendship, her genuine human goodness, now more than we ever did.

Toni was a grown woman in a time when there aren't nearly enough of us to go around. She was devoted to the gospel according to freedom, and that may be her *second* greatest gift, right next to the beauty of her words. Toni didn't just write about freedom. She didn't just think about it or demand it or long for it, *she was it,* and anybody who was moving in another direction had to learn to just mop around her so she could get on with her work and with her life.

In trying to describe Toni, I realize that I've conjured her up in spite of myself, so in closing, I ask your indulgence to address her directly:

Greetings, sister writer, cultural worker, mother extraordinaire, and loyal friend. All here are well. Of course we still miss you each and every day the Goddess sends! Cheryl and Linda did a great job with this book. It does you proud! Much love from those who carry on in your name. Peace & Love, Pearl.

Life/Work

Savoring the Salt: *An Introduction*

Linda Janet Holmes and Cheryl A. Wall

> Salt is a partial antidote for snakebite. Bleeding the wound and applying the tourniquet, one also eats salt and applies a salt poultice to the wound. To struggle, to develop, one needs to master ways to neutralize poisons. 'Salt' also keeps the parable of Lot's wife to the fore. Without a belief in the capacity for transformation, one can become ossified. And what can we do with a saltlick in the middle of the projects, no cows there? — Toni Cade Bambara

Savoring the Salt: The Legacy of Toni Cade Bambara explores the life, art, and activism of a singular woman. Born in 1939, Bambara came of age along with the movements for social justice of the 1960s. She helped shape and was shaped by the Black Liberation Movement, the Women's Movement, and the struggle against the war in Vietnam. She worked to build coalitions among women of color internationally. She belonged to a group of African American women writers who came to voice in the early 1970s. Bambara's art shares much in common with that of Audre Lorde, Paule Marshall, Toni Morrison, and Alice Walker. Widely published, Bambara was the author of two books of short stories *Gorilla, My Love* (1972) and *The Sea Birds Are Still Alive* (1977); two novels *The Salt Eaters* (1980) and *Those Bones Are Not My Child* (2000); editor of the pathbreaking anthology *The Black Woman* (1970) and of *Tales and Stories for Black Folks* (1971); and author of a volume of fiction and nonfictional prose *Deep Sightings* and *Rescue Missions* (1996). After Bambara's death in 1995, her friend and editor Toni Morrison called Bambara's writing "absolutely critical to twentieth century literature."

Best known as a writer, Bambara published her first short story, "Sweet Town," in 1959. Her work was one of the first fruits of the "Second Renaissance" among African American artists. She set her stories in cities, and they bristled with the edgy rhythms of urban life. Several of her most memorable characters were young black girls, who refused to be defeated by their circumstances. Humor and a sharp tongue were their weapons. No one rendered their speech better than Bambara. Throughout the 1960s and 1970s, Bambara published her stories in magazines, including *Redbook* and *Essence*, which reached large audiences. When Bambara's stories were collected in *Gorilla, My Love,* critics applauded a fresh, new voice. The book has never gone out of print. Generations of readers recognize and love Toni Cade Bambara's voice. Although rooted in the urban speech of African Americans, Bambara's language is distinctively her own. As she told interviewer Kalamu ya Salaam, she was "in search of the mother tongue": "I'm trying to break words open and get at the bones, deal with symbols as if they were atoms. I'm trying to find out not only how a word gains its meaning, but how a word gains its power."

That search resulted in *The Salt Eaters,* a visionary novel that enacts the fusion of literary and political, social and spiritual perspectives. Experimental in its nonlinear narrative, it is specific in its representation of the cultural practices of African Americans. But the novel maps a larger world. As it does, it highlights common values—respect for the elders, concern for the children, cooperative economics, functional and collective art, and metaphysical beliefs—among traditional communities of color. It suggests that those values might be the basis for coalitions that would forge a politics for the twenty-first century.

The plot of *The Salt Eaters* unfolds in an afternoon; *Those Bones Are Not My Child* is, by contrast, an epic novel that was inspired—or compelled—by the rash of murders of black children in Atlanta in the 1980s. Its fictional city is drawn in careful detail, and the characters that move through its streets represent a broad cross section of its residents. They are old and young, rich and poor, powerful and powerless. Bambara's ear is attuned as always to their speech. *Those Bones* is one of the most precisely drawn portraits of contemporary urban American life we have.

Her literary reputation notwithstanding, Bambara's importance is not just literary. Indeed, her favorite way of describing herself was as a "cultural worker." She was an activist who worked in Harlem, Philadelphia, and Atlanta. In 1970 she edited *The Black Woman,* a volume that brought together more than thirty women who spoke out on politics, racism in education, stereotypes about black women, and relationships. They wrote poems, short stories, biographical and autobiographical essays, and position papers. Among the contributors were Nikki Giovanni, Abbey Lincoln, Paule Marshall, students, and members of a feminist collective. When Bambara, then Toni Cade, wrote that "it is revolutionary, radical, and righteous to want for your mate what you want for yourself," her words cut through a haze of reactionary rhetoric; they inspired young women to imagine new possibilities for themselves. Still passed from hand to hand in its original paperback edition, *The Black Woman* was reissued in 2005.

Bambara was a teacher, who was one of the first faculty members at the Search for Education, Elevation, Knowledge (SEEK) Program at the City

College of New York, the program that transformed the student population and the university. Later she taught at Livingston College at Rutgers University, Atlanta University, and Atlanta's Neighborhood Arts Center. Throughout her life she was a catalyst for the work of others.

Bambara was also a filmmaker, who collaborated on documentaries including *The Bombing of Osage Avenue* (a film about the attack on the MOVE headquarters in Philadelphia and its aftermath) and *W.E.B. Du Bois in Four Voices*. She was an enthusiastic supporter of the black independent film movement. Julie Dash, writer and director of *Daughters of the Dust*, suggests that Bambara's writing informed her approach to filmmaking:

> The way Toni Cade takes an idea, a thought, weaves it for many paragraphs and then brings it back around, it was just like a regular conversation. It was the way your mother used to talk to you, the way your grandparents would speak to you. I would go as far as to say her work even had an influence on *Daughters of the Dust*.

A teacher of film, Bambara worked with Scribe, a nonprofit film and video center in Philadelphia. In every aspect of her work, she inspired and empowered young people.

Bambara might best be understood as an organic intellectual, who grounded her political and social thought in the lived experience of everyday people. She believed that social change happened from the bottom up, and the intellectual's role was not only to analyze that change but also to participate in it. That participation might take many forms, from explaining to people in the neighborhood how their lives were shaped by the forces of global capitalism to organizing local protests. If the problems were both local and global, so were the solutions. An effective and ethical politics was informed by ideas drawn from progressive movements across the globe. Bambara was a citizen of the world. Yet she understood that the intellectual also needed to speak the language of her community. She had total confidence in the capacity of that language to convey political complexities and moral values.

Savoring the Salt is organized to reflect the multiple legacies of Toni Cade Bambara. Writer, activist, teacher, and filmmaker, Bambara found many ways of doing her work and making her mark in the world. Each section of the book highlights one aspect of her work. But Bambara was too dynamic a woman and artist to be constrained by categories. The boundaries are blurred here, as they were in her life. Following the model that she set in *The Black Woman, Savoring the Salt* mixes genres. It includes personal essays, poems, and critiques, as well as brief reminiscences from cultural workers who knew and collaborated with Toni. It examines Bambara's work—her fiction, nonfiction, and film, as well as her activism and teaching. It honors her resilience and ability to celebrate radical acts as well as her sense of humor and personal grace. Toni Cade Bambara's extraordinary spirit lives on.

The range of contributors to this volume demonstrates the power of that spirit. Their voices are varied and memorable. Seasoned poets take their turns alongside poets who were Bambara's students. Critics who have kept Bambara's work alive in the academy write for the general audience, while activists who were empowered by Bambara's example contemplate agendas for the future. Young filmmakers testify to Bambara's impact on their art.

The weave of voices creates a stunning tapestry. The voice that links them is Bambara's own. In each section, she speaks first. Her words are excerpted from her writings and from speeches she made throughout her life. Several of these pieces are published here for the first time. Bambara's initial statement explains the image that we have chosen for our title. Salt as an antidote for poison, a component of tears and of humor, became for Bambara a metaphor to be endlessly mined. We hope that it can represent for our readers a legacy to be savored.

2

Poised for the Light

LINDA JANET HOLMES

ore than three decades ago at a black writers' conference in Atlanta, someone suggested that I write Toni's biography. I don't remember his name, but I do recall him saying that I might begin by taking notes on my conversations with Toni. I thought then, how could I, Toni's former student, write Toni's biography? Even more absurd was the suggestion that I take notes on conversations with her. That would make me a first-degree snitch to be guarded against. Or so I thought. But, would Toni have minded? Would she have felt invaded? How important was it to mask divergent private and public realities? Or are these my own fears or assumptions?

Toni herself said, "Being honest and frank in terms of my own where— where I'm at a given point in my political/spiritual/etc. development—is not necessarily in my/our interest to utter, not necessarily in the interest of health, wholesomeness."[1] She clearly wasn't interested in being dissected. And her attitude about writing real people's lives into her own fiction becomes even clearer when you read Toni's response to Kaye Bonetti in the American Audio Prose Library series of interviews with writers. "For myself, I tend to leave real people alone. I'm very respectful of people's privacy," Toni said. She reinforced this idea in a conversation with Claudia Tate published in *Black Women Writers At Work*, where Toni explained, "If I wrote auto-biographically, for example, I'd wind up getting into folks' business, plundering the lives of people around me, pulling the covers off of friends. I'd be an emotional gangster, a psychic thug, pimp and vampire." To clandestinely take notes on our conversations, I thought, would have made me the same.

More than three decades later and twelve years after Toni Cade's transition from this life, I can consider writing about her. In fact, it feels vital to do so. One of a small and influential group of black women writers to emerge in the 1960s, Toni worked throughout her life to find new and creative vehicles for courageously expressing her joy in revolt. Her third eye focused on the blueprints that initiated change, refusing to allow her artistry to eclipse her community vision. Although Toni's literary and film work continue to receive acclaim, much more must be done to honor her magnificence as artist and activist.

Then, writing a biographical essay wasn't something I could do. Now I see how that unnamed man could have suggested I write about her. I was not only a former student but also a journalist and friend.

Letters from Toni in my own worn file folders surprised me like bumping into old friends at the supermarket whose phone numbers I had lost long ago. I could recall—even against the distance of time—the anecdotes I remembered from this extraordinary storyteller, those conversations surfacing like pieces of a dream. I called on Toni's friends and family members to share their memories of her, and they spoke as if the events happened last weekend. What follows is a chronicle that includes my thoughts and feelings about Toni and the recollections of many friends, students, and others who Toni influenced.

Community in Harlem

Growing up wrapped in the sounds of Harlem was a biographical fact that Toni liked to make known. She readily pulled from her hip pocket the many gems that came with her Harlem birthright, including her inheritance from Harlem's longshoremen, union activists, communists, the beauty-parlor women and barbershop men, the ladies of the night, tap dancers, be-bop musicians, chitlin' circuit women, the numbers runners, the Rastafarians, the Abyssinians, the church women, the m'dears, the Father Divine workers, the barmaids, and the rappers on speaker's corner.

Born on March 25, 1939, Toni entered the world as Harlem grew in its militancy. Blacks like her great-grandmother who migrated from Atlanta quickly learned that the railway and bus tickets that provided passageways from the Deep South's tyranny of lynching, peonage, and disenfranchisement did not unlock doors to economic equity or political power. Toni's mother, Helen Brent Henderson Cade (Brehon), also left Atlanta for New York where she later joined protesters demanding jobs on Harlem's 125th Street in "don't buy where you can't work" campaigns. Toni once described her mother as a race woman much like Rosa Parks taking courageous stands based on her inherently strong sense of justice.

Helen Cade—as her daughter's writings later did—championed the Harlem that nurtured. Her mother's own artistry ranged from playing organ for Harlem churches to belly-dancing performances later in life and modeled other innovative turns such as managing a reverse migration South from New York to attend school at Clark College in Atlanta. Upon returning to New York, she took courses at Columbia University and taught at P.S. 186, a

Harlem elementary school Toni later attended on 145th and Broadway. Toni often recalled the details of how her mother, wearing a breathtaking Persian lamb coat, felt hat, and suede pumps championed for her, confronting racist teachers who failed to respect her daughter.[2]

Eventually settling into the security of a civil service job at the New York post office with its pensions and nondiscriminatory policies, Helen Cade's quest for housing and quality education meant Toni moved a lot as a child—relocating to Jersey City, Brooklyn, and Queens. Harlem addresses included apartments at 92 Morningside Avenue, 555 West 151st Street, and the Dunbar Gardens, co-op apartments financed by John D. Rockefeller in 1926. Walter Cade, Toni's only sibling, recalled a co-op only becoming affordable to the Cade family when they lucked up on extra money from a big-time hit on the illegal numbers games operated by Harlem street runners.

Even in the midst of family struggles, Toni was never forced to sacrifice the luxury of liberation zones for daydreaming spaces. Toni's brother who now enjoys acclaim as a visual artist and musician also made space for imaginary play as he "entertained (Toni) with long, leisurely, dream-life self-disclosing scenarios with lumps of modeling clay he turned into people, horses, buildings, dramas."[3]

Toni's mother executed concrete plans for her children's education that included taking full advantage of cultural offerings in New York City. Surrounded by bookcases built by her mother that included the works of Langston Hughes and other Harlem Renaissance writers, Toni learned to play the piano from her musically gifted mother and took pleasure in the frequent outings her mother organized to museums and concert halls and to towering black book stores such as Micheaux Liberation Memorial Book store and the Harlem book center of early black historian J. A. Rogers. Helen Cade carefully selected the schools that her daughter attended, including private schools such as the Mather Academy, a boarding school, and the Modern School, an independent black school that survives today at its current location on New York's Riverside Drive. As Toni dignified elders and children in her writing, she also celebrated her mother as the "all purpose swami" who left space for her daughter to recreate herself.

Toni wrote less about her father, Walter Cade II, who left his home in the South as a teenager and eventually absorbed the Harlem life. Frequent trips with her father and brother to the Peace Barber Shop, part of Harlem's Father Divine business community, nurtured Toni's storytelling abilities. Walter told me that he believes his sister's wit and love for humor can be partly attributed to their father, a master of improvisation and informal stand-up comedy.

Toni's childhood interest in film probably came from her father's love for movies. Sometimes he dropped Toni and Walter off on 42nd Street for a day of movies, but most often, similar to the young narrator in one of Toni's best-known short stories, "Gorilla, My Love," Toni and her brother frequented Harlem movie houses, sometimes without adults.

It's hard to imagine Toni ever being called Miltona Mirkin Cade, but that's the name her father gave her, naming her after his employer, Milton Mirkin.[4] Her mom told me that in a simple rebellious pronouncement to her one day after school, sometime around kindergarten age, "Toni named herself." She named herself again in 1970, when she added Bambara to her surname.[5]

Bohemian in Queens

When her mother moved the family to Queens, Toni felt adrift without her Harlem points of reference. The students at John Adams High School in Ozone Park, Queens, the high school Toni attended, contrasted sharply with the elementary school students of her beloved Harlem. In the midst of the larger societal doom and fear emanating from the McCarthy 50s, Toni encountered the ugliness of Ozone Park's rigid demarcations of class, gender, and race. Two decades later, Ozone Park was the setting for the popular sitcom *All in The Family,* where its main character Archie Bunker is a stereotyping bigot.

Eventually, Toni found peers of interest even in Ozone Park. Trina Pearlson (Robbins), who remembered Toni as always having "a degree of hipness," observed, "She didn't look like the tough black girls, who straightened their hair and wore their coats backwards as a kind of gang symbol. She wore golden hoop earrings, and I'd never seen anyone in golden hoop earrings before." When they first met, Trina was poetry editor for *The Clipper,* the high school literary magazine. Today a seasoned writer of comics and books, Trina recalled reading, "Why I am Bohemian," when Toni commented, "That's me. I'm a bohemian." Soon Toni joined the magazine staff and three of her poems were published in the 1955 *Clipper*—"There'll Come A Day," "Femme Du Monde," and the "Devil's Advocate."

Like the South that her grandmother and mother fled, the alien environment of Ozone Park also was a place to leave. Toni's ticket out became the heavier course load required for a January graduation at a younger age than most. Once at Queens College, Toni gravitated toward the Left-oriented hip existentialists who mingled in the school's small cafeteria. Initially considering a pre-med major at Queens College, Toni settled into the theater club and writing courses, writing everything from novels to film scripts. In her junior year, Toni played the role of prostitute in the campus production of William Saroyan's play *The Time of Your Life,* Melvin Wilk, later a poet and professor of English at Simpson College in Iowa, remembered. In 1959, the year Toni graduated from Queens College, Toni received the John Golden Award for her writing. She also garnered the Peter Pauper Press Award in Journalism from the *Long Island Star* for her poem, "Dumb Show."

As some of her new beat-generation friends adopted laissez-faire attitudes, Toni remained connected to protest and communities of color. During her college years, Toni joined with local activist groups opposing U.S. aggression in Asia, Africa, and Latin America. She also stood with black mothers protesting the Korean War and heard from veterans anticipating the war in Vietnam. Toni identified with nascent social movements that wanted to break away from the restrictions of mainstream America.

Still away from her Harlem anchor, Toni moved downtown after college to find an apartment in the numbered streets of Greenwich Village. There, she lived an eclectic life, filling up her many spiral notebooks with story ideas and immersing herself in the local black jazz culture that included hearing Charlie Parker, the Modern Jazz Quartet, and John Lewis at local clubs like the Five Spot. Toni also took time to make music of her own, playing songs on her guitar in Washington Square Park.

Always writing, Toni scripted theater productions to be performed by friends in the large barnlike railroad flat where Martie Siegel and Arnie Goldberg, members of the Queens College set, lived. Siegel, who later became the obituary editor for the *New York Times,* remembered Toni playing her guitar and singing songs that captured her caustic fury, marked largely by a feminist edge. "These songs kept us in shape by totally putting us down all together," Siegel said. Former Queens College classmates also remembered Toni as self-contained and sometimes elusive, simply disappearing for periods of time. Reflecting on these relationships many years later, Toni told her friend Louis Massiah in an interview, "But these were white people at Queens College, and they were not my people either."[6]

Toni married once. She and Tony Batten, an African American documentary filmmaker who graduated from the same Queens high school as she did, joined hands. Less than a year after the wedding, her marriage ended. Unshackled from marriage and free to write, Toni celebrated herself. "I like the quality of things I am writing now and I really believe it's good—even months after and feel really anxious to get rid of the stuff to start on the next batch—rather than hold on to it and fearfully rework and meanwhile work myself up into an anxious fit." Toni and Batten sustained a friendship, however, as years later when living in Atlanta she mentioned Batten along with Ida Lewis as among "media friends whose calls and questions kept me moving."[7]

Despite success, Toni's writing still doesn't pay the bills. At different times between 1959 and 1962, Toni's day jobs included family and youth case worker, New York Department of Welfare; director of recreation, Metropolitan Hospital Psychiatric Division; and program director, Colony Settlement House. The success in writing results in short stories published in the *Massachusetts Review*, *Negro Digest*, the *Prairie Schooner*, and *The Liberator*—but not much by way of material remuneration.

A year after her short-term marriage collapsed, Toni and a friend from Queens College journeyed to Europe. A restlessness generated by the Eisenhower 1950s led several of her friends to seek a reprieve from everyday American repression. Similar to other black writers, Toni goes to Europe to write. She also pursues studies in mime and theater by enrolling in a course of study in Italy. In February 1961, Toni met up with other members of the old Queen's collective in front of the National Assembly of Interior Ministry just as the French military machine began gearing up for the Algerian War.

From an Italian-line freighter carrying only six passengers including her, Toni is stunned by glimpses of Africa and Spain. Toni described her breathtaking experience in another letter to her friend Wilk:

> Today was the most exciting of all. After lunch, great waves splashed around, the sea was very rough to the eye and yet the boat did not as much "rolling and pitching" as times previous. Then it rained briefly and a mist settled between the boat and a very huge rainbow somewhere beyond. Then all of a sudden—Africa! The great mounds of dark blues and purples split through that fog and holy shit, Mel, I was choking.

Harlem Calls

When Toni returned to the United States, the civil rights movement had erupted into Black Power demands. In 1965, the year of Malcolm X's assassination, Toni completed a Masters of Arts in American Literature at the City College of New York and became fully engaged in black revolutionary politics. "Inspired, shaped and sustained by that incredible release of Black energy—poets, dancers, community organizers, health workers, seers, teachers, filmmakers, marchers, healers, historians, comics—I began to discover with greater and greater precision what my work in this world is . . . ," Toni said about coming of age in the revolutionary '60s.[8]

Much later Toni explained, "In the Village I began to run across designers and theater people, artist types, bohemians who had some politics and kind of knew what was happening. But it wasn't until the sixties struck that I really finally felt at home in the world. I finally reconnected with a lot of things from childhood that I had lost. I had lost an edge somewhere while doing those college years, hanging out in Flushing."[9]

City College, a hothouse for militant campus activity, renewed Toni's energies for fostering radical change in the black community. As part of the faculty, Toni made SEEK her base for organizing and demanding change in the racist institutional policies and practices that blocked admission of students of color and perpetuated irrelevant curriculums. Always interested in the arts, Toni encouraged students to establish *Obsidian*, a magazine for black students. In a 1968 interview published in the campus newspaper, she urged students to write for *Obsidian* as an organizing tool in order to connect with black students at other campuses and to the community.

Poet and essayist Adrienne Rich, who taught at City College during the 1960s, remembers Toni and her powerful vision for a community university as one of her most important memories from the period. Rich recalled an article written by Cade in the student newspaper where she championed for a "Harlem University as the students had renamed it—a master plan for a democratized, community-based and community-enriched university, a no-holes-barred act of the imagination which—though I long ago lost the yellowing sheet it was printed on—became part of the store of inspiration—along with the writings of Paolo Freire—that I have carried with me into teaching situations ever since."[10]

More than a decade later in 1981, when Toni returned to City College to receive the prestigious City University Langston Hughes Award, she joined past recipients James Baldwin, Gwendolyn Brooks, and John Oliver Killens. The Langston Hughes Award recognized Toni for her creative writing and saluted her "[o]riginal, vibrant, irrepressible, your voice, whether at conferences, rallies, prisons, or on campus, articulates our deepest insights, surprising us that we should be so wise."

Toni left City College in 1969 to accept a teaching position at the newly opened Livingston College campus of Rutgers University in New Jersey, a rapidly developing haven for faculty interested in creating an academic base for black revolutionary thought. George Levine who organized the English Department at the new college remembered when he first met Toni being "immediately sold not only on her obvious intelligence, but on her shrewdness, her practical sense of what might be involved in teaching first generation college black students in the kind of environment that Livingston was likely to be." At the rank of Assistant Professor, Toni had influence in a wide scope of activities and quickly became one of the architects of the educational experience for black students. "She had to have thought of it both as a personal upgrade and as a wonderful opportunity to do something original and socially useful. She had terrific ideas about education and she was amazingly strong as well as sensible. I didn't even know at that point how serious she was as a writer," Levine concluded.

After going to Livingston, not only was Toni writing, but her books were being published. In 1970, Toni broke new ground with the publication of *The Black Woman*, an anthology that included the work of City College students, an approach to edited anthologies that she continued with the publication of *Tales for Black Folks* a year later. For many, Toni is singularly significant because *The Black Woman* is one of the first publications to lift the veil from gender violation in the black community. Toni wanted workshops stimulated by the reading of *The Black Woman* to become vehicles for confronting rampant chauvinism within and outside the black community. Defining herself as a Pan-Africanist–socialist–feminist in the United States, Toni urged black women to begin deconstructing the myths that lead to their own self-destruction. Nearly a decade later, Toni's first novel, *The Salt Eaters*, made a call "to politicized women artists, especially, to come together with sisters from the Third World and examine sexual politics from an international perspective."[11]

At Livingston College, Toni again dedicated herself to raising black student consciousness about race and gender realities. She supported the activist black student organization and served as an advisor to campus performance troupes such as the Harambee dancers, Malcolm Players, and Sisters in Consciousness as part of efforts to provide creative vehicles for black revolutionary thought.

In her third year at Livingston College, *Gorilla, My Love*, a collection of stories written between 1959 and 1970, was published and soon became a bestseller. Poet and biographer Quincy Troupe still treasures an aging poster announcing his and Toni's joint New York book party at a place downtown on Bleeker Street near 6th Avenue. Quincy celebrated his first book of poetry, *Embryo*, and Toni signed copies of *Gorilla, My Love*.

Toni lived in East Harlem, on 124th Street between 2nd and 3rd Avenues. Recalling his first visit to that apartment, photographer Chester Higgins relayed how Toni negotiated with the local thugs: "After asking around, she found the guy and invited him to her place. She then pointed out to him what she had, being a writer, was not worth a break in. She wanted him to pass the word around to avoid her place. She did not want to return home to see it vandalized and did not want a reason to call the cops on him . . . And there was peace between them." Poet Sekou Sundiata, who moved into Toni's apartment after she had vacated it, describes it as an unusual living space for New York. It was part of a former factory owned by a German American family that had a tool and dye shop on the first floor, Sundiata remembers

> . . . the first floor there was a large living room (with wood paneling the family salvaged from some barn), a small office-type space off

from the living room up front. Going toward the back, there was a medium size kitchen with sliding glass doors at the far end. The floor-to-ceiling bookcases made of the same wood. When we moved in, the bookcases were full of books, probably the ones Toni decided to leave behind . . . enough to make a library. There was a door at the end of the greenhouse that opened into a fairly large patio area. It was large enough to have an outdoor set: food, music, etc.

The commute from Manhattan to Livingston sometimes took hours. Carpooling to Livingston, Toni often rode with fellow instructor, poet, and friend Nikki Giovanni. Racing down the West Side Highway in Nikki's Volkswagen Beetle en route to Piscataway, they talked about the political movements swirling around them; they also shared the new energy in their personal lives. Toni and Nikki were new single moms. Toni gave birth to her daughter Karma in 1970, the same year she began teaching at Livingston, and the same year that Nikki gave birth to her son, Thomas.

In the preface of *The Black Woman,* Toni sent an "especial thanks to my man Gene, Karma's father." Six years older than Toni, Gene Lewis graduated from the same high school as Toni. Occasionally modeling, singing in off-Broadway musicals, promoting jazz, and acting including a bit part in the opening scenes of *Cotton Comes To Harlem,* Lewis also took part-time managing jobs in New York clubs such as Pee Wee's, a popular lower-east-side bar.

In 1973, when Karma was three, Toni made her first trip to Cuba with a group of progressive scholars including Hattie Gossett, her agent for *Gorilla, My Love,* and political activist Susanne Ross who remembered Hattie bringing a supply of *The Black Woman* to give out whenever she could, particularly to women they met. Ross also remembered meeting leading poets, artists, actors, directors and singers along with spending a full three days at the Cuban Film Institute watching Cuban films and dancing at the Tropicana. After her first trip to Cuba, Toni accepted writing as a singularly important way to participate in struggle. By the time of her second trip to Cuba, in 1985 with a group of African American women writers headed by poet Jayne Cortez, Toni is regularly referring to herself as a cultural worker, which she defined as an artist with a strong community base who is committed to organizing for political and social change.

Atlanta's Promise

In 1974, when Toni decided to leave New York, she wasn't looking for a university base or a quiet place for solitary writing. Again, Toni wanted to forge alliances with radical thinkers and activists. She moved to Atlanta with her daughter, Karma, by then four years old, because she believed Atlanta would stimulate both her activism and her writing. Toni's mother, Helen Cade, joined her in this return to her southern birthplace. Where there were once only whispers of defiance, a visible and militant black presence tumbled long-standing walls of white dominance and claimed Atlanta's city hall for its first black mayor, Maynard Jackson. Like Harlem in the 1920s, Atlanta quickly became a haven for a radical black arts movement.

Activist Jan Douglass, previously a dean and one of the architects of Livingston College's vision and later human relations commissioner for the city, made a home in Atlanta and urged her friend Toni to join with the radical black forces shaping the cultural and altering the political climate of the city. Jan recalled, however, that the practicality of Atlanta living finally won Toni over. Jan said with laughter, "Only when Toni saw downtown parking lots for 25 cents an hour by Davison's Department Store in the Peachtree area did she decide to come to Atlanta."

Toni worked at the innovative Neighborhood Arts Center (NAC) where she, with the other original sixteen resident artists, took time to join the 3 P.M. African dancing led by master drummers in the school parking lot. Atlanta activist and writer Alice Lovelace remembered meetings with Toni and Ebon Dooley, poet and lawyer, at the NAC in Atlanta to discuss creating an organization to foster professionalism and networking opportunities for African American writers in the South. "Under Toni's name, we began to hold a series of meetings that resulted in the formation of the Southern Collective of African American writers and a regional conference," Lovelace recalled.

Toni's interest in exploring the metaphysical provided additional reasons for moving South. In an interview, Toni said: "On the rational side—I moved from New York to Atlanta because I had completed that phase of my work, namely, developing a core of young folk at City College and the Livingston campus of Rutgers University, and was eager to relocate to a place where I could sit down and write without fear of starving to death without a job. On the intuitive side—I came to Atlanta because it is a mystic city rich in metaphysical-training possibilities. People adept in clairvoyance, dream analysis, telepathy, healing, and precognition are in abundance here. It is a good place to both expand my vision and the aforementioned repertoire."[12]

The South provided ideal space for Toni to commune with ancestral spirits, traditional midwives, rural herbalists, kitchen-table griots, and porch-sitting elders, all fodder for her fiction. Lean Wise remembered Toni being so deeply involved in her field work that "she talked about laying on somebody's couch somewhere, willing to experiment, free in diving in, similar to Zora Neale Hurston."

Other Atlanta assets ranged from the Martin Luther King Community School, an independent school in the Vine City section of Atlanta, for Karma to attend, to easy access to the Atlanta airport that allowed her to fly across time zones to give an afternoon campus lecture, meet with black students planning self-help programs, and return the same evening, sometimes without changing from her early morning working-in-the-garden attire. She tapped her unusual humor and joy to get rid of pretentiousness and other unnecessary baggage not only in how she lived at home but also in how she traveled. A free spirit, Toni could arrange an overnight flight to Paris just to see films, writer Kalamu Ya Salaam recalled.

Frequently invited to speak at writers' conferences, film festivals, and women's symposiums, Toni "attended literary conferences with a fervency," Eugene Redmond, professor and poet, remembered. Seeing Toni at a Howard University writers' conference chaired by writers Stephen Henderson and John Oliver Killens, Redmond recalled, "On the morning of May 5, 1977, you gave the keynote address and doubled back to balance two brilliant brothers—John O and George Kent—on a fiction panel that afternoon. The force of your folkways and academic elocution galvanized the conferees into a missile of new commitment."

Years later, Toni's boundless energy remained remarkable to her hosts Jessica and Eric Huntley, community activists who ran the Bogle L'Overture Publishing House and the International Third World Bookshop in Elin, England. In a letter to me, Jessica wrote,

> I received a phone call from Toni saying that herself and daughter would love to come to Britain and wondered whether we could offer them accommodation... That evening, Toni spoke for hours about America, racism, the new black writers emerging in the US and about the film she was engaging on Toni Morrison and so on. She did not seem to be suffering from jet lag. I went to bed and left her to my husband Eric to continue solving the ills of the world.

In repeated visits to London, Toni developed ties with the Institute of Race Relations, a unique organization that includes political activists, cultural workers, artists, and academics. She also met with members of the Organisation of Women of African and Asian Descent (OWAAD) and the Brixton Black Women's Group, pivotal in community organizing in response to police harassment and brutality.

An internationalist, Toni's interest in anti-colonial and war-resistance movements led to a visit to North Vietnam with a Marxists/Leninist feminist group in 1975, shortly after moving to Atlanta. As a guest of the Federation of Vietnamese Women, Toni traveled in African cloth and gele with three other American women to Southeast Asia. Laura Whitehorn, an organizer of the trip recalled, "We had to schlep a huge suitcase crammed with illicit medicines, gathered by U.S. peace groups who were trying to fill a tiny droplet of the extensive medical needs of a Third World nation recuperating from years of colonialism and war."

In Vietnam, Toni attended numerous meetings with women, elders, and youth, viewed Vietnamese and Cuban produced films, visited the Museum of Revolutionary History and Ho Chi Minh's house, and learned about hand-icraft and agriculture coops, infant schools, and health programs. When returning to the United States, Toni used lessons from Vietnam to illus-trate the urgency of stepping up organizing activities for a black political vanguard party at home. Her next book of short stories, *The Sea Birds Are Still Alive,* published in 1977, included stories that center on commu-nity and collective political action both inside and outside of the United States.

While in Atlanta, community organizer Leah Wise, then an editor with the Atlanta-based *Southern Exposure,* remembered Toni's intellectual activi-ties having the expected community ties. *Southern Black Utterances Today,* a special publication edited by Toni and Wise, gave Toni the freedom to apply her thematic sense of how things related—intertwining poetry, literary art, photographs, and a list of informational resources "drawn from the com-munity, that is, from the campus forces, the street forces, the prison forces, and from intellectual circles, as they say."[13]

Community in the House

Whether living on Mayflower Street with the eggplant purple carpet, ideal for tucking away slips of paper as part of her unique filing system, or on Simpson Street, also on a hill with a front-yard staircase that climbed to the house, Toni kept her doors open to writers, filmmakers, and activists. Conversations flowed late into the night like jazz riffs. Film historian Pearl Bowser remembered Toni's place as the favorite late-night gathering place after film festivals she helped organize. "Toni usually ended the evening with one of the political fairy tales that she loved to tell in call and response style somewhere around 5 in the morning."

In the Phoenix Afro American Arts Newsletter, Sandra Y. Govan, who has since published widely and is a professor at the University of North

Carolina, described one such gathering, a reception Toni hosted for long-time friend Ishmael Reed. In the newsletter, Govan writes:

> The reception was held at Toni Cade Bambara's place; a house on a hill where one can look down into the city. Toni is a warm and lively hostess. In an unscientific poll of the gathering's guests, I found that most could be divided into four categories: all had come to hear Reed, of course, but some were teachers, some students, some writers (who would later display their wares), and some had come just to bask in Toni's light... As I recall Ujima's boogie, Melanie's Love Song #5, and Osker's Snake in the Grass hit tremendous responsive cords in the audience. The poems had fools laughin' and clappin' and moving with each very different piece.

Toni preferred the informal gatherings, community meetings, and writing workshops of neighbors and artists that she organized at her home to the structured academic life. When Spelman College informed Toni that one of her proposed courses on black women writers did not meet with the school's curriculum objectives, Toni taught the course anyway in her living room, Beverly Guy-Sheftall, director of the Women's Research and Resource Center, recalled as one of the workshop participants.

In a letter that Toni wrote me not long after moving to Atlanta, she relished her easy going freedom.

> Well, Nothin' much to report from this end, kiddo. Been reading newspapers to workers in the factory. Shooting little films about kids. Cutting the grass. Daydreaming about a larger home so I can consolidate my work under one roof. Karma's doin well. A hellafying kid. She keeps me honest. Trying to stop smoking, change a lotta habits, and stay off the campus.

After publication of *The Salt Eaters,* Toni aimed to devote more space and time to film. In the early 1980s, Toni reflected, "But I'm back to paints again, scripts, songs, especially film work. Partly because I need to work in a new language; also because the lumps prying open the shell do not seem appropriate for print. And too, writing is such a lonely business. How novelists do it year after year, book after book is past my brain."[14]

Making films continued to be on her mind as she wrote me in a June, 1981 letter:

Re novel. I'm gonna stick to TV films for a while. The money is attractive and I need to seriously consider my elder/golden years as they say, having not a dime in bank or pension and a kid with grandiose tastes and a mama with all kinds of long-range projects that need bankrolling. Also, scripting a good good way for me to get to that point. I've been under apprenticeship training for years and years—I want to be a filmmaker, I want to poet with an audience that has little habit with & little patience for books. Also, want to open that door to make folks, especially folks not based in L.A. which is a looney town, or NY which is hip but not, after all, the center of the multiverse. Thus far have been instrumental in kicking doors open to some southern writers, actors casting directors, etc and it makes me feel real good to be rebuilding a new constituency. We have GOTTO take over the airways —.

Atlanta events, however, forced Toni to defer much of her film work yet another time. By the early 1980s, mainstream politics, massive corporate land development, and the increasingly middle-class aspirations of African Americans diminished the sense of possibilities and opportunities for creativity that Atlanta once represented. For Toni, it seemed that the best ideas of the 1960s, a period that she defined broadly as 1954 to 1972, were unraveling.

The tyranny of the escalating numbers of missing and murdered children shifted the very ground of Atlanta's black community and rocked the city, threatening despair. As the Atlanta crisis unfolds, Toni aligns herself with those confronting the terrorism. During that time of murder and disaster, more than forty black children were killed. Aptly defiant, Toni chronicled the Atlanta tragedy in her second novel, *Those Bones Are Not My Child*, published posthumously. As she piled up mounds of notes, Toni worked with the street thugs and the homeless, who helped to set up neighborhood patrols, monitor the media, and prop up collages and signage in her yard with community messages and alerts that mirrored the times. At the Library of Congress, when reading from her magnum Atlanta novel in progress then called *When Blessing Comes*, also previously entitled, *Ground Cover*, Toni explained: "The book takes a look at a number of sectors in the Atlanta community by way of trying to share with a reading public what it means to live under a state of siege. What it means to be told everyday about phantom killers and random killings even though many of us who are on the street many of us who are community organizers, community workers, know those two things to be a lie . . . It's a little difficult to explore the possibilities of self-defense if you are responding to random and phantom." About those traumatic times, Toni reflected, "We were all crazy . . . irrational."

Like harbingers that signal environmental shifts, climatic changes, and other planetary disruptions, the signs emanating from the Atlanta murders had to be read. In an undated letter to me, Toni wrote similarly about the anguish: "1) finally finishing up the Atlanta murder children book soooo glad to be able to put this thing to rest done lost all my hair, girl, all my hair."

Karma doesn't remember exactly why they moved to Philadelphia but thinks leaving Atlanta was her idea. "We knew we had to find someplace else. I think we both thought New York was too much." Jane Poindexter who Toni met in Atlanta remembered Toni doing a reading in Philadelphia and coming back to Atlanta excited about Philadelphia "where grocers still write down the price of groceries on the back of a brown paper bag with a thick lead pencil." Toni and Karma moved to Philadelphia, as did Jane and her daughter Sarah.

Toni once said: "Community is not just where you work or go to school, it's where folks live who summon you with endearing terms like sister, mama, daughter, and dahlin' child." Free of geographic boundaries and territorial maps sealed by bloodlines, community could be created anywhere on the planet. That Toni did, always centering her art and work in plans for social change and justice.

In 1985, Toni left Atlanta. First living in a duplex in Philadelphia's Mount Airy section on East Upsal Street, Toni then moved and settled into a co-op apartment, Valley Green, on Wissahickon Avenue in Philadelphia's historic Germantown community. In Valley Green, Toni landed a co-op made up of two apartments combined into one, ideal space for her piano, spacious book shelves, and a maple brown weaving loom left behind by the previous owner, Ida Tucker, Toni's neighbor remembered. The apartment also provided the needed address for her daughter to attend the well-known Philadelphia High School for Girls. With a nearby neighborhood library, easy-to-reach independent bookstores, and community markets with fresh fruits and vegetables in walking distance, this neighborhood quickly became home.

Friend and poet, Sonia Sanchez, living just blocks away on Chelten Avenue wanted to have a "Welcome to Philadelphia Party" for Toni, but they never could come up with a date. "She was right down the street, but we often saw each other more at film festivals or when we were giving talks on the road," Sonia said. "We both went to the same bank. That meant sometimes she just dropped notes in my mail slot saying Sonia, here's a check with a deposit slip, asking me to deposit it in the bank. Then she'd tell me mail back the deposit slip or else she would come by and pick it up. I did it."

Once in Philadelphia, Toni was invited to work at the Scribe Video Center by its founder, Louis Massiah. It became an ideal base for doing exactly the work she longed to do: make films. The reels of endless movies Toni said she produced in her head since birth now had room for expression. Equally important, Toni applied her spirit of nonconformity and political acuity to using media to challenge organizational and societal norms.

At Scribe, Toni's friendship with Massiah grew. In one 1988 letter to me, she wrote:

> I work these days with the brother who was producer/director of the BOMBING OF OSAGE Docu. We work well together and like each other and respect each other's ideas, etc. It's a good collaboration . . . Every once in a while one of us or both of us giggles or squeals or otherwise indicates how pleased we are to be working together. I don't doubt sometime that I can accomplish more (in terms of pages, heft, bulk, amount of typing per day) if I worked alone, but I know I couldn't accomplish half of what (insights, depth, etc) we are getting done, even when we "squander" half the day gossiping or reminiscing or gabbing about umpteen things and cooking up beans and rice and otherwise procrastinating rather than getting down to the hard work of mapping out parts of the script so we can write up sensible and not full-a-shit proposals so SOme DmN BODY will loosen the grip on some money so we can each stop worrying about bills and stop flying all over the place working to get said bills paid.

In Philadelphia, work got done. Toni co-produced the award-winning video *The Bombing of Osage Avenue*, which she narrated. This film documents the 1985 ruthless bombing of a black neighborhood by the city of Philadelphia in an effort to destroy MOVE, a political organization. While in Philadelphia, Toni again traveled to London—this time to narrate and assist in the production of John Akomfrah's *Seven Songs of Malcolm*. She also worked relentlessly with Massiah to see the completion of *W.E.B. Du Bois: Four Voices,* a film where she is the coordinating writer and narrator.

In 1994, Toni appeared in *Midnight Ramble*, part of "The American Experience" public television series, documenting early African American cinema. Produced by Pearl Bowser, Clyde Taylor and Bestor Cram, the film documents the enormous contributions of Oscar Micheaux to the development of early Black film. Interviewed by Bowser on the *Ramble* set, Toni provided an intellectual storehouse of African American, cinematic and women's history that took the project beyond the limits initially set by its producers. Bowser recalls Toni, her mentor, being a director's dream—anticipating questions before she asked them. "By the end of the day, all four of us were in tears," Bowser said.

In her new home town, Toni sustained her long-time tradition of teaching writing workshops. Enrolled in Toni's writing class at the Germantown YWCA where students included a *Philadelphia Inquirer* journalist and a number of poets, Ann-Marie Anderson, marketing director at Temple University Press, recalled grieving her mother's death and writing about it. Anderson said, "It was a difficult time for me. I cried often during the writing but it was made less painful by the desire to write something that Toni would eventually approve. She made me write it over and over, bringing out details that I didn't want exposed. I did finally finish the project to Toni's liking. I wrote about my family's experience dealing with the passing of our mother whom we all loved and respected dearly but didn't always agree with."

Notes of encouragement from Toni also continued to sail through the mail. In 1991, visual artist Tom Feelings received Toni's congratulations for finishing his book, *The Middle Passage*. "One night in NYC a few weeks ago, I had once again conjured up your book during a talk about amnesia-as-a-prerequisite for assimilation . . . and Bam I run into Camille Billops, or rather she attempts to run me over with her bike. I was so pleased to see you'd left New York and found love and light in Souf Cariln. I'm very happy for you, Tom Feelings . . ."

Beginnings in Endings

Masterful teachers constantly shift attention away from themselves. This Toni did: inspiring many to develop the plan, not just vent, and do the work. About herself Toni wrote, "I am always optimistic. Sometimes angry. Concerned. Questioning. Eager for us to resurrect the fighters and builders who have come before us. Eager for us to see all the connections, the ties that bind us to one another. Eternally optimistic."[15] Toni now faced a personal war that challenged her optimism. In 1993, Toni was diagnosed with colon cancer. For a moment, nothing worked—personal advice, self-help books, prescriptions; only Audre Lorde's *The Cancer Journals* made sense, she said. I remember asking Toni about her prognosis and she replied, "When I asked my surgeon, he cried."

Undaunted, Toni regained her balance. She told her friend Louis about the personal significance of writing *Salt Eaters* more than a decade earlier. "If I hadn't written it, I'm not quite sure I'd be sitting here. I was writing beyond myself in that sense."[16]

The impulse to remain accessible and to tirelessly champion the artistry of cultural workers is a lifeline. Toni assisted organizations such as ImageWeavers, a collective of young female video artists, who were launching new films. She also spoke at film festivals, read countless scripts, agreed to readings at women's prisons, contributed to international political movements that challenged colonialism and imperialism, and opened her phone book—an encyclopedic network—to anyone in search of resources.

At home, Toni's guitar is still close at hand for singing songs from the early Village years. When spinning King Pleasure's classic *Moody's Mood For Love,* Toni is reminded of earlier times in Atlanta when she and her daughter danced freely and sometimes stayed up late into the night running out to Wendy's for apple dumplings. Occasionally, Toni walked down the block to a nearby apartment building which housed a bar and restaurant where she could play the piano and sing Cole Porter songs.

By the fall of 1995, spiritual calls—focused prayers, chants, and meditation—intensified in Atlanta, Brixton, Davis, Harlem, Philadelphia, St. Louis, and in other places where Toni galvanized movements. Even though I purchased a monthly Amtrak ticket for making regular trips to Philadelphia, I didn't see Toni as much as I wanted. Meanwhile, Toni urged Karma to go to California to pursue her interests in film rather than sit by her bedside; Karma did not leave.

As winter solstice approached bringing with it nights longer than days, Toni, 56, died on December 9, 1995. The next day a small group met at Jane Poindexter's apartment to plan the memorial. As if flying on the wings of thousands of migratory monarch butterflies signaling a change of season, word of Toni's passing spread. Hundreds gathered for the memorials at the Painted Bride in Philadelphia and later at the Schomburg Center for Research in Black Culture in New York. On December 17th, at the Painted Bride, a Philadelphia venue known for its creative ambiance and for hosting cutting-edge events, speakers and performers included Toni Morrison, Amiri Baraka, Eleanor Traylor, Sonia Sanchez, Bernice Reagon, and Sandra L. Swans, celebration guide. Cultural workers, students, friends, neighbors, and others that Toni influenced to take principled stands lined the walls to tell their Toni stories filled with laughter and tears. Members of the Black Women's Health Project in Atlanta shared memories of Toni's 50th birthday at the Hammonds House that included bathing Toni's feet and anointing her head with oil. Recalling the Philadelphia memorial, Karma said, "You are sooooooo loved!!! I knew you were a genius, larger than life, but damn!"

At Home in the Universe

"What does it mean to me to be a Black woman?" Toni once asked and answered, "It means to share a sense of community with individuals and groups here and throughout the world who are poised for the light, who work daily to rescue and ransom us all from amnesia and fear, who work sometimes wearily-most-times joyously to encourage and equip us to train for the future as sane, whole, governing people."[17]

While walking through an urban park recently, I remembered spending a night at Toni's apartment just before the abrupt shuttling began between nursing homes, rehabilitation centers, and hospitals. After Toni cooked a meal—my first time ever seeing her stand at a stove flipping over stuff—she decided to share with me beautifully wrapped boxes filled with gifts from students at Spelman College. In the midst of opening boxes, Toni did something I never saw her do before—weep. That same night after washing her hair, lengthy twists, Toni told me about the life/death/dream songs of sirens. To my surprise, I heard the underworld songs of sirens for the first time since that night on my morning walk. This time siren songs provided a passageway for me to finish writing this chronicle. While frequently acknowledging the metaphysical, Toni, who many remember in short skirts, low heeled sandals and remarkably sassy earrings, was not saintly or otherworldly. Toni claimed wholeness and freedom for herself and her many interconnected communities here and now.

NOTES

1. Toni Cade Bambara. "What It Is I Think I'm Doing Anyhow," in Janet Sternburg, ed. *The Writer on Her Work* (New York: Norton, 1980), 156.
2. Toni Cade Bambara. "Thinking About My Mother," in Paul H. Connolly, ed. *On Essays: A Reader for Writers* (New York: Harper & Row Publishers, 1981), 69.
3. Toni Cade Bambara. "What It Means To Be A Black Woman," *The Black Collegian* (April–May, 1980): 136.
4. Louis Massiah. "How She Came By Her Name," in *Deep Sightings & Rescue Missions: Fiction, Essays, and Conversations* (New York: Vintage Press, 1999), 203.
5. The term "Bambara" and its more widely used variant "Bamana" refer to a number of related ethnic groups in Mali who have maintained their traditional cultural practices and resisted the adoption of Sufi Islam, the region's dominant religion.
6. Massiah, 222.
7. Toni Cade Bambara. *Those Bones Are Not My Child* (New York: Pantheon Books, 1999), 671.
8. Toni Cade Bambara. "What It Means To Be A Black Woman," 136.
9. Massiah, 223.
10. Adrienne Rich. "Legacy of Struggle—1969 & 1989—Using The Past To Ignite The Future," in *A Newsletter of the Department of Special Programs (SEEK), The City College*, Vol. 15 No. 12, (Fall 1989): 5–6.
11. Paula Giddings. "Toni Cade Bambara on Her First Novel/'A Call to Wholeness' from a Gifted Storyteller," *Encore American & Worldwide News* (June 1980): 49.
12. Deborah Jackson. "Interview with Toni Cade Bambara," *Drum* (Spring 1982): 43.

13. Toni Cade Bambara and Leah Wise. "Introduction," *Southern Exposure, Southern Black Utterances Today,* Vol. III, Number 1 (1975).

14. Toni Cade Bambara. "Salvation is the Issue," in Mari Evans, ed. *Black Women Writers (1950–1980): A Critical Evaluation* (New York: Anchor), 43.

15. Zala Chandler. "Voices Beyond the Veil: An Interview with Toni Cade Bambara and Sonia Sanchez," 353.

16. Massiah, 235.

17. Toni Cade Bambara. "What It Means To Be A Black Woman," 136–37.

3

Toni's Obligato: Bambara and the African American Literary Tradition

CHERYL A. WALL

Toni Cade Bambara belongs to the group of African American women writers who came to voice in the early 1970s, and her art shares much in common with that of Audre Lorde, Paule Marshall, Toni Morrison, and Alice Walker. It, too, makes black female character central; it highlights intraracial rather than interracial conflict, and it represents black vernacular speech and cultural practices. But in its distinctive rendering of that speech, in its insistently urban setting and idiom, and in its feminist/Pan Africanist perspective, it stands apart. Bambara's fiction emphasizes the primacy of the urban experience; it declines to accept the dictum that "the personal is political," insisting instead that politics must be engaged in the public sphere; and it refuses to forego the challenge of rigorous critique in favor of the possibility of spiritual transcendence. Recognizing that "the literature(s) of our time are a collective effort," Toni once described herself as "but one voice in the chorus."[1] Like a musical "obligato," Bambara's is an indispensable voice, an essential component of the composition of its era.

Although she is considered part of the renaissance among African American women writers of the 1970s, Toni Cade's first published story, "Sweet Town," appeared in 1959. Most of the other stories that were collected in the path-breaking volume, *Gorilla, My Love*, were published during the 1960s. Three of them, including the title story, appeared the year before the collection that made Bambara's name as a writer came to print. It was a heady time: the Black Arts Movement was at its height; the Women's Movement in the United States was gearing up momentum, and Bambara was moving at an equally incredible speed. In 1970, she published the landmark volume, *The Black Woman*, a multigeneric volume that includes poems, short stories, and biography, in addition to analytical articles and political position papers. The conjunction of the literary and the political became a hallmark of Bambara's artistic practice. She refused to assign art and politics to separate spheres. Contributors to *The Black Woman* included poets Nikki Giovanni and Audre Lorde; and fiction writers Paule Marshall, Alice Walker, and Sherley Anne Williams. Williams's "Tell Martha Not to Moan" is her first published story. As editor, not only was Bambara a voice in the chorus then, but she helped produce the chorus. In 1971, Bambara published *Tales and Stories for Black Folks,* a volume that juxtaposed short fiction by well-known writers such as Ernest Gaines, Langston Hughes, and Alice Walker; and fiction produced by Bambara's students. A year later Bambara collected her own fiction in *Gorilla, My Love.*

As many critics have observed, the girls who move through the pages of these stories are a new kind of female protagonist: fearless and bold, feisty and articulate.[2] These young characters are angered by injustice of any kind: whether it is the injustice of a theater owner who fails to show the movie that he advertised or the societal injustice implicit in the existence of a fancy store where toys cost more than a worker's annual wage. Children, particularly black children in fiction, had more often been social victims rather than the agents of social change that one finds in Bambara's stories. The sensitive and insightful John Grimes, protagonist of James Baldwin's novel, *Go Tell It On the Mountain,* for example, is barely able to withstand the external pressure of racism and poverty and the internal pain of self-hatred.

Hazel Elizabeth Deborah Parker, also known as Squeaky, the heroine of "Raymond's Run," offers a sharp contrast. As she narrates her own story, she tells the reader right off that she is not like most girls: she does not do housework, she does not like to dress up, and she is an excellent athlete. As she runs, she seems to lay claim to the streets of Harlem, the same streets that terrified John Grimes. Hazel is caring and responsible, so much so that her parents have entrusted her with the care of her retarded older brother. Not only is Hazel able to protect him from the taunts of neighborhood children, she is also able eventually to figure out a role for him that will earn him the dignity that she claims for herself. She sees him in a new way as "a great runner in the family tradition."[3] In the process of achieving this realization, Hazel shows herself to be an acute social critic who recognizes that "girls never really smile at each other because they don't know how and don't want to know how and there's probably no one to teach us how, cause grown-up girls don't know either" (33). By the end of the story, she and her chief competitor, Gretchen, have learned how to smile at each other, because they have achieved the kind of mutual respect that allows them to do so.

Under various aliases (Scout, Peaches, and Badbird), Hazel appears in four stories, including the one that gives the volume its title. In each story, Hazel refuses to yield her sense of right and wrong even when—or especially when—her views are challenged by those in authority. Her moral vision is the source of her self-confidence. Her disgust with the adult world stems from the failure of adults to live up to the standards of honesty, integrity, and self-respect that Hazel demands of herself. In the sharpness of her social critique, Hazel is sister to Claudia, the sometimes narrator of Morrison's *The Bluest Eye*, and to Alice Walker's Ruth in *The Third Life of Grange Copeland*. These first novels, both published in 1970, are coterminous with *Gorilla, My Love*. Though similar in personality to these characters, Hazel faces far more benign circumstances. She confronts challenges; she does not endure physical or psychological trauma.[4]

Bambara's use of first-person narration intensifies the reader's sense that Hazel is speaking her own mind. As striking as what Hazel says, of course, is the way she says it. When one thinks of black female characters in fiction before 1970, Paule Marshall's Selina Boyce in *Brown Girl, Brownstones*, for example, or Gwendolyn Brooks's *Maud Martha*, one thinks of highly self-conscious young women, who define themselves both with and against the community of their elders. Whatever the similarities, those characters, even Brooklyn-born Selina, sound nothing like Hazel. Hazel's voice is inimitable: "And now I'm really furious cause I get so tired grownups messin over kids just cause they little and can't take em to court. What is it, he say to me like I lost my mittens or wet on myself or am somebody's retarded child. When in reality I am the smartest kid P.S. 186 ever had in its whole lifetime and you can ax anybody" (17).

Bambara's perfect pitch for her characters' speech is one of her greatest gifts. She writes the idiom without the punctuation marks that called attention to the nonstandard dialect of black characters in nineteenth and early twentieth-century texts by both white and black American writers. The first-person narration eliminates what John Wideman describes as "the mediating voice" on which black writers relied to distinguish their own more standard language from the dialect of their characters.[5] Even Zora Neale Hurston's justly celebrated *Their Eyes Were Watching God*, written in large measure in what she called "Negro idiom," begins with the voice of an omniscient narrator who does not speak the language of the characters of the text.

Hurston's idiom is black and southern. The "will to adorn" with its profusion of metaphor and simile is not Bambara's. Although a few of the stories, "Mississippi Ham Rider" and "Blues Ain't No Mockin' Bird," for example, are set in the South, most are urban stories that pulse with the rhythms of black urban vernacular. I think of the older woman protagonist of "My Man Bovanne," who protests the tendency of young people including her own children to define her, "And I ain't never been souther than Brooklyn Battery and no more country than the window box on my fire escape" (14).

The urban idiom is edgier, less reliant on metaphor than the one Hurston valorized. It is "in your face"; it is not speech that is overheard, but spoken directly. Hazel's speech is rapid-fire; her repetitions are short phrases rather than elaborate conceits. But her sense of drama, the characteristic of "Negro expression" to which Hurston gave pride of place, is finely honed indeed. Consider the anecdote about her mother that is imbedded in the passage from the story quoted earlier:

> And cause my Mama come up there in a minute when them teachers start playin the dozens behind colored folks. She stalk in with her hat pulled down bad and that Persian lamb coat draped back over one hip on account of she got her fist planted there so she can talk that talk which gets us all hypnotized, and teacher be comin undone cause she know this could be her job and her behind cause Mama got pull with the Board and bad by her own self. (17)

This story extends Hazel's self-definition as the "smartest kid in P.S. 186." The teachers may be reluctant to confirm this fact, but Hazel's powerful and stylish mother can force them to do so. The system may want to impose what the text depicts as a southern docility on their northern students, but parents like Hazel's mother have power within the system and refuse to allow their children to be suppressed. Hazel's mother, like her grandfather, and like the couple in "Blues Ain't Nothin" and Great Ma Drew in "The Johnson Girls" show that the strong sense of self expressed by the stories' young protagonists comes from somewhere. They are connected to the ancestry that Eleanor Traylor describes as "the sum of the accumulated wisdom of the race."[6]

The Salt Eaters is a dazzlingly dense novel that many regard as Bambara's artistic triumph, though others are put off by its nonlinear plot and shifting temporal registers. By any measure, it is a singular piece of writing. *The Salt Eaters* achieves "the boldness and design" that Bambara defines as "black genius." Musicians are the exemplars of genius as they perform "on the stand with no luggage and no maps and ready to go anywhere in the universe together on just sheer holy boldness."[7] Structured like a jazz fugue, *The Salt Eaters* begins with a question, "Are you sure, sweetheart, that you want to be well?" Posed by the healer and singer Minnie Ransom to the suicidal, almost catatonic Velma Henry, the question and its variations resound like an obligato through the novel. "Just so's you're sure, sweetheart, and ready to be healed, cause wholeness is no trifling matter" (10). "Can you afford to be whole?" (106). "The source of health is never outside, sweetheart. What will you do when you are well?" (220). To move through life as the musicians live in music is the challenge that Velma confronts.[8]

The novel's challenges are not only formal. Readers' response to *The Salt Eaters* depends in part on their willingness to take seriously a wide array of spiritual beliefs and practices that the novel argues are fundamental to social and political transformation. Written in the 1970s, *The Salt Eaters* identifies the spiritual as the missing element in the progressive political movements of the 1960s. It argues that to achieve the goals of sixties' idealism and to respond to the new challenges of the last quarter of the twentieth century, including an endangered environment and the threat of nuclear contamination, people of color need to recuperate the subjugated knowledge of their foremothers. By fusing that knowledge with a progressive political consciousness, a spiritually revived people may chart a path to liberation. Even if the group is not ready to mobilize for freedom, the individual carries the responsibility to resist the temptation to despair and to stay healthy in body and spirit. The stakes are huge. As one of the novel's several wise women avers, "There is a world to be redeemed . . . [a]nd it'll take the cooperation of all righteous folks" (92).

Minnie and Velma never move from their location in a meeting room in the Southwest Community Infirmary, where a group of twelve auxiliary healers called the Master's Mind encircle them. But the novel takes up diverse locations, adopts multiple perspectives, and speaks through various voices as the characters who know and care about Velma—even as they do not all know each other—respond to her crisis. The novel fuses their voices, blurs distinctions between past and present, present and future, dream and reality, perception and fact. At once both material and spiritual, music acts as the bridge between these realms. Velma herself rarely speaks, but from the beginning she is "caught up in the weave of the song Minnie hums" (4).

The action in the narrative present lasts less than ten minutes. Velma is healed, through a combination of individual will, communal concern, and psychic power. But to effect the healing, Velma must travel back in time to consider the reasons she felt desperate enough to slit her wrists as well as the reasons she wants to recover. A community activist, she reviews her fraying relationship with her husband, James Obeah (Obie) and reflects on the pressures of working in a movement that many have abandoned. Velma remembers the cutting tone of one lapsed revolutionary who jeered, "You honestly think you can change anything in this country." She also remembers her response, "I try to live . . . so it doesn't change me" (261). Having temporarily lost that battle, Velma strives for renewal. The characters whose lives Velma has touched likewise move back and forth between past and present. Her godmother, Sophie Heywood ("M'Dear"), dreams of Velma as a child and of Velma dreaming now. Her sister Palma travels with a troupe of multiethnic cultural workers called the Seven Sisters who believe that "the material without the spiritual does not a dialectic make" (64); Palma comes across a photo of Velma, dreams that her sister is ill, and takes a mental and physical journey back to aid her. Her character interacts with a range of artists and of workers, notably the troupe's bus driver Fred Holt, who become connected to Velma's healing. Closer at hand, staff and patients at the Infirmary are drawn to the music room, as Minnie calls on "Old Wife," her spirit guide, to assist her. The communal energy buoys Velma's will. The relationship between the individual and the group is reciprocal. Velma's healing is emblematic of the process that the community as a whole must undergo.

The novel shifts scenes cinematically. At one moment the reader is at the Infirmary, where M'Dear, a midwife and union activist, asserts that "we're all clairvoyant if we'd only know it" (13). In that same moment the reader is overhearing an expression of concern for Velma and a protest against sexism at the Women for Action Committee meeting. In another part of town, the reader is at the spring festival, where Meadows, an administrator at the Infirmary, encounters two activists who he mistakes for thugs. He tells them about the healing. Yet Meadows cannot see the men for who they are; neither can he hear their language. When they discover that Meadows has heard "Nadir's" rather than "M'Dear's," they give him a crash course in naming and in black English vernacular: "My name's Thurston, as in need for a beer. This is Hull as in Walnut, called Ml as in rifle. Come on, my man, let's have a beer. Wish we could extend an invitation to grit, but the cupboard's Mother Hubbard's" (189). Despite the fun they have had at his expense, Thurston and Hull leave Meadows feeling "less alone" than he has been for a long time. Meanwhile at a café, two activist women, Jan and Ruby, reflect on the present with a movement consumed by "id ego illogical debates" (199) and ponder the future: "Who could effectively pull together the folks?" (193). Ruby wants a leader and a return to a simpler politics: "Don't anybody talk political, talk black anymore?" "[T]his ecology stuff is a diversion" (242). Ruby is also hostile to psychic phenomena. Jan, by contrast, is conversant with the Ouija board, energy maps, cowries, astrological charts, and Tarot cards. Both are worried about Velma.

Fred Holt, a bus driver for nearly forty years, is definitely concerned with practical matters. He needs to make this run on time so he can pick up an extra trip at the Infirmary. But the bus is delayed, and the passengers get on his nerves. The white women sing hymns, while the black men are stranded musicians, who remind Fred of his unrealized aspirations; a white couple is drunk and fractious, and a young white man in the rear holds what Holt fears is a basket of snakes. He thinks to himself as he observes the Seven Sisters—their T-shirts emblazoned with political slogans and their talk of a performance piece about John Henry and Kwan Cheong, "The Spirit of Iron"—that "if he knew a good psychiatrist to recommend to them, he would" (67). As he drives, Holt sees a postindustrial landscape that is as desolate as the Hoovervilles he has lived in as a child during the Depression. He thinks back mainly on his best friend Porter, recently murdered, who had long been obsessed by his memories of an atomic accident in 1955. "Hospitalized, discharged, no goodbye, get lost buddy, drop dead . . . " (80). Now, Holt thinks, "that might be something to chat about with the T-shirts if the bus broke down" (80). It doesn't. But the reader makes the connections between Holt's concerns and the Seven Sisters'.

Campbell, erstwhile journalist turned short-order cook, rearticulates these concerns with the sharp-edged humor characteristic of Bambara's fiction. As a cub reporter on a small-town newspaper, Campbell published a series of articles on nuclear energy. He impressed his editor with his "ability to discuss fission in terms of billiards, to couch principles of thermonuclear dynamics in the language of down-home Bible-quoting folks" (210). But he had gotten too far ahead of the curve. His aspiration now is to market a board game he has invented and named "Disposal" in which each player starts out with a sum of money, property that includes nuclear reactors and uranium mines, plus 5,000 pounds of nuclear waste to dispose of. To Campbell, the game "incorporated the ferociously acquisitive features of Monopoly with just the right touch of self-righteousness. Best of all, it frustrated and provoked. In short, it was American" (208). Convinced though he is that Disposal is a sure-fire success, Campbell is for the moment serving up lunch for Ruby and Jan.

Velma becomes the figure who brings the workers and the activists, the artists and the psychics together. Far from the messianic figure Ruby seems to yearn for, Velma is the office manager at the Academy of the Seven Arts, the neighborhood cultural center and the wellspring of cultural and political activism. Velma runs the office, manages the books, raises the money, and coordinates the programs. When she falls ill, it takes seven people to replace her. Beyond the Academy, Velma becomes the catalyst for the conversations and (potential) alliances across lines of color, class, gender, ideology, and geography.

The Southwest Community Infirmary as the site of healing has historical resonance. Established in 1871 by "the Free Coloreds of Claybourne," the building stands with its ornate carvings and its motto (HEALTH IS YOUR RIGHT) chiseled across the entrance. Nearby stands the Old Tree, planted the same year by the same freedmen and women as an historical marker and "as a gift to the generations to come" (145). Minnie Ransom, who brings daily offerings of food and water, is one of the few to recognize the spiritual power of Old Tree. Like the Sojourner in Alice Walker's *Meridian*, like the "L'Arbe de la Croix" in Toni Morrison's *Tar Baby*, and like the pear tree under which Janie Crawford experiences a revelation in *Their Eyes Were Watching God*, Old Tree is a spiritual dwelling place. *The Salt Eaters* names the spirits, the loa like their Haitian counterparts, who "danced and stomped unseen by those pretending not to know of spirit kinship, attended each year by a certain few drawn to the tree or drawn to the building, called to their vocation and their roots" (146). But, for the most part the loa in Claybourne are seldom called on, and then for the most trivial purposes like keeping a lover from straying or guaranteeing the number for the day. Consequently, "they were weary with so little to perform" (146). In Velma's individual crisis and in the broader crisis it signals, the loa find a situation worthy of their powers.

If, as Amiri Baraka reminds us in *Blues People*, "the spirit will not descend without a song," the spirits Minnie needs to do her work require a jazz fugue. *Wild Women Don't Get the Blues* changes into Charlie Parker's *Now Is the Time* and Velma, "spinning in music," finally rises from her stool. In this, her "day of restoration," Velma learns the lesson that her M'Dear had taught: "Dispossessed, landless, this and that-less and free, therefore to go anywhere and say anything and be everything if we'd only know it once and for all. Simply slip into the power, into the powerful power hanging unrecognized in the back-hall closet" (265).

A thunder storm announces the descent of the spirits, "summoned to regenerate the life of the world" (249). All of the characters respond, even as they struggle to discern the source of the powerful sound: a nuclear explosion, Damballah, "the roaring of the races underground," the trumpet's sound. What happens next is left for the characters and the reader to decode together. In Eleanor Traylor's[9] eloquent distillation:

> Memory circling, plunging down as though toward the roots of the baobab tree, Velma enters a region where time melds the dead, the living, and the unborn, where the bold act of the imagination weds the actual and the mythical, and where the historical is redeemed by the possible: where 'Isis lifted the veil' (*Salt Eaters*, 246); where Shango presides over the rites of transformation; where Ogun challenges chaos and forges transition; where Obatala shapes creation; where Damballah ensures continuity and renewal...

As Traylor's reading implies, the storm as metaphor for spiritual renewal has antecedents in diverse religious traditions. In African American literary tradition, Bambara's scene echoes passages in Zora Neale Hurston's oeuvre, particularly Zora's initiation as a hoodoo practitioner in *Mules and Men*. There her mentor Luke Turner gives her the name "the Rain-Bringer," and "with ceremony . . . painted the lightning symbol down my back from my right shoulder to my left hip. This was to be my sign forever. The Great One was to speak to me in storms."[10] In *Their Eyes Were Watching God,* of course, the protagonist is transformed during the climatic hurricane. Though the process is not recorded in detail, Janie comes into possession of the word. In recent fictions by African American women, notably Audre Lorde's *Zami,* Paule Marshall's *Praisesong for the Widow* and Gloria Naylor's *Mama Day,* protagonists experience similar passages of spiritual transformation.

In her essay, "But What Do I Think She's Doing Anyway," Akasha (Gloria) Hull makes bold claims for *The Salt Eaters.* She deems it "a daringly brilliant work which accomplishes even better for the 1980s what *Native Son* did for the 1940s, *Invisible Man* for the 1950s or *Song of Solomon* for the 1970s: it fixes our present and challenges the way to the future."[11] Readers did not find the novel in sufficient numbers to justify this claim. But, like Jean Toomer's Harlem Renaissance masterpiece, *Cane, The Salt Eaters* influenced a generation of writers. Experimental in form and mystical in mood, Toomer's book sold a mere five hundred copies. Even those who admired it acknowledged that it was difficult to read.[12] *The Salt Eaters* occupies a similar position in terms of the development of the African American literary tradition at the turn of the twentieth-first century.

Bambara spent the last twelve years of her life completing the epic novel, *Those Bones Are Not My Child.* For a writer who once described herself as an "optimist," who could afford an optimistic outlook because hers was only one voice in the chorus, the decision to focus on a subject that occasioned such despair must have been as painful as it was brave. The novel is based on the series of child murders that terrorized the city of Atlanta in the early 1980s. In this case, "decision" is probably not the right word. To understand Bambara's commitment to this project, one would do well to remember that "obligato" and "obligation" share a common etymology. Bambara felt duty-bound to document "what it meant to have lived in Atlanta in a state of siege."[13] The novel depicts the events that terrorized Atlanta and black Americans more generally, the fear those events engendered, the inadequacy of the official response, and the strength that the community found, ultimately, to take action against the violence that had been inflicted on them. Just as she had refused to turn a blind eye to sexism in the black communities of the 1960s, just as she had called the African American political leadership of Philadelphia to account for the bombing of Osage Avenue, she tackled head-on the most difficult and daunting issues confronting her people. Morrison's observation about her sister writer is apt: "there was no division in her mind between optimism and ruthless vigilance, between aesthetic obligation and the aesthetics of obligation."[14]

A passage in *Those Bones* reflects on the aesthetics of obligation and on the demands of storytelling this particular subject required:

> To be told right, lest it dishonor those who'd live through it and those who hadn't, it had to have a particular beginning. A small, quiet, personal thing was called for—the evil iron that had scorched a collar that morning, exact change lost through a hole in the clothes. Insignificant in the scheme of things, it would be offered as a sign of the teller's humility as confirmation that cataclysms do give warning, for there's an order to the knowable universe, and too, to signal that the teller could not distance himself or herself from communal disaster. (297)

The boot, the missing child's shoe, is the small, quiet personal thing that becomes the metonym for loss in the novel. If it marks the intimate relation of the protagonist to the larger tragedy, it conveys as well the author's sense of obligation both to her subject and to her readers. The subject can never be held at a distance; the reader is gripped by its most familiar details.[15]

The prologue works both intrinsically and extrinsically to connect Bambara herself to the communal disaster. I first heard Bambara read a version of the novel's prologue at a conference in 1982. At that time it was a free-standing first-person nonfictional account of her experiences in Atlanta. I will never forget how she read the passage that describes her watching her daughter in the pool: "Arms spread, legs wide, she facedown in the water in a dead man's float. Can you applaud?" (*Those Bones*, 21). Bambara's voice made the fear in Atlanta visceral. When she finished her reading, the audience sat in silence for a long minute, then broke out in thunderous applause. We knew, of course, that Toni's daughter was safe. But we knew just as surely that this mother/author had lived the fear she wrote about.

Marzala Rawis Spencer is a wholly invented, fully imagined character. Unlike her creator, she is a divorced mother of three and a churchgoer, who is neither an activist nor a woman of the world. She is a seamstress, an artist whose medium is fabric rather than words. Most crucially, she is a mother whose child is missing. But the way Zala works—the notebooks and journals she keeps (journals marked "Missing and Murdered"), the newspapers stories she clips for her files, and the rumors whose truth or falsehood she is determined to ascertain—mirrors Bambara's way of working. Without doubt, the commitment to telling the story as it should be told is Bambara's own. Equally important, the invention of Marzala and her family allows Bambara to personalize the loss the Atlanta child murders exacted, while fulfilling her obligation to respect the privacy of those who were its real-life victims.[16]

Those Bones earns its epic appellation through its depiction of the full canvas of black Atlanta in the early 1980s: from the politicians and city leaders to the lawyers and professionals, the police and the journalists, the mothers of the disappeared and their grass-roots supporters, the political activists like Speaker whose role is to "speak truth to power," to the working class and to the poor. In sharp contrast to the nonlinear structure of *Salt Eaters, Those Bones* adheres to an almost painstaking chronology. As is always the case in Bambara's fiction, the privileged perspective is given to the working class. That perspective is articulated here first and foremost by Marzala (called Zala) and Nathaniel Spencer (called Spence), the parents whose search for their missing son, Sundiata (called Sonny) is the pivot of the plot. Zala works in a barbershop, a setting that is the locus for the subjugated knowledge that defines the communal ethos. At the same time she is a student, taking a drama course at a community college and trying to write a paper on Clytemnestra, an assignment that links the events of the novel to the broadest dimensions of human tragedy. Spence, her estranged husband, is a Vietnam Vet; he drives a limousine, a job that like Zala's allows him to encounter characters from all walks of life. Indeed, *Those Bones* represents a much greater range of class status in African American communities and a greater interaction among African Americans of differing class status than any fiction that comes readily to mind.

As a documentary novel, *Those Bones* has definite precursors in the African American tradition. They include novels as recent as John Wideman's *Philadelphia Fire* and as far back (at least) as *The Marrow of Tradition* by Charles Chesnutt.[17] The latter seems particularly salient. Like *Bones*, Chesnutt's fictional account of the race riot that destroyed the black community of Wilmington, North Carolina, in 1898 drew heavily on contemporary newspaper accounts. Finding himself on the brink of despair, he wrote the novel to protest the violent end of the first Reconstruction. Written in the wake of the *Plessy v. Ferguson* Supreme Court decision that legalized the doctrine of "separate but equal," *The Marrow of Tradition* depicts a cross-section of the white community from the hapless aristocrat to the racist demagogue and of the black community from the working-class rebel to the physician hero William Miller, who is the novel's moral center. Chesnutt regarded with horror the use of terror to reimpose the racial hierarchies that supported the slavery system. He was alarmed by what he understood to be an attack on the racial and political progress of African Americans in Wilmington and throughout the South.

Those Bones focuses on the historical moment when what the novel names the Second Reconstruction is under attack. In this instance the terror seems intended to reimpose the racial hierarchies that the Civil Rights

Movement had finally disrupted. It seemed as well to attack the social and political progress of African Americans by undermining the newly installed black political leadership in the city that had become, in popular parlance, the "Black Mecca." In its most hideous aspect, this late twentieth-century wave of terror targeted children. The novel's concerns resonate with the discourse around the war on black boys and the retrenchment of black peoples' rights during the Reagan administration.

Marzala Spencer is cut from the same cloth as Hazel. Her voice is equally memorable. In the beginning of the novel, as she waits for her disobedient son to return home, she anticipates his arrival: "He would stroll in, take one look, and know she had no good side to get on" (25). Like Hazel too, Zala refuses to yield her sense of right and wrong when—and especially when—her views are challenged by those in authority. Desperate to bring attention to the case, she makes an appointment with a journalist. Smooth-talking and dismissive, the man explains that compared to other news—the revolution in Iran, for example—the Atlanta story lacks scope. Zala responds: "Please! There's terrorism right here in Atlanta. Atlanta, I'm talking about, the 'New International City.' We're not some mail-order postal address you see on late-night TV—smokeless ashtrays, bamboo steamers. Look, mister, children and not just children have been murdered here, and you've got to do something about it. Earl says you're a newsman. Well, this is a news story I'm talking about. Terrorism" (274). Not only can she define the crime, but also she locates her community in the context of global capitalism, where useless commodities get more attention than individual lives. Initially, Zala does not anticipate that her concerns will be ignored. Instead, she expects that those in charge will be eager to help her find her son. Indeed, Zala and Spencer both begin with the assumption that they will be able to gather the information they need to act responsibly.

Bambara once told an interviewer, "as a mother, teacher, writer, community worker, neighbor, I am concerned about accurate information, verifiable facts, sound analyses, responsible research, principled study, and people's assessment of the meaning of their lives."[18] This is the perspective Zala and Spence eventually adopt, once they are past their suspicions of each other and past their initial reliance on assistance from the authorities. They understand slowly what Bambara knew; that is, in certain situations—and almost always for oppressed people—accurate information is hard to come by. The novel enacts this truth over and over again. On her first visit to the Youth Division of Missing Persons, Zala is made to feel like a neglectful parent: "You listed three work numbers. You have three jobs and can keep track of three children? We need you down here conducting workshops, Mrs. Spencer" (66). A later visit to the Task Force is equally unavailing. The list of potential suspects, which includes the Ku Klux Klan, a child-pornography ring, a Vietnam Vet, a police officer, and Wayne Williams, grows ever longer. *Those Bones Are Not My Child* follows false leads. It depicts how various characters come under suspicion and how difficult it is to throw off a cloud of suspicion once it is cast.

Fortunately, Zala begins to define the situation for herself. At a community meeting, she is the one to name the terrorism affecting her community what it is. Her efforts to pressure the authorities to respond with the urgency the situation demands prove fruitless. The FBI fails to do its job; the Georgia Bureau of Investigation (GBI) fails as well. In response, Zala and Spence become self-authorizing agents. They track down rumors, interrogate witnesses, and put suspects under surveillance. In claiming their agency, the couple begins to heal the rift between them and to foster a sense of community among their neighbors.

Those Bones Are Not My Child seems to me to end several times; perhaps as Bambara seeks to achieve a conclusion that is both commensurate with the ending of the actual events, and, better, lacks a definite ending to those events, as well as with her determinedly optimistic outlook. At one point, the novel seems ready to end when it celebrates Sonny's return to the family, but it cannot make sense of the tortures he has endured while he is away. More plots unfold. A moment of reconciliation comes when Mama Lovey confronts her grandson, whose anger, after his return, jeopardizes the family almost as intensely as the fear his disappearance had wrought. In the garden where evening primrose blooms, with its oils that are a cure for almost everything that can ail one, Mama Lovey forces him to open his heart and express some of his pain:

> He heaved the whole of himself at her in a torrent of words that rushed the wind from her lungs. He called himself names, ugly names he'd stored up from the devil knew where burning through the pleats of her bodice. And all she could do was breathe and hold on and declare the love of the blood. A part of her wanted to beat him down to the ground with her fists, then drag him to the road by the nape of his neck and say go on then, go on. But the best part of her locked him in tight while she prayed for a long, hard driving, relentless rain. (569)

The unsentimental depiction of the grandmother and the setting (Epps, Alabama) suggest that Bambara revised her sense of the rural South as a site for docility. Mama Lovey is as tough as any of her urban sisters; she is also true to her name.

The novel seems ready to end again when Zala recognizes the evil that inheres in the glassblower Haynes. When he demonstrates his art to onlookers, explaining that "manipulating is a matter of knowing when to apply heat and when to let things cool off," Zala moves to confront him (588). She suspects that this smooth-talking charmer could have lured away her son and other children. But her suspicion goes unproven. The novel's ultimate ending seems incomplete, yet aptly provisional. We will never know whose voice pulls Zala through the open door. The mystery remains unsolved, but the story is resolved. Zala and Spence have come to new understandings. Significantly, the lessons that Zala especially teaches by precept as well as by example are the ones that Bambara's earliest protagonists intuited.

Zala's second speech brings together the various strands of the novel in one grand "preachment," as Gwendolyn Brooks might have termed it. Aptly enough, Zala turns to Brooks for her epigraph: "We are each other's harvest, we are each other's business." After quoting Andrew Salkey, Maya Angelou, and Alexis DeVeaux, Zala addresses the specifics of the case. She indicts the authorities for their negligence. She confesses her own weakness, when her son's safe return mitigates her concern for the children who are still missing. Then she indicts all of those, all of us, who would stay silent in the face of evil. "In a just order," Zala declares, "crimes against children would be dealt with more seriously than crimes against the state. Because it is more serious. What could be more serious?" (660) Zala urges her audience both within and without the text to take action. The moral of this complex novel is simple. Taking action, moving against injustice whenever and wherever it is met is the most and the least one can do.

The theme is Toni's obligato and our obligation.

NOTES

1. Toni Cade Bambara. "What Is It I Think I'm Doing Anyway," in Janet Sternburg, ed. *The Writer on Her Work* (New York: Norton, 1980), 157. Bambara elaborated on musical metaphor in her conversation with Claudia Tate, "there are no soloists after all; this is a group improvisation," but conceded that she found it difficult to assess the value of her "own particular pitch and voice in the overall chorus." In Claudia Tate, ed. *Black Women Writers At Work* (New York: Continuum, 1983), 37, 14.

2. For critical commentary on *Gorilla, My Love,* see Lindon Barrett, "Identity and Identity Studies: Reading Toni Cade Bambara's 'The Hammer Man,'" *Cultural Critique* 39 (Spring 1998): 5–29; Elliott Butler-Evans, *Race, Gender and Desire: Narrative Strategies in the Fiction of Toni Cade Bambara, Toni Morrison, and Alice Walker* (Philadelphia: Temple University Press, 1989); Mary Comfort, "Liberating Figures in Toni Cade Bambara's *Gorilla, My Love, Studies in American Humor,*"

3, 5 (1998): 76–96; Mary Helen Washington, *Black-Eyed Susans: Classic Stories by and about Black Women* (New York: Anchor Books, 1975); and Susan Willis, *Specifying: Black Women Writing the American Experience* (Madison, WI: University of Wisconsin Press, 1987).

3. Toni Cade Bambara. *Gorilla, My Love* (1972. New York: Vintage, 1981), 38. Subsequent citations will be noted parenthetically.

4. Bambara's early work did not focus on the traumatic. She asserted, "I don't doubt that the horror tales are factual. I don't even doubt that ugly is a truth for somebody ... somehow. But I'm not convinced that ugly is *the* truth that can save us, redeem us." Bambara, "What Is It," 157.

5. John Edgar Wideman. "Frame and Dialect: The Evolution of the Black Voice," *American Poetry Review* 5 (Sept.– Oct. 1976): 34–37.

6. Eleanor Traylor. "Music as Theme: The Jazz Mode in the Works of Toni Cade Bambara," in Mari Evans, ed. *Black Women Writers (1950–1980)* (New York: Anchor Books, 1980), 66.

7. *The Salt Eaters* (1980. New York: Vintage Contemporaries Edition, 1992), 265.

8. Just as the swift changes and dissonant harmonies of free jazz sound like cacophonies to the uninitiated, the discontinuous plot lines and the quickly disappearing characters of *The Salt Eaters* seem like confusion to some readers. According to Susan Willis, for example, the confusion of the opening scene "is apt to overwhelm even the most skilled and persistent readers of modernist texts" *Specifying: Black Women Writing the American Experience* (Madison: University of Wisconsin Press, 1987), 130. In *The Washington Post Book World* (March 30, 1980), novelist Anne Tyler acknowledged that *The Salt Eaters* "is not an easy book to read" and that at times the circuitous plot "actively irritated me." But, she continued, "what pulls us along is the language of its characters, which is startlingly beautiful without once striking a false note" (2).

9. Eleanor Traylor. 64.

10. Zora Neale Hurston. *Mules and Men,* 210.

11. Akasha (Gloria) Hull. "What Is It I Think She's Doing Anyway: A Reading of Toni Cade Bambara's 'The Salt Eaters,'" in Barbara Smith, ed. *Home Girls: A Black Feminist Anthology* (1983. New Brunswick, NJ: Rutgers UP, 2000), 124.

12. Jessie Fauset, who as literary editor of *The Crisis* championed Toomer's career, acknowledged that he was "a little inclined to achieve style at the expense of clearness." Quoted in Cheryl A. Wall. *Women of the Harlem Renaissance* (Bloomington: Indiana UP, 1995), 61.

13. *Those Bones Are Not My Child* (New York: Pantheon, 1999), 521. Subsequent citations to this edition will be noted parenthetically.

14. Toni Morrison. Preface to Toni Cade Bambara, *Deep Sightings and Rescue Missions* (New York: Pantheon, 1996), ix.

15. Bambara's approach differs dramatically from James Baldwin's in *The Evidence of Things Not Seen* (New York: Holt, Rinehart & Winston, 1985), which takes the events in Atlanta as a text for an impassioned sermon on the evils of racism and poverty. Baldwin writes as a witness to the Wayne Williams trial and its aftermath. In contrast, Bambara imagines the fully textured lives of the victims, their families, and their neighbors, particularly of those who were moved to act in response to the crimes.

16. As she had throughout her career, Bambara retained her commitment to writing "straight-up fiction." In the Acknowledgments to *Those Bones*, Bambara lists the dos, don'ts, and maybes that guided her as she wrote. First among the "don'ts: "treat real people as though they were fictional; it's rude, it's confusing, and it ought to be illegal." She notes that only one of the real people who are named in the novel is "an on-the-scene talking presence," and that is Atlanta Mayor Maynard Jackson, whose words are a matter of public record (672–673).

17. John Edgar Wideman. *Philadelphia Fire* (New York: Henry Holt, 1990); Charles Chesnutt, *The Marrow of Tradition*, was originally published in 1901.

18. Bambara. "What Is It," 155.

Writing from Laughter, Writing from Rage

"A Sort of Preface"

Toni Cade Bambara

It does no good to write autobiographical fiction cause the minute the book hits the stand here comes your mama screamin how could you and sighin death where is thy sting and she snatches you up out your bed to grill you about what was going down back there in Brooklyn when she was working three jobs and trying to improve the quality of your life and come to find on page 42 that you were messin around with that nasty boy up the block and breaks into sobs and quite naturally your family strolls in all sleepy-eyed to catch the floor show at 5:00 A.M. but as far as your mama is concerned, it is nineteen-forty-and-something and you ain't too grown to have your ass whipped.

And it's no use using bits and snatches even of real events and real people, even if you do cover, guise, switch-around and change-up cause next thing you know your best friend's laundry cart is squeaking past but your bell ain't ringing so you trot down the block after her and there's this drafty cold pressure front the weatherman surely did not predict and your friend says in this chilly way that it's really something when your own friend stabs you in the back with a pen and for the next two blocks you try to explain that the character is not her at all but just happens to be speaking one of her lines and right about the time you hit the laundromat and you're ready to just give it up and take the weight, she turns to you and says that seeing as how you have plundered her soul and walked off with a piece of her flesh, the least you could do is spin off half the royalties her way.

So I deal in straight-up fiction myself, cause I value my family and friends, and mostly cause I lie a lot anyway.

Straight-Up Fiction: Sitting Down with Toni Cade Bambara's Gorilla, My Love

SALAMISHAH TILLET

I wish I had met Toni Cade Bambara. I wish I had sat down with her and talked about the secret moments that little black girls soon-to-be grown black women soon-to-be elders know only of themselves and others like them. I wish I had learned then that those who live on the fringes, on the barest of corners, on the outskirts of society, create sacred spaces of their own: spaces of beautiful confusion and brilliant chaos, jazz spaces, *Color Purple* spaces, spaces where Girl–Women climb the trunks of rainbows, spaces where Women–Girls defy their invisibility and recover the lost meaning of self.

I wish I had met Toni Cade Bambara because she already knew me. She knew parts of my story, fragmented and funny, before I did. In her short-story collection *Gorilla, My Love,* she recalls the laughter, the awkwardness, and the stumbles of me and of all those like me; and of those who came before us and of those who walk after us, in brown and black bodies, pigtails hanging, braids too tight. If I had met Toni Cade Bambara, she would have pointed me toward a room of my own, told me that it was alright to just sit down and lose myself in the page, *in this very page*; and forewarned that my being black and woman and writerly made all the difference. And it is this difference which is the most beautiful thing of all.

When Little Black Girls Hold the World Upside Down and We Watch Them Win

In Toni Cade Bambara's short stories "Gorilla, My Love," "Raymond's Run," and "The Lesson," the three main characters, Scout, Hazel, and Sylvia, remind me of the little girls that so many of us were prevented from truly becoming: the types of girls who speak when not spoken to, see their bodies as limitless sites of power, and recognize the ceilings of oppression only after they have cracked its glass. We see little black girls like this every once in a while because they stand out brilliantly with their plaited hair, falling in the dirt, running with the boys and not away from them. Girls who scrap their knees so badly when they fall and who never ever pay heed to my mother's warning that we are compromising our god-given beauty by playing so hard. They find the streets more interesting than the stoops and the courts more stimulating than the dollhouse. When we see them, we *pray* they will soon outgrow this stage and become more ladylike because we all know that "ladies" are less vilified by patriarchy. We teach them that when they grow up they must not run in the streets but be afraid of them, especially at night when the boys they used to play with have all grown up, replacing their childhood games of "catch" with their new postures of manhood.

Yet what would these little girls whisper to us if we listen to their ways? What would they teach us about ourselves, about who we can be if we watch them win?

In these three short stories, Bambara tries to share their secrets with us. The first short story "Gorilla, My Love" is about a little girl, Hazel, nicknamed Scout, who witnesses the subtle betrayal that occurs in a world ruled by adults. In this story, Scout and her three brothers attend the local movie theater, the Washington, to see the film with the catchy title, *Gorilla, My Love*. Instead, the manager of the Washington plays the film *King of Kings*. In response to this abrupt and unannounced substitution, Scout leads a minor rebellion, in which the child-filled audience rejects the authority of the movie theater by "yellin, booin, stompin, and carryin on," (15). For Scout, the clumsy exchange of films from the mysteriously titled *Gorilla, My Love* to the all-too-well-known crucifixion story, *King of Kings*, symbolizes the paternalism of "grown-ups" who "figure they can just treat you anyhow" (15). In response to this cinematic sleight of hand, Scout confronts the manager and asks for her money back:

> So I kick the door open wider and just walk right by him and sit down and tell the man about himself and that I want my money back and that goes for Baby Jason and Big Brood too. And he still trying to shuffle me out the door even though I'm sittin which shows him for the fool he is . . . So he ain't getting up off the money. So I was forced to leave, takin the matches from under his ashtray, and set fire under the candy stand, which closed the raggedy ole Washington down for a week . . . Cause if you say Gorilla, My Love, you suppose to mean it. (17)

Here, Scout expresses her disappointment with the movie theater and its refusal to either play *Gorilla, My Love* or reimburse her for their false advertising. However, instead of quietly submitting to the manager's authority and watching the wrong film or subtly exiting the movie theater, Scout invents a new plot of honor and retaliation. As a child, Scout can neither lead a formal protest nor complain to a higher authority. Her only site of resistance is something as childlike and innocent as the candy stand. And when she sets it on fire, she engages in a fight against both movie industry greed and adult hypocrisy, ironically proving to herself and the world that corporate deceit has dire (even if only for a week) consequences.

In the short story "The Lesson," Bambara again takes up the theme of corporate avarice; however, here the ultimate moment of epiphany is not when the main character Sylvia is betrayed by an adult; rather it is when she recognizes that she has been betrayed by the larger society. The plot of the story "The Lesson" is simple enough. It begins in the predominately black world of Harlem and with Miss Moore who "was black as hell, 'cept for her feet, which were fish-white and spooky," taking a group of children into midtown Manhattan on a field trip to a toy store. However, by taking them to FAO Schwarz, Miss Moore enables the children to recognize the economic and racial disparity between the black Harlemites they see everyday and the wealthy whites who repeatedly shop for "toys" at this store. Like the candy stand in the story "Gorilla, My Love," toy store simultaneously embodies innocence and loss. When the children initially arrive at the toy store, they are unaware of their *invisibility* and socioeconomic inferiority. But as they read the various price tags on the toys, they quickly realize that their parents would never be able to afford these toys. The various toys include a microscope, a semiprecious-stone paperweight, and a fiberglass-handcrafted sailboat priced at $1,195. These Harlem children see these toys as impractical and too expensive, and Sylvia on learning the price of the toy sailboat exclaims: "That money should last forever... What I want to know is... how much a real boat costs? I figure a thousand get you a yacht any day" (92–93). Initially, when Sylvia assumes that a real boat costs less or as much as the toy boat, she asserts her agency through mocking disdain of the toy store. Unfortunately, Sylvia immediately deduces that her parents' inability to purchase this small toy boat also means that they could never afford a real boat. Ironically, it is in the make-believe world of FAO Schwarz that Sylvia's self-contained world of Harlem begins to crumble.

And yet in response to this glaring reality of race and class distinctions, Sylvia concludes that it will not "beat" her. Rather than remain at the store with the other children, Sylvia rejects the socio-economic authority of FAO Schwarz by running away from the store. However, as Sylvia runs toward Harlem she reinstates her all-black community as her epistemological center. And even though both Miss Moore and Bambara's more worldly readers know, she will eventually have to confront the limitations set forth and symbolized in FAO Schwarz, for a brief moment Sylvia chooses to defy those limitations, run home to Harlem, and never look back.

While running away connotes defiance in "The Lesson," in "Raymond's Run" it also represents opposition and solidarity. The story "Raymond's Run" chronicles the adventures of Hazel Elizabeth Dorothy Parker and her brother Raymond. Hazel is a sprinter who annually wins at the May Day Races but who must now defeat a new and equally talented competitor named Gretchen. Hazel is of course nervous before each race, but that anxiety is always tempered by the fact that she could beat anyone or anything that stood in her way. Her invincibility climaxes when her older brother Raymond is threatened. She tells us, "if anybody has anything to say about Raymond, anything to say about his big head, they have to come by me. And I don't play the dozens or believe in standing around with somebody doing a lot of talking. I much rather just knock you down and take my chances" (23). Even with the seeming handicaps of size and weight, Hazel uses her body to defend her brother and herself against the blows of the outside world. But as you read the story, you can't help wondering, where in the world did this little black girl learn that she could use her body to fight injustice?

Perhaps Hazel worshipped Wilma Rudolph. Or maybe she did what I did, and simply always wanted to be the fastest, boldest, girl-soon-to-be-woman body out there on gravel. I suppose my being the only girl on the winter track team in high school made Hazel even spectacular to me. At the age of thirteen, I *should* have known that boys always are faster than girls. That we should not and cannot play on the same courts, tracks, and fields as our opposite sex. And yet, somehow I missed that lesson and kept on running, until finally, in the dead of winter, I learned never to think that I am less than a boy because someone somewhere told him that he was better than me. Similarly, even within the confines of male privilege, Hazel always believes that she is the baddest runner out there and always knows that the only person who could beat her, and *only* on a good day, is her father.

It is only when Hazel meets her main competitor for the May Day races, Gretchen, that she begins to doubt herself:

"I always win because I'm the best," I say straight at Gretchen... Gretchen smiles, but it's not a smile, and I'm thinking that girls never really smile at each other because they don't know how and don't want to know how and there's probably no one to teach us how, cause grown-up girls don't know either." (27)

Hazel's insight reveals that there are inexplicable silences between her and Gretchen that translate into a smile. The blank space between them longs for the knowledge, that essential ingredient, that will help them reaffirm the humanity of the other. And yet how does one smile when the word girl is synonymous with prohibitions, limitations, and vulnerabilities. Hazel's mother would rather Hazel finally "act like a girl for a change" (27) and participate in the May Pole dance rather than in the May Day races. And for Hazel, "act like a girl" means liking dolls, the color pink, or dresses. Unfortunately, too many of us heard that same restricting expression as we tried to be ourselves. I especially heard these words when I would dress in pants for Sunday morning Baptist church and was sent back to my room to change. I always argued that God probably didn't care what I wore, but I lost my moral crusade to church-sanctioned skirts. I then, as Hazel thinks now, felt that our mothers should "be glad her daughter ain't out there prancing around the May Pole getting the new clothes all dirty and sweaty and trying to act like a fairy or a flower or whatever you're supposed to be when you should be trying to be yourself" (27). To be yourself, to be ourselves, means being the type of girl we wanted to be rather than the type of girls that our mothers and grandmothers, in their most protective gaze, hoped we would be. If girl means being something that every girl is not, then how could we smile at someone else when we weren't even allowed to smile at ourselves? It is only when Hazel and Gretchen compete that Hazel gains knowledge that her rival Gretchen is "good, no doubt about it" (32). Although Hazel wins the race, she and Gretchen find mutual admiration and learn how to smile:

> We stand there with this big smile of respect between us. It's about as real a smile as girls can do for each other, considering we don't practice real smiling every day, you know, cause maybe we too busy being flowers or fairies or strawberries instead of being honest and worthy of respect... you know... like being people. (32)

The true victory here is not Hazel's individual medal; it is that she and Gretchen have learned to bow and to smile to each other in love and support. To recognize that standing across from you is your mirror, yourself; with different strides, different tastes; but confronted with the same painful reality that growing up black, and female, is not an easy race.

On the Bridge of Our Teenage Backs

Thanks to the feminist movement, the war for the chastity belts has been on a steady decline. Women and girls continually feel more comfortable articulating their own sexual needs and desires. Our sexual liberation consistently asks us to re-define the word and the act of SEX. Slowly but surely we form new sexual battles over reproductive rights, same-sex unions, and the right to refuse. Ironically, as we painstakingly name our bodies as ours, the black female body continues to be paraded on BET, MTV, and *Flava of Love* in the tradition of the Black jezebel and whore. We are taught that our desirability is directly linked to our accessibility, and that the ideal is to be both a lady on the streets and a freak in the bed. Within this labyrinth, black girls must create even more resilient sexual egos. I remember the first time I learned what sex was: I mean real sex, not the type that my parents would tell me about using polysyllabic terms like spermatozoa and fallopian tubes; but the kind of sex that my parents wished I didn't have until I was *happily* married; the type of sex they forgot to teach you about in sex health; the sex that takes place in the adolescent mind, uncensored, unknowing, and utterly curious. Not necessarily what Lil' Kim, Shawna, and Trina rhyme about, because I did not know those parts of my body existed. I learned what sex was on a bus ride home from school from the words of a young classmate of mine who had been having sex since ninth grade. She told me in short words what she and her boyfriend did at least three times a week—in our classrooms, parties, and sometimes if they were really lucky, in her bedroom. I suppose it was her graphic description, that ever-so-seductive fruit of knowledge that sparked my interest. I suddenly wanted to try what I had learned with somebody somewhere. And it is this unbridled curiosity that plagued me during the summer before I went to college that Bambara both encourages and warns against in the short story "Sweet Town."

In "Sweet Town," the adolescent character Kit confesses that she lost her virginity to B.J. when she was fifteen years old. The story itself is a testimonial of sexual self-discovery: "My mother calls it sex and my brother says it's groin fever time. But then, they were always ones for brevity. Anyway that's the way it was. And in this spring race, the glands always win and the muses and the brain core must step aside to ride in the trunk with the spare tire. It was during this sweet and drugged time that I met B.J. ... " (122). Kit falls in love with B.J., and as he departs she longs to find their sweetness again. When he announces that he and his friend Eddie are taking off for the West Coast, she recreates the *Romeo and Juliet* balcony scene. Instead of declaring his eternal love, B.J. states, "It's been real great. The summer and you... but... maybe next summer" (124–25). The seasons, like their love, are temporal and transitory. While Kit intends to proclaim her undying passion for her B.J. and that she is "great, talented, good-looking and going to college at fifteen" (125), she actually just reveals her anger and calls his friend Eddie a "shithead" (126). In one fast motion, Kit falls from the cliffs of romanticism to the brute reality of waste and "shit" in which first love is dramatically betrayed. As B.J. leaves Kit, she resolves, "Days other than the here and now, I told myself, will be dry and sane and sticky with the rotten apricots oozing slowly in the sweet time of my betrayed youth" (126). "Sweet Town" now symbolizes the simultaneous innocence and loss of Kit's female adolescence; a place of former comfort and present experience; a knowledge of sex and its consequences, of what happens when young girls are drugged with the nectar of their own bodies, the smells of the other, inside and outside of themselves. Sadly, I never had the "Sweet Town" balcony scene, just a few words of consolation and a peck on the cheek saying "maybe I'll see you on campus some time."

For me, being a teenager was the most impossible stage to survive. By survive, I mean to get through the day-to-clay realities of body spurts, social clicks, and mad family drama; articulated silences; articulated shouts; articulated politics; unarticulated self. All of those things appear to be subsumed by age and gender and inexperience. Your friends partly listen to you. Your parents listen to themselves bounce off of you. And you struggle with trusting your own inner voice. And within all of this, you gain the knowledge of peer pressure, anti-drug campaigns, and sex. So the impossibility of it all occurs each time you look into the mirror, daring you to take the next step.

The next step, of course, is breaking silence with voice. Like the fifteen-year-old narrator in the short story "The Basement" who testifies that her best friend Patsy lies about sex. Patsy constantly confesses that she "did it on the roof with James Lee" (147) in an unsuccessful attempt to prove her self-worth. Patsy not only testifies to her own sexual experiences but also lies that the apartment building superintendent regularly sexually harasses her and her friends. When Patsy tells her mother of the superintendent's alleged exploits, she appears to break the building's silence around the sexual behavior of older men toward young girls. In response to her confession, Patsy's mother then proceeds to beat up the "flasher" superintendent, and he is temporarily marked as an assailant. The narrator warns the reader "to stay out of Patsy way 'cause she sex crazy and talk nasty'" (145). This warning automatically challenges Patsy's narrative authority. Each time Patsy describes her sexual encounters, the narrator undermines her story: "Patsy scared too cause she always makin up stuff on top of the real stuff" (145). The real stuff is the layer that the narrator chooses to share and speak out against Patsy's multilayered lies. The narrator chooses to speak for herself and "just tell her [mother] the truth and take the weight and let it go" (147). The truth that she visited Patsy, that Patsy lied, and that "Patsy Mother is beatin the hell out the super" (147). But what she does not confess, what she "leaves out" (147) is that "Patsy pulled her drawers down and her dress up and put her hand there" (147) in a desperate attempt for friendship. She leaves it out because it only confirms the absurdity and crazy talk of Patsy of which her mother warned her. While the narrator omits this episode to her mother, she does admit it to the reader and ends the story with this image. Through this articulation, she not only disrupts Patsy's narrative but also reveals her unexplored sexual curiosity. On one hand, Patsy represents the overtly sexual girl that the narrator wants to distance herself from; yet on the other hand, she also symbolizes the sexual spaces that the narrator longs for but is afraid to enter and claim. As such, "The Basement" reveals those uncomfortable moments of adolescent female sexuality—when we are both uncertain of our desires and driven by some unforeseen need to search through another, the taste, the touch, and the smell of our own humanity.

When the Other Mother is the Self

Many of the stories in *Gorilla, My Love* describe black girls and women whose individuality and nonconformity lead to their heroism and marginality. Yet, in the short stories "The Survivor" and "The Johnson Girls," the main female characters can only find their individuality within a larger community of black women "other mothers." Our other mothers are not mothers in the strict sense of the word. They are not biologically ours but are required for our survival. They were our beauty-parlor poets, our aunts, and our mothers' sister-friends. They used to sit up late crying and laughing with one another when they thought we were sleeping and confess the sins of their husbands and their fathers to one another. They would tell us how beautiful and trifling we were in the very same breath. These were black women friends who loved one another more honestly and intimately than they loved anyone else. They were understood only by one another and bringing daughter-spirits into the world.

In the story "The Survivor" the "Other Mother" characters Miss Candy and Miss Cathy help deliver Jewel and her baby into the world. Because the story travels back and forth between fantasy and reality within the mind of the main character Jewel, the story splits our own consciousness in half. While Jewel tries to compress the memory of her late husband Paul, her pregnancy and acting career into one tightly woven narrative, she cannot. She is unable to avoid both the pain of these memories and of her present situation. For example, she tries to leave out "once, after their fiercer arguments ... he broke the caps off her two front teeth" (101) or that "he had told her that he'd been right in the first place. She should've gotten rid of the kid in the beginning" (109). Jewel tries to supplant her abuse with suffocating silence in which she mourns the loss of her violent husband rather than grieves for her abused body. Although Paul's fatal car accident plagues the beginning of the story, Jewel's own story of healing emerges once she enters the home of her grandmother, Miss Candy. Her healing begins when Miss Candy confronts Jewel:

> "Tell me something, Jewel," said Miss Candy, perching herself on the edge of the couch so she was in profile and not looking at her. "Why did you stay on with him after so long?... Like I said to Cathy... when a woman lives with a man for ten years she is not being abused. You understand what I'm saying, yes? How do feel... about it all? You mustn't blame yourself. People always do of course. That's what it means to be the survivor." (109–110)

When Miss Candy tells Jewel that she was not abused because she stayed with Paul for ten years, she forces the wife/actress Jewel to understand that she had some agency even in the confines of her financial and professional dependence on her husband/film director Paul. Miss Candy also provides refuge for Jewel, for she is the first person to name Jewel a "survivor." Miss Candy creates a space in which Jewel can drape her body in wool blankets, hot soup, and premarital memories. The time before Jewel was a survivor. And the time in which she hears herself laughing. As "Other Mothers" Miss Candy and Jewel's niece, Miss Cathy, not only help Jewel heal but also deliver her baby. The baby represents Jewel's own rebirth in which she will revel in herself and not subjugate that self to Paul. In her daydream, as she delivers the baby, Jewel imagines herself as a film director who witnesses her own journey to the water underworld. With the lenses of her self and her two other mothers, Jewel can now envision a self-sustaining community in which one of the few ways to survive is to choose to be reborn.

And that is just what my friends and I thought we were creating, a community of self-sustained women, when my best friend walked in on her boyfriend having sex with another woman. We rallied around her and spit out lyrical words that buried his tales of dishonesty. Like Kit, we were no longer virginal and adolescent and curious. Like Jewel, we were primed for the betrayals of adulthood. Man leaves. Woman cries. Not quite "Other Mothers," sistah-friends shake heads in disbelief, not sure where to go from here. Girl–women ready to fight? And with whom? Sistah-friends holding one another's hands and wrestling forgiveness out of one another's hearts. Looking to Bambara's "The Johnson Girls" for sound advice.

The Johnson Girls soothe their sister Inez when her partner, Roy, leaves her. The story is the last in the collection because it is the culmination of all the female voices in the preceding stories. They are the chorus and invite the readers into an expression of female agency and solidarity. The solidarity reaches its peak with Roy's absence. When Roy leaves only a note for Inez saying that he has left for Knoxville, the Johnson Girls commune as Inez packs to visit him there. The Johnson Girls are not there to deter her from her chase; rather they are there to help her recognize and acknowledge her choice. Even as they respect her choice, each sister shares her insight into Roy and the larger community of men:

> "First, you gotta have a fuckin man, a cat that can get down between the sheets without a whole lotta bullshit about 'This spiritual union' or 'Women are always rippin off my body' or... "
>
> "Amen," says Marcy.
>
> "Course he usually look like hell and got no I.Q. atall," say Sugar.
>
> "So you gots to have a go-around man, a dude that can put in a good appearance so you won't be shame to take him round your friends, case he insist on opening his big mouth... "
>
> Course the go-round man ain't about you, he about his rap and his wardrobe and his imported deodorant stick with the foreign in-gredients listed there at the bottom in some unknown tongue. Which means you gots to have a gofor."
>
> ... "Like when you crazy with pain and totally messed around and won't nobody on earth go for your shit, you send for the gofor cause he go for it whatever it is."
>
> ... "You gots to have your money man, that goes without saying. And more importantly, you got to have you tender man." (168)

The tender man differs from all of the other types of men because he is the only man that is not substitutable. The tender man may be "painting your bedroom a dumb shade of orange, cause just so happens that you need that dumb shade of orange in your life right now. Or holding your head while you heave your insides into the toilet" (169); he is the mixture of charm, loyalty and intimacy and is the blue-plate special in the Johnson Girls discourse. Roy, though missing, is posited as the tender man, a "rare bird" (176) who deserves "the super heavy plottin" (176) to reconcile him and Inez. As each woman lists her different types of man, she engages in a call-and-response with the other Johnson girls and with the larger narrative of the book. They call to each of the female characters to form a private space of women-voices in which they create and mold themselves and the men who surround them. This list can only be found in the secret conversations women have behind the backs of men. In the pages of our communal journals. In the nightly conversations which sistah-women note because many of us have imagined boy–men like these before. All of these men exist in Bambara's stories in one form or another. However, her stories focus not on them but on themes of female solidarity and independence. The Johnson Girls believe in Roy and Inez because they "need a Nez and Roy in life to keep the blue-plate special on the horizon" (177); the blue-plate special is the fantasy of forever and love and commitment. But it is also the fantasy of self-preservation, self-contradictions, and self-love. As we did, they seem to base their communal strength in what seems like a desperate male-centered hour of need but in fact found themselves carrying each other through the laughter of their own love.

We End Where We Begin

The short story collection *Gorilla, My Love* begins with the short story "My Man Bovanne," which is about a sixty-one-year-old woman, Miss Hazel, who dances with her blind neighbor, Mr. Bovanne, at a neighborhood fundraiser. Bambara begins the collection with the voice of an elder to shape the larger narrative of black woman exclusion and resistance. Miss Hazel dances with Mr. Bovanne, even though her adult children chastise her because he is a "tom" whose "feet can smell a cracker a mile away and go into their shuffle number post haste"(6). For her children, her dance partner compromises the integrity of their post-civil-rights Black Power struggles. Her dance, which eventually leads to her apartment, indicates her sexual independence because she continues to dance with Mr. Bovanne in spite of the glaring eyes of the onlookers. As Miss Hazel leaves the party with Mr. Bovanne, whose blindness hides him from seeing the contempt of her children, Miss Hazel reflects that she is "just like the hussy my daughter always say I was" (10). To be a hussy here means to be sexually free, in control of one's body and able to assert that control at all times. Miss Hazel invites Mr. Bovanne into her home as an act of resistance and an exercise of choice. Bearing the name Miss Hazel, she appears to be the grown-up Hazel of "Raymond's Run" and brings the young Hazel's budding characteristics of outspokenness, refusal, and truth telling to maturity. She leaves the party, politics in one hand, Mr. Bovanne on the other.

While Bambara begins the book with this short story, I chose to end this essay on *Gorilla, My Love* with "My Man Bovanne" because I wanted to trace the trajectory of black womanhood from girl to teenager to adult woman to older woman. The book follows each stage of female development by highlighting the journey of protagonists to find comfort and solace in their courageous individuality. A journey that we as readers are invited to witness and experience. A moment in time in which we are allowed to sit down with

Toni Cade Bambara and laugh and sigh like never before. She tells us that we are still brilliant, and beautiful, and visible.

I learned a lot from sitting down with Toni Cade Bambara. I learned that traveling to and from our sister souls can be pleasant and difficult all in one breath. That there are black girl–women who long for another world in which there are new rules of inclusion, and difference, and faith. One in which we can come in all forms and still be considered human. And equal. And free. Only in the coded language of her stories did I learn the secret of my own woman-self.

Hussy. Outsider. Runner. Writer. Actress. Johnson Girl.
Hazel. Sylvia. Jewel. Inez. Scout. Kit.
All parts of each other.
Are made into a whole woman.
Black woman.

There to keep one another sane. In the middle of muffled chaos.
Threads holding each closer than ever before.
Burnt on the sheaf of narrative sounds.
Beginning in the end.

Moving in and out of our reader heads with victory dances.
Never looking back to see who we were supposed to be.

5

Searching for the Mother Tongue: An Interview with Toni Cade Bambara

KALAMU YA SALAAM

Kalamu ya Salaam [KS]: Are you consciously trying to do anything particular with your style of writing?

Toni Cade Bambara [TCB]: I'm trying to learn how to write! I think there have been a lot of things going on in the Black experience for which there are no terms, certainly not in English, at this moment. There are a lot of aspects of consciousness for which there is no vocabulary, no structure in the English language which would allow people to validate that experience through language. I'm trying to find a way to do that.

KS: Do you see yourself, then, essentially in search of a language?

TCB: That's one of the things I'm trying to do.

KS: Why hasn't this happened before? Do you think other writers have tried to do this and been unsuccessful?

TCB: I don't know. I do know that the English language that grew from the European languages has been systematically stripped of the kinds of structures and the kinds of vocabularies that allow people to plug into other kinds of intelligences. That's no secret. That's part of their whole history, wherein people cannot be a higher sovereign than the state. At the time when wise folk were put to the rack was also a time when books were burned, temples razed to the ground, and certain types of language "mysteries" for lack of a better word—were suppressed. That's the legacy of the West.

I'm just trying to tell the truth, and I think in order to do that we will have to invent, in addition to new forms, new modes and new idioms. I think we will have to connect to language in that kind of way. I don't know yet what it is.

KS: Do you see any models of any path breakers?

TCB: I think most poets play with that. I think musicians are far more successful with their language. It's become an obsession with me now. I'm trying to break words open and get at the bones, deal with symbols as if they were atoms. I'm trying to find out not only how a word gains its meaning, but how a word gains its power.

KS: Do you see a difference between writers trying to deal with their craft, with words which are part of their craft, and your attempt, and the attempt of other writers, to create a written language in English that can express the African American experience? Is it simply a technical question dealing with craft or . . . ?

TCB: No, I don't think it's a technical question. It's beyond a technical question. I don't know what the term is for that kind of exploration, that kind of obsession, that kind of quest.

KS: Have you seen any examples of this in other writers of the Third World, particularly the decolonized Third Word?

TCB: Amos Tutola, for example, for the kinds of areas he is exploring, has to invent, has to mediate between whatever language is characteristic of the way he moves in the universe and that other language, the colonial language. That's true of anybody dealing in a language other than their mother tongue, obviously.

KS: Strictly from the African American experience, in your opinion what language would be our mother tongue?

TCB: The language of Langston Hughes, the language of Grandma, the language of "mama say." Mama say don't let cha mouth get you into what, *etc. etc.*

KS: What problems have you had with publishers and editors in getting them to accept this search for a new language. With *The Salt Eaters,* were there any problems with . . . ?

TCB: No, the problems are with me in terms of my own editing. When I edit, I have to decide whether I'm editing for readability or am I editing for that questing. Sometimes I have to compromise or play games.

KS: What does that mean?

TCB: Sometimes it's necessary to edit for readability, in which case I have to let go.

KS: In other words, to maintain a bridge to the audience you have to pull back a bit?

TCB: Yeah.

KS: But, you didn't have any problems with the editors or publishers?

TCB: No. Well, they raise the usual kind of copy editing questions such as, "Do you mean to drop the 'g' off of doing; is this a typo or is it an expression of your community; is this a 'coined' phrase or does it have currency?"

KS: Which is interesting because usually when they say "coined phrase" they mean it's counterfeit, whereas if it has current usage, if it's commonly in use they say it has currency.

TCB: Yeah. Like the word artifice; to make art is to be phony.

KS: When you were doing *The Salt Eaters*, in the process of actually writing it, did you at any time consider yourself in a state of altered consciousness?

TCB: I think that when I write at any time I'm in a state of altered consciousness in the sense that I am self-remembering; that is, I'm acutely aware of a dialogue that is going on between me and characters which are conjured. I am acutely aware of myself as a reader. I actually am aware of the relationship between what's going on in my head and what I can do with my hands, and that is not the state that I normally walk around and fry the eggs in.

KS: How do you prepare yourself for that?

TCB: Sit down and be still. Unplug the phone and be quiet.

KS: Do you do any type of research for your fiction?

TCB: Not in any conscious, deliberate sort of way, but I'm reading all the time, and traveling a lot . . . I jot down notes. Sometimes I will pursue . . . for example, the original manuscript of *The Salt Eaters* was a short story about a Mardi Gras society that elects to reenact an old slave insurrection [. . .]. Some of the characters began speaking Portuguese; I don't speak Portuguese. I had originally set it in some place like New Orleans, or kind of like Galveston (Texas), and the scene shifted, so I went with it and wrote it out. I then found I needed to verify what this was. In about three months I began to do a lot of reading on Palmares and felt maybe that was where the story was going to take place except I don't have any . . . (interrupting herself) there are no words. I was going to say "control," but that presupposes I was trying to get control and I don't, so that's not the word, but, get a "handle" on it, that's the best way to say it. Sometimes I will do that kind of research. As a rule, I don't do a lot of research.

There's a scene in *The Salt Eaters* where Nilda, the sister of the corn, was thinking about Barnwell and about the jackrabbits—contaminated, radioactive and glowing in the dark. I thought that this was a good metaphor and a nice image but I seriously doubted if radioactive animals glow. So, I had to look that up and found that they didn't. But I liked the image, so I figured, well, I'm just going to go ahead and keep it.

This thing I'm working on now requires a great deal of research. I'm trying to put together a Harper's Ferry script. I've never been satisfied with the movies, particularly Hollywood versions . . .

KS: That reference you have to Harper's Ferry in *The Salt Eaters*—does that have anything to do with this project?

TCB: Yes. That's to remind myself of what I'm doing next. I've had a hunch for a long time that Mama Pleasant and Marie Laveau, in addition to the work they did that we know of, I have a feeling that they had put together an intelligence network and were very much into the underground railroad. Nobody has documented that yet. I keep waiting and throwing it out there, hoping that someone else will go and do the research. I'm researching that now and that requires a lot of time.

I'm not a good researcher. I'm a good research teacher because I'm a detective and I'm nosey. I'm willing to go anywhere to get the information. But I'm not a trustworthy researcher because I reconstruct and most reconstructing means fictionalizing.

KS: Fictionalizing in the sense that you use the basic events to create a new or future scenario?

TCB: More than that. I lie. I make jump cuts, absolute leaps.

KS: Does that have anything to do with your interest in film?

TCB: Yeah, but I didn't mean to say "jump cut," I meant to say quantum leaps. For example, with Mama Pleasant, she had a girl, a laundry worker, who pops up in a couple of other people's diaries as being retarded. Yet, Mama Pleasant used to send her far afield. She was in Lawrence, Kansas, at one time, and she was in another place in Kansas. Around that time John Brown's raids broke out. I have the feeling that Mama Pleasant bankrolled John Brown's raids. So, in my research, I'm looking just for that one thing to confirm this so I can forget about it and do my work. That's not research.

KS: Actually, you're already looking for something to validate a conclusion you have already made rather than just gathering information.

TCB: Right.

KS: Ideally, what would you like *The Salt Eaters* to accomplish?

TCB: Based on the kind of feedback that I've gotten from letters and phone calls, more than the reviews—only since Jerry (Ward) and a few others have started writing have "folk" been giving me some critical feedback: the reviewers in *Newsweek* and *Time* and *The New Yorker* have not been particularly intelligent or informed—but the feedback I've gotten from writers, I would say younger writers but rather up-and-coming writers, is that *The Salt Eaters* breaks new ground. For people who live with a comfortable molding of the physical and the metaphysical but don't know how to talk about it yet, and don't know whether they have to find a metaphor for talking about spirit, vibes, for talking about what people call psychic phenomena or whatever, they have called up to say, "Hey, you handled it in a kind of nonchalant way. I feel better. I'll just go head and do it."

The other thing, I think is more important, is that there are three kinds of calls I'm making in *The Salt Eaters* through the three institutions in Claybourne that are governed by Black people. In the Academy of the Seven Arts, Obie is attempting to bridge the gap between our medicine people and our warriors, and that's a call. I don't think it's terribly important whether I got it nailed in the book. I explore it, I bring it up, but I don't have anywhere to put it or push it. But I think, if it's done by organizers then that's the accomplishment. The other kind of call through the seven sisters is that they are obviously bridging the...

KS: Third World gap.

TCB: Yeah, that, but also the political worldview and the artistic worldview, which has always been a tradition in our community. They are obviously reaching also for Third World coalitions, which is the struggle we really haven't explored. When we talk about coalitions, it always seems to be about Black and white. I think that's a real waste. So, that's another kind of call. And, three, is the Southwest Community Infirmary. Those workers are attempting to merge the best of so-called traditional medicine with the most humane of so-called modern medicine.

When you say, "What am I trying to accomplish?" I think the questions I'm raising or the gaps I'm pointing to become an assignment, so to speak, for community organizers. If that message is clear to people who work on the streets and who work with groups, then I've accomplished what I set out to do.

KS: Looking at those three calls briefly, there have been attempts and some successes at Third World coalitions. And having traveled throughout the Third World yourself, I'm sure you know that in the Third World there are a lot of people who feel an affinity for the struggles of African Americans and in the case of people such as Robert Williams, that affinity has been an actual working together. With that in mind, do you think that part of your call for what is needed is a validation that this is not something that is foreign to our experience? In other words, we are not asking people to do something new...

TCB: ...that's so strange. Right. Because, certainly there has been with the runaway captives...

KS: The Seminoles...

TCB: Yes, the Seminoles. During the Sixties we had the Young Lords and the Panthers on the East Coast, and Asian student unions working with the Black student unions and that kind of thing, but I'm trying to get at something a little more than that. It's not only a common...well, it's not only a call to unite to wrath or to unite to vision, but there's also an awful lot in our own cosmology that is so similar that it's really striking. That suggests to me that if the warriors and the medicine people were merged that you would tap into a potential that is stunning.

KS: So, you're saying then that you're not calling for a union of two different groups, but rather a recognition of the commonness in the two? Going to the question of merging of the warriors and the healers, is this part of the meaning of the Korean masseur in the Academy of the Seven Arts?

TCB: He functions in a number of ways. Everything in the book, the way it's structured, the avoidance of a linear thing in favor of a kind of jazz suite, the numerous characters, the potter and the masseur, everything becomes a kind of metaphor for the whole. We have to put it all together. It deals with all the senses and also different kinds of ways to meditate, different ways to tap into the center. The masseur, in my mind, is the other half of the potter, in the sense that to raise the clay you've got to get the clay centered. The potter's wheel is part of the whole discussion of circles, prayer circles and being in a circle. The masseur says, "My dance is the meditation." He's trying to get Obie center[ed] as Obie keeps sliding all around the table. It's just another way at trying to get at the need to get centered. It's repeated throughout the book.

When Velma is in the marshes and she thinks how did she get there, she was talking to Jamahl whose answers to the so-called problem always lie in someone else's culture. She is convinced that the trip is in the people and it's to stay centered in your own best traditions that will keep you in touch with the best of yourself.

KS: Which goes back to the point that you're not actually calling for a coalition as much as a recognition of commonness. For some people, the attempt at a coalition has resulted in a denial of self and adoption of a whole alien culture.

TCB: of someone else's interests, someone else's agenda.

KS: Which is exactly the opposite of what you're calling for?

TCB: Right.

KS: Do you think fiction is the most effective way to do this?

TCB: I don't think fiction is the most effective way to do it. The most effective way to do it, *is to do it*!

KS: Well, what makes you think that fiction is an effective way to lay this call out there? For example, why didn't you write an essay?

TCB: Because I don't know how to write an essay, seriously. It's not that I think literature is a "deep, paramount tool for transformation," but I think it has potency and it's what I know how to do. Literature is what I do.

It took me a long time to get around to that. I never thought... well, writing seemed like a frivolous way to participate in struggle. It wasn't really until I went to Cuba—although I certainly had been writing for years and publishing for years, and taking some things rather seriously, and being embarrassed about the amount of time I used to spend trying to learn how to write—but in Cuba everything was confirmed. People made me look at what I already knew about the power of the word, which is something I certainly knew, having grown up on 125th Street and Seventh Avenue. I think it was in 1973 when I really began to realize that this was a perfectly legitimate way to participate in struggle. I don't have to be out there running in the streets or at the barricades. This counts too.

KS: So then, to talk about your career as a writer, this phase is more than just a search for a new language, it's a search for a language to be able to say something meaningful...

TCB: ...to enlarge a certain kind of vision that I've been getting at in little pieces. From *Gorilla* to *Seabirds* was a five-year span. In that five years a lot happened. I went to Cuba, I went to Vietnam. I got more deeply into community organizing. I got a certain amount of miseducation behind me and got a more serious kind of self-education. I think what is most noticeable in the widening of the lens is that in *Gorilla* those kids share with us those lessons that they learned on the block as though we the reader and writer were neighbors on the block. When I get to *Seabirds,* I'm looking at more than that. I'm looking at those forces that impact on us, particularly socioeconomic and political forces. But then, by the time I get to *Salt,* which is a two-year difference, I'm not satisfied with just the physical forces. I want to look at all the forces that impact.

KS: One person I know commented that there no white people in the novel, which is not quite true.

TCB: ...no, it's not...

KS: But that was the sense they got. I also got a sense that this was a very expansive but still interior sort of conversation or meditation. What you were talking about was not so much what others do to us and how others do it to us, but rather what we must do for ourselves.

TCB: Yes.

KS: The colonial response: first, you have colonialism and then you have anticolonialism, which is still not affirmative of yourself because you're just reacting to your oppression and are still using colonialism as a reference.

TCB: I think that's the politics of despair and I don't ascribe to that at all. There was something before colonialism and there is something that persists in spite of it. It's that core that interests me. Colonialism was just a moment in our history. It's a very temporary thing.

KS: What you're saying then is that as long as we consider colonialism the major aspect of our reality we have in fact missed.

TCB: ...we have in fact collaborated...

KS: ...with colonialism because then we are implicitly saying that's where our history started...

TCB: ...saying that this is our reality. It's not our reality. One of the things that...I think it's Fred the bus driver, who is very much off-center but there have been enough people in his life to kind of spin him back, well, he's thinking about Jimmy Lyons. Jimmy Lyons would say, "colored people,

Negro people are fours." The thing about fours is that if they invest too much time looking at how they are boxed in on all four sides they never look up and know that they can build upward. To constantly be looking at those four sides is to stay in prison, is to collaborate with your captors, indeed, is to lend them energy, which is the same thing as providing them with the power to keep you locked in.

KS: In our music there has always, at certain points, been innovators who have provided the key which, once that key is presented, we can go to another level...

TCB: They broke it open, yeah. That is characteristic of our everything here. You don't accept the constraints. You try to break past. Coleman Hawkins picks up the sax and rescues it from the vaudeville nonsense role that it was supposed to play. He liberates the sax from that role. He had to liberate the instrument from its own constraints in order to break something open. Jimmy Blanton picks up the bass and he opens it up for everybody. It's a whole new thing.

KS: Yeah, there're more than three octaves.

TCB: It's a whole new thing. That's true of everything. It's true of the music; it's true of our literature.

KS: The question I'm getting at is: do you think that, because of some very real constraints which were not spoken to directly enough in the late Sixties and early Seventies, do you think that it will be some of the women writers who will knock the hardest at trying to find some of these keys?

TCB: I don't know but I'm somewhat interested in what Black women and other women, particularly young women... I'm interested in that particular voice and stance that they're trying to find. I think that perhaps they have a greater stake in trying to find a new vocabulary of images...

KS: ...in making change.

TCB: Yeah. I think they have a really tremendous contribution to make because no one else has their vantage point. No one moves in the universe quite that way, in all the silences that have operated in the name of don't know what: "peace," "unity," and some other kind of bogus and ingratiating thing...

KS: You mean from the self-silences to the "shut-ups!"

TCB: Yeah. Yeah. Once you break that silence, then anything is possible. There's no telling where it might go. It's stunning, it's very stunning.

KS: My evidence of that and the data I'm building on is not simply what has happened in literature or the case with *The Salt Eaters,* but also if you look at film, particularly what happened with Cuban film where it was Sara Gomez (a Black lower-class Cuban woman filmmaker) who really...

TCB: ...broke that open. Yeah.

KS: It is the Third World woman of color; in fact the lower-class Third World woman of color who has, after all the various liberation movements have gone on through the late Sixties and Seventies...who still remains oppressed and exploited and whose voice is still not fully heard.

TCB: Yes. They have the greatest stake in finding a new mode, a new idiom...

KS: ...a new language.

TCB: Yeah.

KS: And we will all benefit from it.

TCB: Right.

KS: Thank you.

Commentary

In her novel *The Salt Eaters,* Toni Cade Bambara touches us. She addresses themes and discussions which are necessary to be raised if we as people are ever to reach the higher levels of love and life that some of us try to attain. The questing for language is a central issue confronted by Toni's book.

Peter Nazareth, an Ugandan of East Indian ancestry, in an essay entitled "Afterword: Toward Third World Literature," wrote, "In order to survive, Black people in the United States had to use every resource at their disposal, preserving their African folk traditions underground and having to 'mask' their intentions, having to use the language in a way 'The Man' would not understand." Toni believes that this language that Nazareth describes is the African American mother tongue. However, the problem is how to transform what is predominantly an oral language into a written language. This has been a major, although often unacknowledged, preoccupation of *nationalist-*oriented, African American writers.

Achieving a written language is not simply about duplication, or even about "replication," of the language we *hear* in our communities and neighborhoods. Because, like our music, as of this moment there is no adequate form of written notation which can fully render our sound to paper. The struggle of the committed African American writer is to create the written forms that can adequately translate the reality and visions, the past, present, and hoped-for future, into black and white on the page.

In an effort to give "currency" to our mother tongue and its "folksy" essence, some of our writers have taken to attempting to write in a way that mimics or mirrors African American speech. This process, at one time called "dialect," is characteristic not only of African American literature but also characteristic of most of the literature of African people who have been colonized in the Western hemisphere whenever diasporan-African writers attempted to give *voice* or *be the voice* of the particular people from which they originate.

In the United States, the most frequently cited paradigm of this process and style of writing was the "negro" verse of Paul L. Dunbar. During the sixties, trying to get down to it, we would "be" droppings g's and adopting a ditty-bopping style which was better understood and appreciated when *heard* than simply *read*. The elliptical spelling and speechlike patterns of Ntozake Shange are probably the best-known example of seventies dialect writing. But words change; sounds change; tempo, rhythm, and the gestures associated with talk: all of that changes; thus, I suggest that "dialect" alone has only a surface relationship to the actual quest for the mother tongue, for an African American language.

In the Caribbean and in Central and South America, this process, the use of "dialect," generally is referred to as using the local *"patois."* The *patois* is generally the Africanization of the colonial language. What is sometimes referred to as " Black English" is actually African American *patois*.

In a context within which the use of African languages was strictly forbidden (either *de jure* or *de facto*) and actively discouraged by force, our people's use of *patois* reflects, not, as has been mistaken by some, the attempt of the ignorant and illiterate to speak the English (or French or Spanish or Portuguese) language; rather the significance of *patois* is that it reflects the will of our peoples to inject our African root and essence into everything we do and say, and especially into the way we communicate with each other. *Patois*, in our case, Black English, is not the bastard tongue of aliens and slavers imitating the master. *Patois* is the affirmation of the African presence in the Western hemisphere.

Furthermore, language is not *just* style, it is not only "how" we say or write something. What makes one language fundamentally different from another is not how it sounds, but indeed its actual "structure," which is derived from the users' worldview, that is, how the users of the language view themselves, other people, and the world. The creation of any language which is *fundamentally different in worldview* from the colonial language is the most subversive act, short of actual revolution, that any colonized people can conceive and carry out.

Unfortunately, most of us who are literate in the colonial tongue, especially those of us who are nonpolitical- or apolitical-oriented writers, have generally failed to understand the importance of establishing the mother tongue. Too many of us as writers have spent irretrievable time attempting to demonstrate that we had mastered the colonial language. Thus, much of our "writing" has an "outside" quality vis-à-vis our own people. We write from the outside looking in; we write as observer/voyeur who is explaining to others (those who are equally "literate" in the colonial language) what these "people," our own people, are all about. It is essentially a pimp/peephole/act/art.

In fact, the very act of writing and publishing in the postchattel slavery period is often considered a sign that some writer has "made it," that is, collaborated with and been accepted by the colonial master.

The importance of *The Salt Eaters* (hence, Toni's dismissal of establishment critics and her desire to garner response from our "folk") and before it books such as *Cane, Invisible Man,* and *Their Eyes Were Watching God,* is precisely that these books, whether intentionally or not, are a form of written *patois.* They are among the best examples of African American literature in the novel form. They present the African American experience from the inside and presuppose the legitimacy of African American culture and the malevolence of the colonial context.

These books, and others like them, also demonstrate that "dialect" is at best only a subset of *patois,* only a linguistic attempt at rendering certain speech patterns and sounds into a written form. There is more to our mother tongue than how it sounds; hence, these books also display inventiveness of form and structure, of presentation and logic.

Central to all of the books cited is the nonlinear exposition (*Invisible Man* begins with the ending) and the emphasis that any "understanding" of reality is dependent on the understanding of the "context" or reality. Other aspects of importance are the separation of questions of morality from questions of truth: truth is "what is," reality, and morality, is a value judgment of truth. And, of course, all of these books deal dialectically rather than dualistically. There are no born heroes who are "heroic" from beginning to end. No absolutes. Also, in a very important sense, there is no tragedy. (See Cheikh Anta Diop's *Cultural Unity of Black Africa* for a brilliant exposition of the concept of tragedy as a Eurocentric worldview.). Each character has not only human strengths and weaknesses, but moreover the combination and degree of strengths and weaknesses is the essence of said character. Thus, in one context, the person who is a "savior figure" can become a mortal menace in another context (Tea Cake in *Eyes*).

What we have is a worldview that accepts that, although conscious characters can alter their social and material conditions, human beings are basically defined within their context and conditions. The revolutionary vector of the worldview, particularly as expressed in *Eyes* and *Salt,* is that social transformation is possible—people working together can change themselves and bring about change in their conditions. These two books are optimistic about our ability to grow and transform ourselves. In a period of depression, anxiety, alienation, and confusion, such as these times are, achieving this optimism in a convincing manner is no small accomplishment. The necessity of healing is at the core of *Salt*.

When Toni comments that being a writer is serious business and a socially responsible aspect of revolutionary struggle, she is sounding a major point. The Establishment mass media is intent on hiding the reality of African American and Third World life and struggle. American electronic networks, publishing concerns, and cinema industry present historical, deliberately misleading, falsified events in conjunction with official statements from the U.S. government perpetrated under the guise of originating from "responsible sources," and filtered through their own ideological sieves—this is the maze through which the Third World and all other news and events are presented to watchers of television, listeners of radio, readers of major periodicals, and viewers of cinema. A significant responsibility of *revolutionary* Third World writers is to cut through this crap, to expose the coverups and ideological/material interests inherent in these presentations, and, most important of all, our responsibility is to offer analysis, inspiration, information, and ideas which we think/feel work in the best interest of Third World defense and development.

Third World writers ought to be about the business of addressing the hard questions, about the business of freeing us, as a people, from illusions and misconceptions about our ourselves, other people, and the world. Again, *Salt* is instructive and to the point. For example, Toni successfully raises the nuclear power issue, an issue that many of our people have not yet grasped as important. Toni also addresses why Black women are so upset about the way Black men have treated them in the past, *particularly in the context of the Black liberation movement*. These are only two examples, however; the novel is full of such probing presentations.

The analysis and vision of progressive, working-class-oriented, Third World women of color (and similarly, of those Third World men of color who attempt to understand and identify with what our progressive women are struggling to achieve) are both a challenge and a valuable addition to our struggle for beauty and betterment. The work of revolutionary writers, such as Toni Cade Bambara's *Salt*, is a significant contribution to the body of Third World literature, a literature that will be the future literary standard of progressive peoples all around the world.

The Language of Soul in Toni Cade Bambara's[1] Re/Conceived Academy

ELEANOR W. TRAYLOR

> **Old Wife:** I'ma get my walkin shoes soon, Min, cause them haints fixing to beat on them drums with them cat bones and raise a rukus. So you just leave me here and I'll talk to you after while. I can't stand all that commotion them haints calling music …
> **Min:** Old wife, what are you but a haint?
> **Old Wife:** I'm a servant of the Lord, beggin your pardon.
> **Min:** I know that. But you a haint. You dead ain't you?
> **Old Wife:** There is no death in spirit, Min, I keep tellin you [that]. Why you so hard head?
> You just rip them fancy clothes off, Min, and thrash out into them waters, churn up all them bones we dropped from the old ships, churn up all that brine from the salty deep where our tears sank, and you grab them chirren by the neck and bop'm a good one and drag'm on back to shore and fling'm down and jump to it, pumping and cussing, fussing and cracking they ribs if ya have to to let'm live, Min. Cause love won't let you let'm go. (*The Salt Eaters*, 61,62[2])

A sense of the wonderful—the pervasive atmosphere—informing the fictional universe of Toni Cade Bambara is achieved through a language alive with self-confidence as it invents

> … new possibilities in formation
> new configurations to move with … (*SE* 293)
> the need for legend and fable,
> for the extraordinary so big,
> the courage to pursue (*SE* 268)

It is ever alert to and adept at testing its own trustworthiness:

> The dream is real, my friends.
> The failure to make it work is the unreality … (*SE* 126)
> It requires "exacting ceremonies," Min. (*SE* 145)

It points to the way it has forever existed as music, lore, saga, poetry, oratory, rhetoric; as a core of ideas and beliefs and values and literature[3] and humor and fun. It is the instrument of creation itself:

> ... And God said,
> I believe I'll make me a world ...
> And God said: *That's good*![4]

It signals pride when it records its transitions as it defied and continues to defy the muzzle since the time when it said,

> I must navigate my way through circumstance
> that will otherwise destroy me.[5]
> I set out with a firm purpose to learn.[6]

It expresses impish glee when it recalls its willfulness—its vulnerable though intrepid impulse to gaze in the face of conventional wisdom in order to ensure posterity:

> Git down offa dat gate-post! You li'l sow, you! Git down! Setting up dere looking dem white folks right in de face! They's gowine to lynch you, yet. And don't stand in dat doorway gazin out at 'em neither. Youse too brazen to live long.[7]

Loving its amazing powers, this language connects two interacting worlds: *Aye* (the tangible and visible world of living beings) and *Orun* (its invisible companion, the ever-present otherworld of spirits, ancestors, and gods). It conflates tenses to sound in a present moment the voices of the past and the prescient voices of the yet unborn. This language is "clairvoyant, clairfeelant, clairaudient, and clairdoent" (*SE et passim*). It is the stubborn, enduring, deeply textured language of Toni Cade Bambara, alias TCB, alias the swamp hag, alias the loa of the yellow flowers, alias Miz Hazel, alias the "she" who with her "Afrafemcentric" co-conspirators–"shes" of literature and of film creates a language called *she*:

> And she learned to read the auras of trees and stones and plants and neighbors ... And studied the sun's corona, the jagged petals of magnetic colors ... And then the threads that shimmered between wooden tables and flowers and children and candles and birds ... She could dance their dance and match their beat and echo their pitch

and know their frequency as if her own... She knew each way of being in the world and could welcome them home again, open to wholeness. (*SE* 48)

This she-language—confident of its self-chosen, life-saving, life-enhancing, corrective, and healing purpose—understands everything there is to know about the arbitrariness of signs. The questions it asks are these: Who is controlling the sign? Is some glib and hypocritical HUNCA Bubba[8] or some meanspirited, self-deprecating Miz Turner[9] breaking the heart of Little Hazel Elizabeth Deborah Parker or Little Luther—dashing their dreams and aspirations by wielding a sign reading grown-up-common-sense-wisdom: the ability to "mis-inform, mis-direct, smoke-out, screen out, black out, confound, contain, intimidate" (BE 78)? Are the children of "Bovanne's" Miz Hazel under the sign of "we hipper than you" refusing "home-tongue proficiency" (BE 78) in favor of some "unattached," "unobliged," "psychically immature, spiritually impoverished, and intellectually undisciplined" (*SE* 133) hype?

These and similar questions regarding the nature of language had received by 1972 a stunning and rigorous response from Toni Cade Bambara in "Black English," where she corroborates James Baldwin, following Max Weinreich's observation that people who raise powerful armies are said to speak a language; those who do not are said to speak a dialect. Many premises of twentieth-century linguistics and semantics, of course, support this observation, but two in particular are the focus of Bambara's "Black English." One is that, in her words, "language is the single most important political institution in a culture" (BE 78). The other, as W. E. B. DuBois and other scholars laying the foundation for more recent thinkers knew it, is that language is "a political institution that functions in the interest of the ruling class" (BE 78). As TCB reminds us, the political way of looking at and speaking about language is "not the way schools approach language" (BE 78). She continues:

In school, we have focused on how language operates as grammar, diction, vocabulary. We have focused on language as noun (namer) not on what or who is named or on who is doing the naming; we have focused on language as verb (generator of action or situation of) not on what kind of action is being generated or on who or what is situated in what kind of state of being. In schools we do not emphasize the real function of language in our lives: how it operates in courts, in hospitals, in schools, in the media, how it operates to perpetuate a society, maintain a social order, to reflect biases, to transmit basic values. In schools we focus on vocabulary, diction and grammar, but not on the implications of words, not on the use to which words are put. (BE 78)

In her 1972 essay, she raises the question, which has only recently (ca. 1998) been aired in the National Media: "What is Black English Anyway?" (BE 77). She muses:

Is it ghettoese, a sloppy variation of proper speech . . . is it what many teachers, Black and non-Black describe it to be, slang, profanity; a language that demonstrates the intellectual deficiencies of Black folks, or that demonstrates perhaps sheer perversity on the part of the student . . . is it, as some parents describe it, something shameful, disgraceful, the language of low-life, unambitious folk? . . . or among the pedagogues, . . . those who get their Ph.D.'s hustling Black stuff— there is the notion that the whole issue can be summed up [in a question]: Are Black students bidialectal or bilingual? Bidialectal meaning that the language of the home is a variation of a standard. Bilingual meaning that Black English is a language . . . foreign, perhaps. (BE 77)

Old Wife: It won the Nobel, didn't it, Min. Whatever dey call dem prizes.

Min: Please, old wife, remember that you are a haint.

Old Wife: Min your brain is a sieve. I told you ain't no death. You just pull off dat red suit and bop em. (SE)

In her short fiction, collected in *Tales and Stories for Black Folks*,[10] *Gorilla My Love*, and *Deep Sightings and Rescue Missions*,[11] and in her novels *The Salt Eaters* and *Those Bones Are Not My Child*,[12] Toni Cade Bambara perfects a narrative mode and appropriates the language of "our music, poetry, stories, and intellectual discourses" (BE 83) to write against the language of another mode. That mode, "the myth of the official version" (*Those Bones* 666), has been characterized as "a school, an overwhelming volume of literature, theory, arguments, hypotheses and accepted belief" as Toni Morrison observes. It is a school that finally betrays, abandons, the teacher (as in James Baldwin's "Sonny's Blues"[13]), and plunges the student into the void of homelessness. Countering this school, TCB constructs a universe of intelligence—an Academy—in which a language, "kept alive by our caretakers and custodians—our writers and teachers and singers" (BE 83), resists colonization and loves itself:

> I want to talk about language, form, and changing the world. The question that faces billions of people at this moment . . . is: Can the planet be rescued from psychopaths? . . . And the challenge that the cultural worker [engaged artists certainly within my community] faces . . . is that the tools of my trade are colonized. The creative imagination has been colonized. . . . And the audience—readers and viewers—is in bondage to an industry. (*Deep Sightings* 139–40)

So, this language, reinforced by the "ideological maintenance" (BE 83) of a host of contributions and having "nothing to do with illiteracy of any kind," is what Miss Bambara calls Black English. And for the Academy that she specifies in *The Salt Eaters* and implies elsewhere, its discourses characterize contemporaneity itself.

Quite like the jolt that "stunned" Campbell to awareness in *The Salt Eaters,* the words *infotainment* and *even*, appearing in Sam Lipsyte's review of Jenny McPhee's first novel, sent me reeling down through the years to the earliest critical responses to TCB's first novel. Lipsyte tells us:

> Here in the age of *infotainment even* the novelist must have the facts to survive. Today's fiction reader will just as likely exclaim how much he "learned" from a certain novel as much as how he felt, so it is incumbent on the *writer* to head straight for the bookstore or search engine to stock up on data.[14]

As TCB would put it, the gap between availability and discovery or between practice and recognition can be piercing. By 1983, more than twenty years ago, Bambara's earliest readers had called attention to the "fact-o-fictive" world of *Gorilla, My Love; The Seabirds Are Still Alive;* and *The Salt Eaters,* noting that "as story, *The Salt Eaters* is less moving tale than brilliant . . . rite of transformation quite like a jam session."[15] As Gloria Hull has put it:

> Although everyone knows instinctively that Toni Cade Bambara's first novel, *The Salt Eaters,* is a book that he or she must read, many people have difficulty with it . . . *Salt* is long, intricately written, trickily structured, full of learning, heavy with wisdom—is, altogether, what critics mean by a "large" book.[16]

By the early nineties, inquiry of Bambara's first novel had turned to class-room approaches, as in Margot Ann Kelley's essay which relates the response of her students to scientific investigation of the novel. She writes: "... after providing the class with a brief introduction to chemical dissipative systems (a topic that combines thermodynamics and the law of time), the students immediately, clearly, made numerous connections to the text that give them access to Bambara's ideas" (480).[17] And by 1996, we receive, in Janelle Collins's "Generating Power: Fission, Fusion and Post-Modern Politics in Bambara's *The Salt Eaters,*" an examination of the novel as it "simulates the postmodern condition" (37) and as it characterizes postmodern experimentation:

> ... *The Salt Eaters* combines fabulism and realism, adapts a non-mimetic form of representation, rejects linear history in favor of a *flattened, one-dimensional chronology of events*, displays multiple angles of vision rather than either a first person or omniscient perspective, presents a decentered subject rather than unified subjectivity ..., offers a labyrinth of events instead of a plot to follow, and rejects closure in favor of open-ended meaning" (36, italics added).[18]

Of course, the re-conceived Academy of Bambara's fictional universe, poised to investigate past and present usage, would question post-words *thermodynamically.* And when we consider its curriculum as Gloria Hull has pointed to it, then we might want to scratch such evaluations as "a flattened, one-dimensional chronology of events" as descriptive of her poetic practice. As Hull suggests, "many avenues of knowing pervade the Bambara textual world":

> telepathy and other psychic phenomena; astrology; dream analysis; numerology; colorimetry; the Tarot; past life glances and reincarnation; the Ouija board; reading auras, palms, tea leaves, cards, and energy maps; throwing cowrie shells; herbal and folk medicines; voices, visions, and signs; witches, loas, swamphags; saints, djinns, and divas; the "ancient wisdoms"; the power of prayer; "root men ... conjure women ... obeah folks"; divination; demons; and so on. (220)

And its knowledge base is drawn from

> ancient and modern history, world literature, anthropology, mythology, music, astronomy, physics, biology, mathematics, medicine, political theory, chemistry, philosophy, and engineering. Allusions to

> everything from space-age technology through Persian folklore to
> black American blues comfortably jostle each other. (226)

What, to me, is compelling in Collins's essay is contained in its fourth
footnote. In support of her focus on the novel's "resistance to the cultural
logic of capitalism," Collins recommends readings that offer "a theoretical
complement to Bambara's fictional treatment of the possibilities of post-
modern politics" (46). And yet, one might argue that in the Academy of
The Seven Arts that Bambara constructs in *The Salt Eaters,* indeed, in the
Academy that seems to characterize, as hypogram[19] (a structure pretext or
thematic complex, according to Michael Riffaterre), her fictional universe,
the distinction between the poetic (or fictional) and the theoretical, since
both serve as metalanguages and deal in possibilities, is erased.

In any case, *infotainment,* if a new coinage, is no new practice in Afro-
American fiction and certainly intensifies, self-reflexively, in the fiction exemplified by Toni Cade Bambara and her Afrafemicentric colleagues (men
and women) by and since 1970. As readers of this fiction (mentioned here,
and others who offer modes of access) have suggested, it is this practice that
drives readers "to head straight for the bookstore or search engine to stock
up on data." And these *readers* sustain an inquiry which participates in a
design quite like the conception of an Academy that the world of Bambara's
fiction builds. That conception is not unlike what Martha C. Nussbaum
describes as the literary imagination:

> I shall focus, then, on the characteristics of the literary imagination
> as a public imagination, an imagination that will steer judges in their
> judging, legislators in their legislating, policy makers in measuring
> the quality of life of people near and far. Commending it in the pub-
> lic sphere is difficult, since many people who think of literature as
> illuminating about the workings of the personal life and the private
> imagination believe that it is idle and unhelpful when the larger con-
> cern of classes and nations are at issue. Here, it is felt, we need some-
> thing more reliably scientific, more detached, more sternly rational.
> But I shall argue that here, all the more, literary forms have a unique
> contribution to make . . . [G]ood literature is disturbing in a way that
> history and social science writing frequently are not. It inspires dis-
> trust of conventional pieties and exacts a frequently painful con-
> frontation with one's own thoughts and intentions . . . Literary works
> that promote identification and emotional reaction cut through those
> self-protective stratagems, requiring us to see and to respond to many

things that may be difficult to confront—and they make this process palatable by giving us pleasure in the very act of confrontation.[20]

In "Salvation Is the Issue"[21] Toni Cade Bambara had capsuled this point as the purpose of her fiction:

> Stories are important. They keep us alive. In the ships, in the camps, in the quarters, fields, prisons, on the run, underground, under siege, in the throes, on the verge—the storyteller snatches us back from the edge to hear the next chapter. In which we are the subjects. We, the hero of the tales. Our lives preserved. How it was; how it be. Passing it along in the relay. That is what I work to do: to produce stories that save our lives . . . In *Salt* most particularly, in motive/content/structure/design, the question is, do we intend to have a future as sane, whole, governing people? I argue then and in "Faith" as well that immunity to the serpent's sting can be found in our tradition of struggle and our faculty for synthesis. The issue is salvation. I work to produce stories that save our lives. (41–47)

The story that is told in *The Salt Eaters* continues in *Those Bones Are Not My Child* (hereafter, *Bones*). Underneath the topical matters that urge the surface action in both novels is a deeper movement informed by an ancient or archetypal story whose motifs register variously over time and over place. It is a story accompanied by music (the constant *hums* one hears in *Salt* and *Bones*) of the sort Douglass heard in the deep woods or the shout Zala hears rising up "through the grate" (*Bones* 529). In *Women Who Run With the Wolves* (hereafter *WWW*),[22] Clarrisa Pinkola Estes calls one mode, the sorrow songs, "*hambre del alma*, the song of the starved soul;" the other, the shout, she calls "the joyous *canto hondo*, the deep song [sung] when we do the work of soulful reclamation" (4). This music *under-grounds* the consciousness of Velma (*alma*), the sorrowful, focal character of *Salt*, and Marzala (a savory olio, though *de-classe*), focal character of *Bones*.

Velma and Marzala (Zala) sign "the modern woman [engrossed] in a blur of activity . . . pressured to be all things to all people" (*Bones* 2). Their daily lives may be measured by the tempo, intertextuality, and *largesse* of a jam session, but both arrive at a moment when the tune springs its rhythm, dissipates; its parts refuse to work together— melody, no longer a song, becomes a scream, or in Old Wife's term, "a *rukus*." Velma and Marzala, for Bambara, Clarrisa P. Estes, and us, are "the creative, the gifted, the deep women" (*WWW* 4); for Estes, the *cantadora* and Jungian psychoanalyst; and for Bambara, the professor–novelist, "Traditional psychology is often sparse or entirely silent about deeper issues important to women: the archetypal, the intuitive, the sexual and cyclical, the ages of women, a woman's way, a woman's knowing, her creative fire" (4). For both the psychoanalyst and the novelist, it is *story* (more than accepted, we might say approved, forms of psychology) that addresses, mediates, and medicates these "deeper issues." Bambara's Velma in *Salt* slits her wrists and thrusts her head into a gas oven because "[s]omething crucial had been missing from the political/ economic/ social/ cultural/ aesthetic/ military/ psychosocial/ psychosexual mix. And what could it be? And what should she do?" (*SE* 259). What is missing is explained by Clarrisa P. Estes as a disconnection: "We lose touch with the instinctive psyche . . . a knowing of the *soul*, we live in a semi destroyed state, and images and powers that are natural to the feminine are not allowed full development" (*WWW* 7–8). As Bambara put it " . . . there is a split between the spiritual, psychic, and political forces in my community . . . It is a wasteful and dangerous split" ("What It Is I Think I'm Doing Anyhow" 165).

Twenty years before the publication of *Women Who Run With the Wolves,* Bambara's *The Salt Eaters* had *poeticized* its major concepts: the significance of the *Wild Woman* archetype, its sign for soul, and its implications for healing. Nor were these concepts missed in *Salt*'s earliest reviews: for example, in Traylor's attention to the manner in which "Velma's soul goes gathering" (Traylor, 62; see footnote 15) and Hull's recognition that Velma's attempted suicide is the price she pays for "blotting out the mud mothers" (Hull, 225; see footnote 16).

By 1990, in Joanne Braxton's *Wild Women in the Whirlwind: AfraAmerican Culture and the Contemporary Literary Renaissance,* these concepts guide theoretical premises and critical evaluations supplied by the poetic practice of black women crafting fiction. Yet while Doctor Clarrisa P. Estes includes in the bibliography of *Women Who Run With the Wolves* such writers as Maya Angelou, Gwendolyn Brooks, Toi Derricotte, Gloria Hull, Jamaica Kincaid, Ntozake Shange, and Alice Walker, the names of Toni Cade Bambara and Toni Morrison—novelists who anticipate her thesis—are strangely absent. The split between availability and recognition is as much a challenge, certainly in the Academy, as is the split between the conscious and the unconscious. On any day, one may receive a Campbell-like jolt when, for example, one reads a headline heralding a new direction:

AT GWU, A
HEALING SPIRIT
A NEW INSTITUTE SEEKS TO
REESTABLISH THE LOST

CONNECTIONS BETWEEN
MEDICINE AND BELIEF
BY LOUISE LEVATHES
Special to
The Washington Post (August 7, 2001).

One learns that Dr. Christina Puchaiski, director of the George Washington Institute for Spirituality and Health, has convinced her colleagues that

> ...Health care needs to be delivered by a community of people, including extended families, friends, priests and spiritual counselors. It's a community our culture seems to have lost in recent years.
>
> At one time, we lived near relatives and friends, priests and rabbis, who all came to our aid when we became ill. Now many people live alone without family or friends to help them.

One's "wild" nature rears and bares its teeth as one recalls the opening lines of the 1980 novel of Toni Cade Bambara: "Are you sure, sweetheart, that you want to be well?" It is a novel, as its readers know, whose spiritual and medical healers conduct a rite of healing that is the novel's *plot*. As her readers also may agree, what I am calling Toni Cade Bambara's Re/Conceived Academy exemplifies and requires "a fuguelike interweaving of...voices" (*SE* 214), which is the antidote for the split between the cognitive and intuitive, or psychic (soulful) and other ways of knowing, and between availability and recognition that remain our condition today.

NOTES

1. The first part of this essay, presented at the 1996 meeting of the MLA, was published as "Black English: The Counter Narrative of Toni Cade Bambara," *Revelations*, 3rd edition. Teresa Redd, ed. (New York: Simon & Schuster Custom Publishing, 1997).

2. Toni Cade Bambara. *The Salt Eaters* (New York: Vintage 1992). Hereafter all references are to *SE*.

3. Toni Cade Bambara. "Black English," in *Curriculum Approaches from a Black Perspective* (Atlanta: Black Child Development Institute, 1972). Hereafter BE.

4. James Weldon Johnson's "Creation," in *God's Trombones* (New York: Viking, 1927, 17).

5. Olaudah Equiano. *The Interesting Narrative of the Life of Olaudah Equiano, or Gustavus Vassa, the African,* in Henry Louis Gates, Jr., ed. *The Classic Slave Narratives* (New York: Penguin, 1987, 281).

6. Frederick Douglass. From *Narrative of the Life of Frederick Douglass, an American Slave*, in Henry Louis Gates, Jr., ed. *The Classic Slave Narratives* (New York: Penguin, 1987).

7. Zora Neale Hurston. *Dust Tracks on a Road, an Autobiography* (Philadelphia: Lippincott, 1942, 46).

8. Martha Naussbaum. *Poetic Justice: The Literary Imagination and Public Life* (1995) excerpted in David A. Richter, *Falling into Theory*, (New York: Bedford/St. Martin's, 1999), 356–65.

9. Toni Cade Bambara. *Gorilla, My Love* (New York: Random House, 1972).

10. Toni Cade Bambara. *Tales and Stories for Black Folks* (Garden City, New York: Zenith, 1971).

11. Toni Cade Bambara. *Deep Sightings and Rescue Missions* (New York: Pantheon, 1996).

12. Toni Cade Bambara. *Those Bones Are Not My Child* (New York: Random House, 1997).

13. James Baldwin. "Sonny's Blues," in *Going to Meet the Man* (New York: Dial Press, 1965).

14. Sam Lipsyte's review appears in the "Book World" section of *The Washington Post* July 15, 2001.

15. Eleanor Traylor. "Music as Theme: The Jazz Mode in the Works of Toni Cade Bambara," in Mari Evans, ed. *Black Women Writers (1950–1980): A Critical Evaluation* (Garden City, New York: Anchor-Doubleday 1984, 69).

16. Gloria Hull. "What It Is I Think She's Doing Anyway: A Reading of Toni Cade Bambara's *The Salt Eaters*," in Marjorie Pryse and Hortense Spillers, ed. *Conjuring* (Bloomington: Indiana UP, 1985), 216–32.

17. Margot Ann Kelley. "Damballah is the First Law of Thermodynamics: Modes of Access to Toni Cade Bambara's *The Salt Eaters*." *African American Review* 27:3 (Fall 1993): 479–89.

18. Janelle Collins. "Generating Power: Fission, Fusion and Post-Modern Politics in Bambara's *The Salt Eaters*." MELUS 21.2 (Summer 1996): 35–47.

19. Irene R. Makaryk, ed., *Encyclopedia of Contemporary Literary Theory: Approaches, Scholars, Terms* (Toronto: U of Toronto P, 1993, 554).

20. Nussbaum, ibid.

21. Toni Cade Bambara. "Salvation Is The Issue," in *Black Women Writers* [noted above].

22. Clarrisa P. Estes. *Women Who Run With the Wolves: Myths and Stories of the Wild Woman Tribe* (New York: Ballantine Books, 1992).

7

Translating the Salt

ANNE WICKE

T ranslation was indeed not my first choice as a professional activity, even though my training was literary. I studied American literature and decided to write my "Doctorat d'Etat" dissertation on the works of Herman Melville, preparing myself to become, with humility and awe, a specialist in the American Renaissance. Then I started translating modern American novels, but it was not until I came across *The Salt Eaters* that I really and deeply realized that this activity would eventually occupy a very important place in my personal and academic life. So this paper is not so much to be read as a scholarly appraisal—which it is not—but as a short narrative of an important and meaningful encounter.

When a French publisher[1] asked me whether I would be interested in the translation of Toni Cade Bambara's novel, I had, so far, never translated any book on my own; I had always worked in collaboration with another translator, a college friend who also specialized in nineteenth-century American literature. We had decided that after one more book, we would try to go ahead and work alone. *The Salt Eaters* was going to be that one more book. So the two of us translated the novel, and I then translated Bambara's collection of short stories as well as *Those Bones Are Not My Child* on my own. I must also add that, at that time I had never even heard the name of Toni Cade Bambara. The reading of *The Salt Eaters* was for me a revelation; of course, as a student in American literature and as a reader I knew a number of African American writers, but here I immediately had the feeling I was being confronted by a very specific voice, or rather by a multiplicity of voices woven together in a text that, to this day, remains something like a shock to me.

As students of American literature in the seventies, in a Parisian university still vibrant in the wake of May 1968, we had been presented with the major African American voices of the century, we had been told about the importance of writing as a political gesture and as a form of commitment, we had been taught about the aesthetics of politics and history—or maybe should I reverse the phrase and speak of the politicizing of poetics and aesthetics, and we had thus learned to conceive of African American writers as spokespersons for their community.

Yet, I have always had the feeling that this vision, as respectful as it may be of the works and of the authors, remains risky, in the sense that it maintains a kind of discrimination, which, even though it is here positive, seems questionable as another form of essentialism. I would like to think that, without denying what also constitutes the very nature of this literature, without any attempt at reappropriation, we could try and read these works as belonging to a wider patrimony, to a community I could also belong to, the community of those who wish for and work for another way of viewing the world and considering relations among people.

To return to Toni Cade Bambara and *The Salt Eaters*, I found in that book what I had previously appreciated in other novels written by African American writers. I must say that humor—that can be as devastating as it is warm and loving—is also certainly part of what attracted me to that novel and to the universe of Toni Cade. Indeed, I laughed a lot when I read, and also when I translated the book. And this is surely part of the salt that we all savor and cherish.

All that is not to imply that everything was easy when we started that first translation: despite my universalizing tendencies, I knew—and I still do know—that denying the specific problems of a French translator meets when working on African American texts would be a most serious mistake. For these problems are real and the translator has to try and find solutions.

First of all, one could mention the lexical aspect: when we started translating *The Salt Eaters*, we soon realized that we constantly came across words or phrases that we did not understand, or only vaguely understood, not clearly enough, anyway, to be sure of our translation. The phonetic transcription of a word uttered with a certain accent or intonation suddenly became a riddle. Phrases and words coming from various origins (urban, rural, southern, northern, etc.) were also problematic for us. The different terms, idioms, and vocabularies used by the African American community that appear in the novel and in the short stories also raised questions: these words and constructions, constituting the language of a group, are often difficult to understand for people who do not belong to that group, and even when one starts possessing knowledge of it, it always remains a sort of passive knowledge (one understands the word or phrase but does not use it).

Syntax brings other kinds of questions. In *The Salt Eaters* in particular, but also in the other texts, one is confronted by a great number of elliptical sentences (with the omissions of subject pronouns, or of auxiliaries, for instance) and to very long sentences without any internal punctuation, creating a rhythm that is always very difficult to bring forth in French. That, allied with the use of monosyllabic or very short words alternating with longer ones, create a musicality that the French language is not really equipped to convey. I am thinking here of the beginning of a sentence in *The Salt Eaters*. "The raga reggae bumpidity bing zing was pouring out all over Fred Holt...": though we immediately feel the music behind the words, we immediately know we are in trouble, for it will be most difficult to find words, and an association of words, that will convey the meaning, the rhythm, and the music (in the text and referred to by the text). This is certainly essential, as music plays a major role in Toni Cade's writing (as a network of references, and as a conveyor of themes and of cadences, among other things), and most importantly since Toni Cade's writing is itself highly musical. One might add, here, that it is exactly the same with the dialogues in her stories: we all know the part played in her books by oral language and its written transcription. Because of her extraordinary ability to capture the spoken word, Toni Cade's dialogues are most difficult to translate, but translating them is also one of the funniest and most pleasant activities there are. We often spent a marvelous moment laughing over the original dialogues and what we were trying to find as a good translation.

But at that point I would be tempted to say that these problems are also those any translator is confronted by; when translating, one always has to appraise and come to terms with the language, within the written universe of another person. It is the job of the translator to try and get as near as possible, knowing all the time that an irreducible distance will remain, that an inevitable loss is part and parcel of what we set out to do. One way, though, of bridging gaps and reducing the distance was to explore all the references I came across when translating Toni Cade: what can I do, for instance, with "a Nedick's nigger," if I do not know that Nedick's is a fast-food chain, a cheap one, which qualifies the character in question as the type of man "who invites you to dine, then takes you to a corner fast food chain for a hot dog/frankfurter and a watery orangeade served in a paper cup—and expects the date to find it all very impressive" (Toni's explanation)? Once I got the reference, I could start working, because, as a woman, I then knew what Toni Cade had in mind when she chose that phrase. (Of course, then another problem is to decide whether your translation is going to be too explicative—which to my mind it should not be—or whether you will leave an element of "exoticism"—keeping Nedick's, for instance—for the French readers to find out for themselves).

Similar problems arose when I was translating *Those Bones Are Not My Child*. To give just a couple of examples: Zala is thinking of her missing son, and there is a link made between what could still be thought of as a voluntary running away and the fugitive slaves; we have then a very beautiful and pregnant long paragraph focused on the word "runaway." That paragraph ends with: "Run away. Not snatched, not choked, not dumped, but run away. Run away, Sonny. Rail line, hot line, steal away home." I did not know that "Rail line, hot line" came from a slave song, and that "steal away from home" came from a spiritual. It was certainly important for me to be able to read the lyrics of the songs, the circumstances of their composition, in order to make my choice afterwards.

What are, then, the various means one can use to tackle these problems? Dictionaries and glossaries, of course, slang dictionaries, reference encyclopedias, historical studies, or the Internet, to get information or simply to check what you think you know. If I was more at ease with the references dealing with the civil rights movement, I must recognize that I was very easily at a loss when confronted with references to Afro-American folklore, or to Voodoo, for instance. I also felt it necessary to read books on the missing and murdered children of Atlanta. Because of the documentary aspect of *Those Bones Are Not My Child*, I had to find specific tools (plans, maps, information, statistics, etc.). Yet, thinking of my personal experience, I am convinced that what helped me most was the ability to ask questions to American friends, or even better, to the author herself. Between 1991 and 1992, while I was translating the two collections of short stories, I got in touch with Toni Cade and asked her as many questions as I wanted, with Toni offering me, each time, very documented and often hilarious answers. During the translation of *Those Bones*, I was lucky enough to be able to do the same with Toni Morrison, who was always very generous with her time and with her patience. She should be heartily thanked here, once again, for editing the original American edition of the novel and for the help she gave me.

This kind of dialogue taught me a lot, and I am not only speaking of facts, of course; though I am quite embarrassed when I reread the first batch of questions I sent to Toni Cade (she must have been appalled, thinking of the ignorant person that was supposed to translate her work into French!). As I advanced in the translations, as I got more and more familiar with the universes of the stories, I learned not to trust myself systematically, I learned to be suspicious, to suspect that, in the case of such-or-such phrase, things might not be that simple, that there might be more to it than what appeared at a first reading. This is why, probably, Toni Cade once wrote me that she did not mind the number of questions I asked her: "No, Anne," she wrote me, "I'm not worried by the number of questions; Would be worried if there were few, hysterical if there were none." She was aware that translating *The Salt Eaters* was no easy task: "I'm so glad," she wrote in the same letter, "you didn't find SALT a nightmare piece of work. It's dodgy enough in English. The Japanese translator, rumor has it, went berserk."

I would like, at this point of my narrative, to share a few of Toni Cade's answers to my questions, to provide yet another occasion of savoring the salt.

- "feet smell a cracker"[2]—a cracker, or reconstructed peckerwood, is a European American, who having failed to rise above his/her supremacist training, persists in aggressive/delusional/ugly racist behavior—feet with a sense of smell refers to [the] "ability" of African folk, well trained in the lunacy of "race relations" to code switch in behavior and play bear (as in brer bear, stupid as opposed to brer rabbit, rebel) that is—to shuffle (or in extreme cases "cut a caper" or dance foolishly) and otherwise engage in kinesics that signify obsequiousness.
- "playing the dozens"—a word ritual engaged in for the purpose of displaying language wit on the part of the speakers and en-durance/restraint on the part of the spoken to, that is in the actual ceremony, two or more parties begin cracking on each other, sling-ing insults, casting aspersions. It's a one-upsmanship transaction. The above refers to people in the know, who are aware of the duel, share the same language/values/codes, are part of the same com-munity. In the text, refers to people who malign w/o ceremony, who engage in it w/o recognizing/acknowledging the rules so that they may appear "innocent." Teachers playing the dozens behind colored folks are EuroAm teachers who malign without a contract, without ceremony, without shared values ... just insults.
- "Sweet town"—"Sweet" is one of those words that pops up in reveries, reminiscences, as in 'That was one sweet man' (doesn't mean he couldn't also be mean or a pain in the ass; mostly means the speaker is enjoying the backglance) 'Did you see him dunk that ball, it was sweet (how wonderful it is to witness artistry and then share the memory and the appreciation with someone).' "She was one sweet angel chile (meaning I'm real sentimental about who she was and who I was back in those days)." The word is used not only for the meaning of "sweetness" (as in sugar, candy, desirable) but also for the sound of it ... it can be drawn out, made delicious, then punctuated percussively with the final consonant. If a speaker sounds the word with appropriate drama, the hearer is compelled to applaud it, as in: "It was a good job. Paid well, didn't humiliate me, and flexible hours too. Plus there was this woman on the job ... Uh huhn. Tha job was sweeeeeTTT." "Honey dripper," would be the answer, a response and a prod to say more about the woman.

In the story, it's part of the overall hyperbolic style of the obviously young (but thinks she's grown and wise) protagonist/narrator. Thus it is ironic, for she's just a kid trying to be sophisticated and world weary.

There's a street in Atlanta, Georgia that the post office calls Auburn Avenue. Old timers call it Sweet Auburn because the memories of the clubs, the lodges, the talent, the fun is sweet (poignant, perhaps bitter sweet considering what else was going on in those days). If a young person called the street Sweet Auburn, the elders would tease, "Ahh what do you know about it, Youngblood?"—meaning, it is not altogether appropriate for a young person to claim a history who was not part of it; that youngblood is speaking beyond her/his years. It's a grown up word, in short, used to signal reverie.

- "Johnson Girls"—women who have their things together, have style independent cool unimpressed nobody's fool—actually, "Johnson" is a synonym for any noun the speaker is avoiding either because its scatological or corny, or overly obvious or so complex it defies easy capturing/description. In the story, means both obvious and mysterious summation of womanish qualities.
- "Jitterbugs"—not excited people, just a name that recalls/evokes the jitterbug or Lindy Hop era; meaning, people whose gestures and postures are manifestations of Ebonics, African kinesthetics/just a common expression of that day meaning "folks."
- "Flyboy"—not literally necessarily, he makes the most of white-perceptions-of-Blacks-as-pitiful victims-needing-help. In the period of the story (40s/50s), the urban environment was loaded with posters, billboards, ads featuring working class poor children of color with the directive Send This Poor Child to Camp. Major do-gooder campaign.
- "Dirty Red" (no connotation of nasty// just as "dirty rice" does not mean unclean// an agricultural people do not think of soil, earth, loam, or dirt as negative, merely descriptive) red-hair and ruddy-brown complexion.
- "Bad William"—the herb called Sweet William was/is a favorite of elders (windowsill pots//sachet in the drawer); because of the herb, actual living Williams usually get a tag—Sweet William, Mean William, Bad William—doesn't mean they aren't nice, loveable, cherished . . . just so people won't get them confused with some other William.

Now that I have a longer experience of literary translation and of relations with authors, I must say that my epistolary relation with Toni Cade[3] remains unique: the generous thoroughness of her answers, the friendly and warm tone; these are things I have rarely experienced since. She was the first author I wrote to, and I am still happily surprised today when I read her letters.

Thanks to that encounter with Toni Cade's books, I also learned a lot more about American studies and literature, I discovered artists and activists that I would never have heard of, were it not for her, and this, in turn, modified my views on both teaching and translating American literature. I taught *The Salt Eaters* to third-year English majors who, despite the difficult reading, were all enthusiastic and had the feeling of having discovered an author, a companion, not only a subject for final exams. We organized in France the first Toni Cade Bambara conference in 2003, and this was another opportunity for meeting people who love her and her work, people whose lives were enriched for having met her. One Toni then led me to another, since I had the privilege of meeting Toni Morrison when I was working on *Those Bones* and I was asked, afterwards, to translate her 2003 novel, *Love*. There is no doubt my encounter with Toni Cade Bambara and her work was a fundamental opportunity for me.

She once wrote me, "I hope you're having at least 1/10th of the fun translating as I did writing." So much more than 1/10th, Toni, so much more...

Thanks, Toni.

NOTES

1. The French publisher of Toni Cade Bambara's works, Christian and Dominique Bourgois, remained firm in their determination to publish Toni's four books of fiction, especially *Those Bones,* without consideration of commercial parameters, because they thought, as we all did, that these books should come out in French.

2. Inside quotation marks are the words or phrases from the short stories that I asked her about. We had finished the translation of *The Salt Eaters* when I was able to write Toni. I have respected here Toni's presentation in her letters (dated August and October 1991).

3. I only met her once, at her place in Philadelphia, in November 1991. To this day I cherish the memory of a very pleasant and warm evening, among piles of LPs (she was in the course of organizing her collection of records). We talked about everything: our lives; our passion for writing, for literature; her work as an organizer; our children; the political situation in the States, in France, in Africa; and most of all we laughed a lot.

"She was just outrageously brilliant":
Toni Morrison Remembers Toni Cade Bambara

VALERIE BOYD

In an October 1999 interview, author Toni Morrison talked about her long literary friendship with Toni Cade Bambara, and about editing her "magnum opus," *Those Bones Are Not My Child*—the novel Bambara worked on for the last 12 years of her life.

Set in Atlanta in the early 1980s, *Those Bones* places readers at the center of that awful atrocity that came to be known as the Atlanta child murders— the period roughly from 1979 to 1982 when more than 40 black children were abducted or killed. But the novel isn't about the tragedy in an abstract way: it's about a particular family and what happens to it when a son doesn't come home one night.

Bambara lived in Atlanta in the late 1970s and early 1980s, and she became actively involved in the drama of the missing and murdered—attending community meetings, clipping newspaper articles, taking notes.

In her prologue to *Those Bones,* Bambara reports that she began her first journal on the cases in September 1979, "with nothing particular in mind, journal keeping a habit." Soon, though, her journal ballooned into several volumes of notes for a novel, and into an obsession of sorts. By December 1995, when Bambara died of cancer, she had completed her novel—all 1,800 pages of it.

When Bambara's daughter, Karma Bene Bambara, decided to publish the book posthumously, Morrison, a former editor at Random House, quickly secured a contract with Pantheon, a Random House imprint. She also committed to editing the book herself, with all proceeds going to Bambara's estate.

In this interview, Morrison discusses the process of editing the book, as well as personal aspects of her friendship with Bambara, who lived in Morrison's New York City apartment for a short while during her final days—when she apparently was as vibrant as ever. "She called all her friends and they all had a party . . . People who visited her have told me about that," says Morrison, who stayed at her Hudson River home during this period, giving Bambara free run of the apartment in the city. "She had a good time. I think she really liked the place. That pleases me that she was happy there, really happy . . . She knew that was her place, for as long as she wanted it."

In some ways, it's still Bambara's place. "There's a lot of her in that apartment," Morrison says. "I left all that stuff. All the food she bought when she was there, all the notes she was making to herself, all that's still in that apartment."

Also, Morrison never got back her key. It was a distinctive key, she recalls, with a blue head. After Bambara died, Morrison called around looking for the key, but Bambara's daughter and friends couldn't find it, Morrison recalls, laughing. "So I said, 'Well, I guess the girl wants the key.'"

Valerie Boyd [VB]: When and how did you and Toni Cade Bambara meet? Will you describe that first meeting and your first impressions of her? And how did your relationship blossom from there?

Toni Morrison [TM]: She came to my office at Random House with the woman who was then her agent, Hattie Gossett—the first black agent that I'd ever met. Toni had published *The Black Woman* and had also published an anthology for black children. They were interested in her publishing her own stuff primarily, so they came to Random House.

They were both fierce and seemed so clear and they had their hair cut short, like crew cuts, and they were very beautiful. This was in, oh my, the '70s—the early '70s. *The Bluest Eye* I know I had published, and maybe even *Sula,* and that was '73, so somewhere around there.

So we had a very funny, fun, interesting conversation, without the preliminaries that normally you get from artists, would-be writers, people looking for a new publisher, or a new editor. She had a number of stories already, so she was not coming in asking to be considered as an author who was *going* to do something. She came in with manuscript, or saying she had it. And that was extremely gratifying . . . And I was very busy at that time trying to find writers that agents did not have—you know, the routine, obvious people—which meant I was particularly interested in unpublished, or minimally published, black female writers. And here was one.

And we hit it off rather instantly, I think. And she turned in these stories which were amazing to me . . . They were sooooo sophisticated, so far beyond the kind of literature that was being published at that time. It wasn't harangue, you know. It was beautifully political without being pedestrian. So I immediately got a contract for her. That was no problem . . . And that first book we did, she had some idiotic title for it. She always did. So I used the title of one of the stories, which captured her wit in an extraordinary way, that story called "Gorilla, My Love." The book is still in print . . . They were just marvelous pieces. She was a genius. Perfection seemed effortless in the writing. That's what you look for. Not that struggle to say something ornate, or the struggle to say something simply.

That one was successful. Then we did another one, *The Seabirds Are Still Alive* [another collection of short stories].

At the time we met, Toni was living in New York, uptown. Her daughter was young, maybe three years old . . . Then she moved to Atlanta. She had a woman who read a map and told her what latitude or longitude she should have been in; Atlanta was in the column. From then on, I would see her when she came to New York, or occasionally when I went to Atlanta.

The Salt Eaters [Bambara's first novel] was the third book I did. It was very, very hard to edit that book—meaning make suggestions—because she's so tight . . . You can't take anything out without the whole thing collapsing, you know. She's very, very intricate, and almost cunning, in her structure. I used to complain a lot because I said she never waited for the lame and the halt, the reader. If they weren't with her, she left them behind. (Laughing)

The Salt Eaters was well-reviewed, but it didn't sell well . . . Once you surrendered to it and just did it (as a reader), you were so amply rewarded, but it's hard any way to get readers in large numbers to put in that kind of service.

While working on *The Salt Eaters,* I was moving to the house that I'm in now. It's right on the river, maybe 40 or 50 feet from water. My sister and brother-in-law and some other people came to help me move and all we did was sort of open a box, then go sit on the swing for hours, then come back . . . Toni was in town and she had the time to go over the book with me. She'd write and I'd edit some. So she did that; she stayed here about three days. It was total chaos. She would go upstairs and work, then she'd run down the stairs and say, "What about this?" Then I would sit down and go over that, then she'd run back up the stairs. It was the most amazing—but certainly extremely efficient, for us—way to do it, because she was so clear. She could focus in immediately. I would just have to grunt and point and she knew exactly what I was suggesting.

VB: How did the idea of the novel on the Atlanta child murders evolve?

TM: Right after [*The Salt Eaters* was published], the business began to distract everybody in Atlanta . . . She knew she was going to do something about it—a documentary or a book. I signed her up for that. She spent the next dozen or more years off and on doing it.

I resigned from Random House, maybe a year or two after signing her for the Atlanta book, and turned her over to another editor, but told her that

I would do whatever she wanted me to do... Toni and I by that time were friends, and she knew that she could count on me for whatever.

VB: I know Toni Cade worked on this book for several years and had done at least three drafts, according to what she writes in the acknowledgments. What was the state of the book when she died?

TM: Pretty good actually. You know, fair copy. I had seen it in various stages, but it was soooo long. It was about 1,800 pages. And all while I talked to her, even before she got sick, she said, "I have to cut this," or "I'm restructuring this." One of her problems was that she didn't have an ending. And she didn't want to have an ending that wasn't as close to the truth as possible. So she was sending me articles off and on about the Klan and all sorts of things trying to figure out how to close the book. She didn't know whether the boy was gonna live or die, and if he did either, under what circumstances. And she did not want, and never did want, any of her work to end in despair. That was extremely important to her. So she wanted not just survival at the end of her work but kind of a refreshment at the same time. Because that was part of her teaching, the political as well as cultural point of what she was doing. And it was very strong in her.

She was an unreconstructed rebel—I mean, beautiful in every aspect of that. And there were a lot of such people, but they didn't have the talent. (Laughing) Hers was just outrageous. She was just outrageously brilliant.

So that stymied her for a while—just the execution of how the narrative would shape itself. And when she learned what that would be, finally, she finished it. But there was so much to say about the life in this culture, so many kinds of people, black people, in it.

She loathed, as I do, the sort of simplistic reduction of black people. And loathed, as I do, that notion that all the black people are goooood, and there's no difference, and everybody can eat off their grandmother's floor... There's the negative image and then there's the positive image, and neither one holds anything that is like a complicated, interesting black life. And it was that that she was so marvelous at eliciting from her characters. You laugh, you weep, and you disagree, but you *recognize*. And it was the recognition and the play and the dead seriousness of everything that suffused her work.

And here in the Atlanta scene she was able to pull out all the stops, and do things with class and do things with all kinds of people—in the community, out of it. But the major genius is just that simple narrative line.

I have never read a book—any book—that had a representation of an African-American family that is so, on the one hand, accurate and on the other joyful as well as hard. It's just a beautiful rendition, with not one stereotype in it. I've always been astonished by her. Just astonished.

VB: In your preface to *Deep Sightings and Rescue Missions,* you talk about some of the challenges of editing: the paragraphs or pages that may need to be written, the sentences that may need to be recast. What particular editing challenges did you face with this book?

TM: The actual editing of it was a nightmare because of the size. And you've gotta cut. You have to. So you're gonna take away half the book...I said, "One of these days, somebody should publish that book as done." You know, a big 2,000 pages.

VB: How did you go about editing 1,800 pages down to 600?

TM: Well, I went through it a couple of times, made some changes, notations, marginal cuts and things, but I kept losing the book because I wasn't editing it. Every time I started, I would *read* it, which is different. I'd get caught up in it—which is a marvelous sign of the power a book has. But at the same time, you're not doing your work, which is to look at it with a surgeon's eye, or to look at it coldly and be unimpressed, unseduced. If you start loving it, you're not gonna cut it. (Laughing)

VB: So, other than being long, it sounds like the manuscript was in good shape when you got it?

TM: I was so happy to find this huge thing of well-typed stuff, because over the years, when Toni would revise, she'd have notes clipped and penciled sentences that curl up and down the page and wind around. But this was fair. It was all done.

The funniest thing happened: I had some old pages of this book from various stages—you know, parts of it: 200 pages here, 200 pages there. Anyway, when I got the manuscript, after the prologue comes the first page of the text, right? That wasn't there. The first page. I called up everybody. Who typed it? Nobody knew this, nobody knew that. So there were about eight months there when I didn't have the first page. I had the second page. (Laughing) You can fudge a lot as an editor, but you cannot fudge the first page. That has to be there! So I just thought, "What kind of trick is she pulling on me?" You know I had a huge fire in my house [in 1993] and lost a lot of things, so I was digging around in boxes and old file cabinets, and I did find a very early, early early version of the book. Not even a version—it was like 50 pages. And it also included the first page, which had not changed...So that hurdle was solved.

And when I found myself reading and not editing, I called up the in-house editor [at Pantheon] and said, "I really need a first-rate copy editor," someone I hoped could read it without my baggage and my seduction. And she did. She made the copy-editing kinds of marks—when names are spelled five different ways, that sort of thing. That was helpful. And even with that, there were lots of problems...So I had to do some research. You know, find out whether it was Tanya or Tonya, that kind of thing. And then there were acronyms, some of which were peculiar to Atlanta, but some were just organizations that no longer exist. So anyway, there was a lot of that. And I just would not let them off the hook. We just had to find out. So there were a lot people that I needed to put on the case: "Go find out what this is."

The novel part of it, the fiction part of it, that family, has *got* to rest on publicly verifiable information. Otherwise it doesn't work. We can't make up streets. Is it the Bowen Homes or the Bowen Community? We had to go and find out what it is . . . But everybody who read it—from the copy editor to the production manager—everybody was riveted, absolutely.

VB: Did you have to do any rewriting, as part of the editing process?

TM: Cutting requires rewriting. Once you cut her things, you have to do it in an elegant way so that the cuts are not obvious. But it didn't take the kind of heavy rewriting that some books do. You might have to change a verb tense, introduce another sentence in another way.

If it were just a question of cutting and then going on, it would be simple, but it's never that—certainly not with her. You have to find out whether you're bleeding or not. Suddenly, other references, to very small things, to things like Kleenex, become important, because people are moving and doing things. Toni's very cinematic. Nobody ever is just sitting there talking. They're all picking up things, moving things, sewing, ironing, cooking, whatever they're doing.

It was like a read-through at least 12 times, just to make sure. And every time, you'd find something else. But that's what it took.

VB: As a reader, I found the editing to be rather seamless. Your voice never intrudes, and it was in no way obvious that this book had been cut down to a third of its original size.

TM: I have to say that I'm very good at that. (Laughing) Editing is, I suppose, like teaching in a way, because you really are trying to make certain that the *author's* voice is clear and it's what the *author* wants, what the text is demanding, in that style, in that fashion. What would this person say? What would this author say if she had her lifetime to do this? How would *she* say it?

VB: Are you pleased with the way *Those Bones* turned out?

TM: I am outrageously proud of it, because of the hard, hard work that went into sort of pulling it together. And also, I always felt at the beginning, when she first started, that this book was so *absolutely* necessary that I just couldn't imagine its never being published. And when what's his name's book came out—Tom Wolfe, *A Man in Full*—I didn't have these outrageous expectations for that book, but it sort of stamp-paid to that idea of Atlanta as a fictional milieu. You know, you have *Gone With the Wind*. (Laughing) Then you have whatever you've got. Then you have this Tom Wolfe book. And that's Atlanta. Boom. Over. And his was highly racially charged. And I thought, "No, no, no. No one is talking about Atlanta from the point of view of these people who knew it—not the political way, not the way the marketers knew it, but, you know, on the street, in the houses, in the schools. That sort of thing." And to have it about this unbelievable situation of these slaughters...

So, it just seemed to me, absolutely, the history of the world was incomplete if this book wasn't published. And obviously it's a major contribution to African-American literature, and to American literature. I'm convinced of that.

VB: In the preface to *Deep Sighting and Rescue Missions,* you mention "the hilarious title struggles" you and Toni used to have. Did she choose the incredible title *Those Bones Are Not My Child?*

TM: She changed the title about four different times. She talked it, and I said, "That's the name for the book," and she said, "Yes." So she used it for a little while. Then she changed it to *Ground Cover*. And then her final title was *Blessings*. And I understand the reasons for all those titles, but they're not capturing. So I just went back to the original title... It's amazing. It's just—boom.

VB: For me, reading *Those Bones* was similar to reading *Beloved,* in that it was a very hard book for me to finish because of the subject matter. Yet it's clear that it's a very necessary novel. Do you have any concerns about this book finding a substantial and appreciative readership, given its subject matter?

TM: Always. It's there, that question, because most people read not to confront anything like that, but to escape. And also, there's a different kind of reading going on... The biggest problem is having to look without blinking at something that is that dreadful—in addition to what happened to the families and the children, but the indifference with which they are met because they are black and poor. Just having to look at that—not have it intimated, but see the consequences of it...

This book will last forever, I am certain. It will be read in every possible course in African-American literature—I mean, I *know* that, but that's over the long haul. But as far as making an early or immediate impact, I just don't know, because there's such shying away from books like this for the easier thing—you know, the sort of spectacular thing. The same impulse that operated in the book of "let's get it over with" will operate with the reader who doesn't want to feel that again. And in *Beloved* the same thing: Nobody wanted to remember slavery. But too bad. I mean, there it is. (Laughing)

Now, the reviews have been very strong. Some people have complained about it being preachy. But I say whenever black folks have something to say it's called preaching. When they have something to say it's called ideas, I guess. (Laughing) So that part doesn't trouble me.

VB: I know Toni Cade had been fighting cancer for some years. Had you two discussed what TO DO IF SHE DIED BEFORE THE BOOK WAS FINISHED OR PUBLISHED?

TM: No. I talked to her a lot during, and she was winning for a long time. And then when she got sick the last time, I just let her know anything I could do to help . . .

I never broached the subject because that would mean I would have to talk about all kinds of stuff. Instead of "What is to be done to make you well," I would have to talk about "Since you are not going to be well . . ." I never really . . . I guess the rational part of my mind, when I saw her last, was clear, but she never let you stay there, you know? She was taking painkillers and laughing and cussing people out and stuff when she was in the apartment [Morrison's apartment in New York City]. She was calling the shots, which is the way it should have been, about that. She was very, very proud, very private, for a public person. She talked about it as a mean disease . . . but I never talked to her about that.

So I was quite hurt—devastated—when she died because, you know, you just don't think about it. And that was somebody who was so full of life, you couldn't even imagine. So no, we never talked about that. If she had brought it up, I would have . . . but I was determined to do it [to get *Those Bones* published], some kind of way.

I didn't think there was anybody around who could do it but me. And certainly there was nobody who was gonna negotiate a contract and just make those people do what I said. (Laughing) I didn't ask them: "Would you do this?" I said, "Look, this is what we're doing and this is what it is, so there."

VB: Was there any resistance?

TM: Nope. Not one iota. I mean, I wasn't even raising my voice. I just called 'em up and said, "This is what's happenin'. Great."

VB: Did Toni have any more manuscripts she was working on at the time of her death?

TM: Yeah. There was some old and some recent stuff that I saw when I was putting together the stuff for *Rescue Missions*. But the other stuff is with [filmmaker] Louis Massiah. I suspect there's quite a bit actually. Toni wrote a lot . . . If they ever dig up something and say they want to do that, I would certainly help. But this is the big one.

VB: What did you know of Toni Cade's writing discipline?

TM: She was like me: she was a rush artist. It's there, you know it, you do it. This is why she was such a good short story writer. I don't write short stories, but I work the same way in terms of the scene. You know, if it's there, you have to do it. And I don't care if I don't write for months. That's why writers think they have blocks, because they think they have to write every day. But I don't like what happens when you write through a block. Let it arrive. And then I rewrite a lot, as she did. She did a lot of that. And they were *all* improvements.

But there were times, I know, when she was writing every day on things, long periods, and then she would stop and not do it for another long time . . . You just have to figure out how you work best. Some people work best by writing two pages every day, and at the end of the year, they've got 600 pages. But I don't—because it's not cumulative in that sense to me. Sometimes you get up and there's nothing to say. (Laughing) Why cover the page with stuff you know you can't use or, if you're smart, you'll throw out?

I've always said that I had enormous powers of concentration because I could write under adverse circumstances. I didn't need silence, I didn't need just whatever writers think they need, because I didn't have it and I was writing anyway. So I never developed those habits where if I don't have a cup of coffee, if I don't have a whatever . . .

I think her life was active enough and responsive enough—she would respond to calls, go travel and read and so on. And she was very devoted to her students and to her friends; she would take time out . . . almost at the drop of a hat. And then there were periods when she would take the phone off, and that was it. Or she would go off somewhere and then you would not know where she was. I don't think those, the going off, were writing periods, those were recharging periods.

She used to put all of her writing material, in the latter days . . . in a shopping cart. You know, like a grocery-shopping cart? She would put manuscripts in there and notes and things, so that she didn't have to jump up and run over here to get something. (Laughing) It was all in the shopping cart. She could tool around the house. And I thought, "Now isn't that smart?" I have snatches of paper everywhere . . .

VB: What's your own writing schedule?

TM: I know that I'm smarter in the morning. I usually get up around 5 o'clock and go to work. And then if I work till 11, I've put in a good day and then I can do stuff that I don't like to do or junk stuff, or real stuff—it doesn't matter—because the book I have addressed already. I just know that's better for me. I'm not good at night. I have very country hours I keep.

VB: What did you admire most about Toni Cade Bambara?

TM: She had this keen, keen intellect, absolutely on-target intuition—and humor. She was so funny, and she could be deadly in it. But that wide-spiritedness and her willingness to have and almost be amused by her own errors in judgment. As keen as her intuition was, she made these outrageous mistakes—I don't mean the work, but I mean in her judgment about people . . . She would keep me up all night, and we'd just be weak, weak, with laughter. She read the world in the way I tend to do also, but she really read it—its symbols, you know, the things behind things. She was very, very, very adept at that.

VB: One thing I admired about her was that, as someone put it, she "suffered fools gladly"—that is, she would talk with *any* one very seriously about writing or filmmaking or any kind of art or activism. She seemed to take each person seriously, whether they were an obvious genius or a clear knucklehead. Did you find that to be true of her also?

TM: She had a lot of patience that I don't have . . . One likes to think one is like that, but in actual fact, I have to be up for it, and she didn't. She would do it whether she was up for it or not . . . She's a big void in my life.

VB: What do you miss most about her?

TM: Talk. Knowing that I cannot just pick up the phone and spend a couple of hours with her, or 20 minutes. I mean, real giggling—and enlightening—time. And that absence is fairly profound. For me personally, there are not a lot of friends that I've known over time that you don't have to explain things to. They know who you are and where you're coming from. They know your history and you know theirs, so there's a whole lot you don't have to say, but everything is colored with your knowledge of that and also where you are going from there. And fresh. She was always fresh. I don't expect to find a duplicate of that. When friendships are like that, you can have other friends but nobody can replace that, and so you are always missing it . . . My mother died about five years ago and every now and then I think, "Oh, Ma's gonna like this." You know, you almost make the gesture to the phone—not quite, but you feel your little mind dwelling that way. So it's that. It's that.

VB: Does her spirit still speak to you?

TM: I'm not able quite yet to talk to her the way you do with people whose spirits are there. Working on the book, I felt, was a kind of homage. I thought that was the absolute best thing to do. And I knew all while I was working on it . . . I guess I talked to her then, saying, "What are you doing? I have something else to do, please." As I said, when I didn't have the first page, I said, "Toni, puuh-leazzz, what is this about?" . . . But what you're talking about—no, I haven't done that yet. I may be able to now. Now that I have finished this *work*, maybe I can have a decent conversation.

I know that was first on the agenda, I know that was my work, and I know she gave it to me, and I know she wanted me to do it. *That* I know. There's never been a question in my mind. And it was extremely important to me but I know it was extremely important to her that I finish that. I didn't really have to ask her. It was as clear as daylight to me.

VB: Is there anything else you want to say?

TM: I just hope that that little resistance to work by black women that so many black men seem still to feel doesn't surface in that awful debate that's not about anything, but that keeps coming back. That the transgression of actually writing a book (Laughing) is, in some quarters, so severe that you don't get to talk about the book, to talk about the thing itself. I keep thinking, "Oh that's gone," and then I go somewhere to give a talk or a lecture and then somebody drags me back into, "How come black women are the only ones who get the attention in the writing world?" You know, that kind of thing.... Sometimes just that residual...I guess it's envy—gender envy—among us hurts the discourse about a book. If you have an imperfect man, which is to say a human man, who is not running around with guns being the hero, some people get really mad, because (for them) it's very much about re-presenting certain kinds of typical answers to a negative stereotype.

But it's all addressed [in *Those Bones*]. You can feel when you read Toni Cade's book that she's talking, she's not closing out anybody, but she's addressing African-Americans. Her respect and her love and her seriousness about us is so overwhelming and is so irresistible that she brings you up to her level. She never plays down. And if the reader wants to be played down to, he should read something else. I think, working on the book, all this time, every time I read it, I felt better, even though I had looked into those terrible dark places.

Anyway, that little alarm is probably unworthy of her, but still having been in publishing all these years...I don't want there to be any hesitation, any resistance.

This is some place where we need to be. This is the kind of art that we have delivered in practically every art we've ever entered—at *this* level. Everywhere we go, we just change the rules...It's always amusing to me when people talk in the newspapers and on television about lowering standards. And it's just so obvious that everywhere we have been, we have *raised* the standards. Everywhere. All the terms are changed now. Whether it's Michael Jordan or Toni Cade Bambara. It's all different now. The little girls [Venus and Serena Williams] in that tennis match. Over. Out. Brand new. (Laughing)

I always wanted to write that way, for readers like me. I mean, black readers. And it meant that I had to do better. I couldn't snow [those readers]. You know you can't play those games. And sometimes you read and you see it—you see people just slumming, as I call it. And when you see something like this book, you say "This is it. This is the real deal here."

She's done it. She has done it. And I thought, "If this book is not published, that whole period [of the Atlanta child murders] would just be a little anecdote in the history of the country." But now it's not.

9

The Making of Paper
(for Toni Cade Bambara)

NIKKY FINNEY

In the early '80s, I spent two years in a writing workshop that Toni
Cade Bambara held in her Atlanta home. Anybody in the community who was writing was welcome. I adored the opportunity to sit
at this great writer's feet who knew so much about so much. In 1990, she
moved to Philadelphia and was later diagnosed with cancer. We talked on
the long-distance line when we could. I would always ask if there was anything she needed that I could send. She usually answered no. But in our last
conversation, which took place one week before she crossed over, she held
the phone a little longer. "Maybe," she said, "maybe you could send some
paper and what about one of those fat juicy pens?"

Imagine that,
you asking me for paper.

For the record let me state
I would hunt a tree down for you,
stalk it until it fell
all loud and out of breath
in the forest.

Much as I love a tree,
fat, tall and free.

As anti-violent and pro-vegetarian
as I am.
Never been much
for strapping a gun
to any of my many hips,
for any reason whatsoever,

but on the copper penny eyes
of my grandmother, I tell you
this: I would hunt a tree down for you.

And when found
I would pull it all the way down the road
through congested city streets all by myself
and deliver it straight away
to your hospital bed,
one single extra-large floral arrangement,
something loud and free,
with red and purple bow.

Or better yet,
this tree loving
gun hating Geechee girl
would strap a wild west
gun belt machete
around her hips
enter the worst part of the woods alone
and go trunk to trunk
until the right one appeared
growing peaceful in its thousand-year-old
natal pot.

Look it
right in its
round rough ancient eyes
and confess away,
tell it straight to its woody face,
my about to do deed.

I'd even touch it
on its limbs,
fingers begging forgiveness,
give as much comfort to it
as I could, while trying to
explain the necessaryness
of its impending death;
me standing there,
my *Gorilla My Love* eyes

spilling all over everything,
sending up papyrus prayers
that all begin with,
"I'm so sorry but Toni Cade needs paper."

Only then would I slash its lovely body
into one million thick black cotton rag sheets
just your uncompromising size.

Send you some paper?
Oh yes,
paper is coming Toni Cade
wagonloads
in the name of
your sweet Black writing life,
from Black writers everywhere
refusing to leave
the arena
to the fools.

Paper is on the way.

"Making Revolution Irresistible"

From The Vietnam Notebooks (1975)

Toni Cade Bambara

In late May, I received an invitation from the Women's Union of the
Democratic Republic of Vietnam to make a three week visit to the
North as a guest of the Women's Union. At that time, I made some
attempts, not terribly organized, but I made some attempts to contact a
number of organizations in the Black community and to put myself at their
service as a mailman. Again, while I wasn't terribly organized in doing this,
it was important to do because as most of us know, the White Left has a
virtual monopoly on trips like this. All too often, we're not able to send
papers abroad, to inform other people, our allies, as to what we are doing
in this country as part of the worldwide anti-imperialist movement.

We are not always able to send expressions of solidarity, but between
the four of us, that is to say, the other three women in the delegation and
myself, we were able to take lots and lots of posters, literature, letters from
prisoners such as from H. Rap Brown and from organizations such as the
Institute of the Black World and the February 1st Movement that provided
some sense of what stage of struggle we are in from a Black perspective—
crucial.

By the end of June, I was in touch with the three other women who'd
been also selected on the basis of their involvement in the anti-war
movement. In mid-July, the four of us met in New York for the purpose of
trying to pull ourselves together as a group and to establish some discipline
and understanding of what we were about to do and begin to establish
some kind of mechanism by which we could keep each other cool.

Anybody who has ever gone abroad with a delegation knows how very
difficult it is to establish a collective habit with folks who are products of
this society in which narcissism itself is an obsession and individualism is
raised to some kind of metaphysical principle. But we managed in two days
to establish some ground rules for how we would operate as a group. We
also used the time to pull together collectively a presentation on the state of

Courtesy of Karma Bambara.

affairs of the U.S. at the time. That is to say, what is the state doing and how the people are responding, and what stage of struggle are we in?

We arrived in Hanoi on Monday, July 21st and we were met by the Central Bureau of the Women's Union. There, we were presented with flowers and given a most unusual concoction of beer and papaya juice which I've since become addicted to. We were warmly thanked at the airport as we were thanked everywhere we went for the antiwar effort of a significantly large section of the American population. It was a very good time, needless to say, to be in Vietnam in the summer of '75. The people were celebrating the 45th anniversary of the Party, the Vietnam Workers' Party, which was established in 1930 and has as their first political thesis equality between men and women. Just as the Party was established in February of 1930, so too the women's organization was encouraged to form. Out of the many Party organizations, Women against Imperialism, Women for the Defense of the Country, a lot of patriotic bourgeois women's groups, as well as rank and file worker's groups, they finally merged and became the Women's Union.

The Women's Union too was celebrating its 45th anniversary. The Vietnamese were also celebrating the 30th anniversary of the Republic. In 1945, recall that Vietnam declared its independence and also drafted its Constitution. The Vietnamese were also celebrating the 30th anniversary of the Women's International Federation. Bear in mind that the Indochinese Communist Party during the thirties with all their constitutions laid out specific articles regarding the status of women. In many ways, the 1945 Constitution changed the status of women from slaves to citizens. The Constitution enabled them to vote, to run for public office, to be active in every field, to be eligible for education, for job training and the job, to have free choice in marriage, to have a voice in the family, that is to say, the democratic family was the legal model. The non-democratic family was illegal. Maternity leave and maternity allowance and child care allowance were instituted. Through the efforts to emancipate the woman, progressive legislation that benefited everybody immediately occurred such as social security and free medical care.

The country was also preparing to celebrate the 85th birthday of the late president Ho Chi Minh. And, of course, it was International Woman's Year. Needless to say, the country was absolutely jubilant over the spring victory over U.S. imperialist aggression. It was a very good time to be in Vietnam.

In the next ten days we learned a great deal about the efforts of the Women's Union to mobilize, organize, develop and defend women and their interests. We learned too about some of the earlier women's *organizations, the precursors or prototypes of the Women's Union, and their efforts to recruit and train women, and to encourage women to be masters of their destinies—to take real responsibility for the running of the country. Bear in mind, we're talking about women who had experienced two thousand years of feudalism under the Chinese, the Mongols, the Chinese again, then 80 years of colonialism and foreign aggression under the French and then later the Japanese in '45 and the French again and then finally a fantastic war with the most powerful military machine, the most powerful counter-revolutionary force in the world, the United States.*

Unlike a lot of other delegations that go to different countries and are able to get a history lesson, an economic lesson, or who visit the schools, our trips were designed primarily, if not exclusively, to acquaint us with the work of the Women's Union. At first we thought that meant not being able to realize our agenda, the itinerary we had drafted together. We didn't fully appreciate how wide ranging the Women's Union is. They cover everything. They are everywhere. There is not a single aspect of national life that is not the domain, the concern of the Women's Union. So we were able to get a thorough-going tour just through traveling from one Women's Union branch to another, from one district to another, from one province to another branch of the Women's Union. We visited many handicraft coops, both state run and community run, as well as agricultural coops and infant schools, both state run and community cooperatives.

Thai Binh remains in my mind because of the women we met there. The Vietnamese women in general are a hellifying group of women and the Thai Binh women in particular were quite stunning, very strong, warm, and gracious. I was just composing a letter the other night trying to thank them for a gift they gave me. They gave me back my grandmother in the sense that being in the presence of these women renewed your whole love affair with your grandmother, and with all those other women that we know who kept on keeping on. You're in the presence of Vietnamese women for five minutes and you recall, yes, Harriet Tubman, right Sojourner Truth. They gave me back my grandmother.

Toni

Amiri Baraka

Ah, there is a steadily more greedy shadow alienating us from our memory. That comes with time, which consumes us finally, to make us history.

The consciousness of this, we mark by the completeness of our perception, rationale and use of the world. But also by the hostility and sadness pressed upon us by death. The death of our friends. Especially of those whom we agree were, in some way, wondrous. Those who have left the brain prints of their minds and visions upon our lives and upon the world's.

Particularly, for a people deprived of the primitive normalcy of bourgeois democracy and self determination. Particularly, for a people identified by their physical appearance as slaves, those "who can be slapped," those whose torture provides the wealth, philosophical measure and social stability of a world, my grandmother said, God let be ruled by the Devil.

I know now why old people seem so removed from the tipsy gibberish of topical surfaces. They grow lonely, through the years, because the people they are closest to, the ones they have loved, laughed and reasoned with, have passed. With the absurd quickness of the years.

Witness our friend here, Toni Cade Bambara, who would make us smile when we saw her. Who would make us feel more significant in the world. Because she was one of those wondrous presences who could prove her and all our, being, by being a living site, a conscious profile of creating.

Harlem born, Harlem Hip, Toni was always direct when you saw her, but the ironies of what she could see spread her words into a splash of narrative invocation. The quick flash of inference. She had a kind of drollery I match with the city. So she was always with us. At the front. No matter where she was. Toni was never Blank to the world. She spoke back to it. She was engaged with it, mind and person. A woman of evocation and imagination. She was, like Jimmy or Margaret, a witness, but on her own terms. Spinning the matter with the due west breath of the new world.

Bambara, she dug out of her family's reflections. For she was with us in embracing Africa, as the place of origin of what she was, but although she called herself a nationalist and a feminist some years ago, the rush and spirit and tone of democracy, as quest, certain as love, confused as distance, was always there.

So that she felt the balance of our world. The union of our two historic selves. The African. The American. The Black and Blueness of our Am.

Last night, Amina remembered Toni, though self identifying as Black nationalist and sensitive to our culture, still was never as wild a cultural nationalist as some of us! But she was born in the Big Apple, an uptown Griot and learned from the street's memory the corniness of atavism. Toni was surprising because she would take independent looks at "Dis" and still shoot out the Bull's eye.

Toni was part of the rush of Black women writers that flowed out of the Black Arts '60s, a smoking magma of the real. Who converted the concrete dialectic of out struggle into a complex reflection of people's lives and minds.

But she was on the case. Not with a fiery pitchfork, but an insistent rationalism. She wanted to give our feelings names and addresses. So we could better understand how many and diverse are the ways and paths of revelation.

Toni knew what all the advanced know. That we are circumscribed by what we are as well as what we are not. That America has never been a democracy, and we have never been citizens!

She gave a living cast to our real life struggles. A contemporary human dimension to our dreams and our torture. She wrote of Black people, women, men, children, as workers, mothers, wives, husbands, sons and daughters, revolutionaries, militants, community organizers, nationalists, their families, the participants, the onlookers, bystanders... innocent or otherwise. She created a cast of the real people of our world. The selves and their consciousnesses, of where we were and wanted to go to. Our grace and our backwardness. The strength and the fragility it becomes when denied. What are the lives of conscious, progressive Black people, beset by themselves as the illness of captivity, the psychology of resistance as well as submission. She got up close on Black men and women, as a precise observer, who is a woman, advocating we get real, narrating the layers of unrealness our oppression, our ignorance, our denial, our opportunism, our momentary victory, can produce.

Her women are advanced intellectuals, as working women, activist sisters resisting Brothers insisting on locking them up in their own male delusion. Women, mostly Black, who are strong as, and mostly stronger than, their Black men. Who must convince themselves not to reveal it, even to themselves. But who must, even down to the smallest benediction. The conversational goodbye, as explanation of our movement, of Her and Him, We and Them.

But she asked, "Are you sure you want to get well?" to us all. Why was her great creativity, like all of ours, not tied by us, all together, more tightly? So many of us gone, going soon. So much pain whizzing around. More than enough!

Our bright revolutionary generation. And its fantastic desires. Its beauty. Its strength. Its struggle. Its accomplishment. Its legacy. What will that be?!

Because, like the Bambara, we must use our highest flights of vision and creativity as the intellectual headquarters of our struggling nation. For Toni knew, so well, the truth of this oppressed Afro-American Nation. We worked together with Thulani Davis and Wesley Brown in Louis Massiah's Du Bois film. When you see it, notice how clear she is. How matter of fact about the meaning and motion of history. Listen to her. What we know, if we find a precise use for what we have already given a name.

The very removal of our friends and comrades. Large and small. All those, who like Toni, used their vision to explain the world to us, so we could change it.

Before the deadline of our lives, the experience and maturity, the moving art that Toni created, is part of the direction we must travel as a collective consciousness. Because we are in a world where even the leaders of our struggle can oppose democracy with religion and its baggage of feudalism packaged as militance. Where an intellectual activist and veteran of our struggle, a great warrior artist, can be dismissed from the struggle as a gesture of "atonement" and love. Where Angela Davis, who, a long time ago, proved her revolutionary courage, can be booed by the backward as some grim patriarchal patriotism (same word). And we, by the millions, ride the tail of our own desire, a cynical riderless horse.

We must, in the next period, begin to transform our vision and desire into living blueprints of unity and organization for self-determination, as the first necessity of democracy. Like Toni, we must create the vision, the image, but also begin to actively intervene in the politics of Black people and the advanced of the whole of the Afro-American and oppressor nation.

We must begin to create the collective organization of ourselves, the artists and intellectuals, as an act of self-determination, so that we are free to tell Toni's life and our own. And our history. One hundred of us could create a network of collective self- reliant Black Art and the necessary organization to begin to nationalize our greatest weapon, ourselves and the invincibility of our truth, our history and the very plan for our liberation. Our Art. Our Minds. Revolutionary Art. Democratic and Beautiful. Revolutionary Art for Cultural Revolution.

The United Front for Afro-American Self-Determination, the "Man March" must become, should be consolidated only with the intervention of revolutionary Black intellectuals and artists. Like Toni Cade Bambara, we must turn our analysis and criticism into action. For the most valuable aspect of our culture is our creativity, mobilized by true self-consciousness.

We are great artists, the sons and daughters of great artists. And from the conscious self organization of that art, as a method of national development, as education, employment and the expression of our lives, we can use our art to revolutionize our lives and our people's and America's. We must create a national network of artists and intellectuals, to nationalize Afro-American Culture as a total resource for Self-Determination.

Revolutionary Black intellectuals must unify and organize a national union of Afro American Artists and Intellectuals. As the creators of and catalysts for revolutionary change, upon Black people and the world. In every city or community where we are. Create. Communicate. Unite. Organize. We are given opportunity by the abuse of our enemies. Whose glitzy emptiness has long since abandoned Art, Truth and Reality for Money, Lies and Power.

Instead of whining, asking why—why can't we be all of ourselves in the world and tell our story and say how we live our lives? Then laugh at the gullible Bloods who rooted for OJ (but not Mumia). Who have no question for the Minister, or the others who admire foolish Negroes and cruel whip crackers. The cultural canon of national oppression, its philosophy, influence, psychology and stolen wealth, must be neutralized and prevented from stealing more of our soul's wealth, and misdirect, condemn and doom our people.

In every city, there is a Motown! A collective of the city's history and heartbeat. We must provide an economic base for ourselves, collectively and take intellectual responsibility for our people's level of development, not by cynicism and alienation or being a drowned fly in the sour buttermilk of "white america," the oppressor nation.

Stop bowing to our enemy! Communicate! Organize! Produce! Unify the Afro-American political culture with the development of a national Black Artists and Intellectuals Network, for self determination, self-consciousness, self-reliance and self-defense. Use the art to provide resources, education, employment and political unity. We can fight in the superstructure. The class struggle in the realm of ideas.

Let us begin, before we lose another wonderful friend. "We have a better future than that," Toni said. That's what Toni was saying. Be Clear. Understand. Act! Make the Revolution!

* * *

(At the National Black Arts Festival in 1994, Toni, Amina, Wesley Brown, Michael Simmons and I sat up most of the night in the lobby of the Marriott kicking these ideas around, as we have done before. Then we started singing.

We went from the sorrow songs become Freedom songs, and then for the last couple hours, Toni and Wesley and Amina started singing Oldies But Goodies, into the Gems of American Popular Song. Toni played piano and sang and She and Wesley wailed. Man, was that hip!

I should ask Toni, now, if she remembers. Toni is saying, "Make the Revolution!")

1995

11

Cuba

JAYNE CORTEZ

In early January 1985, Toni Cade Bambara, Rosa Guy, Verta Mae Grosvenor, Audre Lorde, Gloria Josephs, Mildred Walters, Mari Evans, Alexis DeVeaux, and I arrived at Jose Marti airport in Havana, Cuba. Poet Nancy Morejon and members of the Union of Writers and Artists of Cuba (UNEAC) met the delegation. This was the Black Women Writers Cultural Tour to Cuba arranged by *Black Scholar Magazine*. After checking into the Havana Riviera Hotel we went to the offices of UNEAC to meet with translators and go over details concerning the tour. While in Havana we met with the Federation of Cuban Women, with writers, filmmakers, visual artists, and a central committee representative. We toured the old part of the city, which was under reconstruction, the Vedado area, the countryside, and attended music events, book launchings, and an awards reception for young writers. We visited Ospal Poster Center, Casa de Las Americas, Ernest Hemingway's house, a new hospital, a day care center, museums, art galleries, and the Club Tropicana. We were in the sunshine of Havana for about ten days.

TONI

She was
    who she was
With that shy smile of
    a little girl from Harlem
With that frown of
    a mature writer of fiction
With that pace of a hip New Yorker
    jumping barricades and
Making entrances into marshes with
    Seabirds & Salt Eaters while
Singing a theme song of
    Mother clan solidarity within

Collective intonations of
   revolutionary blackness
She was that magnetic teacher &
   marvelous mediator
With the busy headdress &
   Bamana known as Bambara

12

Toni Cade Bambara, Black Feminist Foremother

BEVERLY GUY-SHEFTALL

In 1974, Toni Cade [Bambara] had recently moved to Atlanta and was one of the first persons with whom my departmental colleague Roscann Bell and I consulted when we began conceptualizing our anthology, *Sturdy Black Bridges: Visions of Black Women in Literature,* which would be the first collection of black women's literature in the African diaspora.[1] Bambara's now-classic text *The Black Woman* (1970) had been in print only four years. I also felt strongly that Bambara's contribution to the development of contemporary black feminism, feminist theory, and women's studies had not been adequately documented by scholars, though it is the case that *The Black Woman* has begun to garner the attention it deserves in mainstream narratives of American feminism.[2]

When I think of the beginnings of women's studies, especially Black Women's Studies, not necessarily academic feminism, I think of Toni Cade Bambara, whose anthology *The Black Woman* was as important in the development of this new interdisciplinary field as Kate Millett's pioneering and more celebrated *Sexual Politics,*[3] though Bambara's work has rarely been seen in this context by white feminists. *The Black Woman* was significant because of the value it attached to hearing the distinct voices of black women, arguing that our experiences were different from both black men and white women. Cade's work preceded by two years Gerda Lerner's influential 1972 documentary history, *Black Women in White America,* which is often erroneously cited as having ushered in Black Women's Studies. Frustrated with the priorities of the new women's movement, which was in process during the writing of her preface, Bambara asserted, "in the whole bibliography of feminist literature, literature immediately and directly relevant to us wouldn't fill a page."[3] By "us," she meant black and other Third World women, for example, sisters in Vietnam, Guatemala, Algeria, and Ghana.

Rather than simply complaining, she advocated a radical agenda for women's studies and the women's movement (inseparable, from her vantage

Excerpted interview courtesy of Beverly Guy-Sheftall.

point), which if it had been taken seriously, or even noticed, would have altered the course of "second-wave feminism" within and without the academy. Her plan was to:

> set up a comparative study of the woman's role as she saw it in all the Third World nations; examine the public school system and blueprint some viable alternatives; explore ourselves and set the record straight on the matriarch and the evil Black bitch; delve into history and pay tribute to all our warriors from the ancient times to the slave trade to Harriet Tubman to Fannie Lou Hamer to the woman of this morning... interview the migrant workers, the quilting bee mothers, the grandmothers of the UNIA[4]... outline the work that has been done in the area of consumer education and cooperative economics... provide a forum of opinion from the YWCA to the Black Women Enraged; get into the whole area of sensuality, sex; chart the steps necessary for forming a working alliance with all non-white women of the world for the formation of, among other things, a clearing house for the exchange of information.[5]

Commenting on the profound impact of Toni Cade's ground-breaking anthology on her own "revolutionary feminism many years later," bell hooks also captures the significance of *The Black Woman* for other black women like me who, in the early 1970s were claiming feminism as a legitimate vehicle for understanding black life, and who were working within the academy to transform it:

> Singlehandedly, *The Black Woman* placed black women at the center of various feminist debates. "On the Issue of Roles"... was one of the first essays on feminist theory that looked at the interlocking relations between race, sex, and class. It legitimized looking at black life from a feminist perspective... it helped to create an intellectual climate where feminist theory focusing on black experience could emerge. Without the publication of this anthology, later feminist works focusing on black life might never have been written.[6]

Toni Cade Bambara would have as well a profound impact on my own career as a feminist scholar/activist. Because of the historical significance of *The Black Woman* and her importance as a writer, educator, feminist critic, and community worker, the interview with Toni was critical to the vision of *Sturdy Black Bridges,* my first publication. Roseann and I believed it was imperative to mark the visionary thinking of early black feminist scholar/activists such as Toni Cade who would continue to have a powerful impact on younger women like myself and bell hooks. When I inquired about the possibility of black and other Third World women forming alliances around the eradication of both race and gender oppression, Toni revealed her involvement in what we would now call a global women's movement. A year later (1975) she would travel to North Vietnam having been invited by their Women's Union with a delegation called the North American Academic Marxist-Leninist Anti-Imperialist Feminist Women. She believed that feminist movements should not be narrowly focused on the evils of patriarchy but rather on eliminating all oppressions, including that experienced by the colonized Third World and poor people in the United States. She also bemoaned a missed moment in the early 1960s when what she called a national black women's movement could have been multicultural and multiethnic if African American women had joined Puerto Rican women and Chicanas "who shared not only a common condition but also I think a common vision about the future." In her usual prophetic fashion, she also anticipated that in the last quarter of the twentieth century, African Americans would begin to forge critical ties with other communities of color, which, she believed, was also critical for white women involved in the women's liberation struggle in the United States. When I asked her whether it was a dilemma for her to be both a feminist and a warrior in the race struggle, which for some black women and men was an oxymoron, she asserted unequivocally, "I don't find any basic contradiction or any tension between being a feminist, being a pan-Africanist, being a black nationalist, being an internationalist, being a socialist, and being a woman in North America." This was precisely the message many of us young black feminists needed as we found ourselves increasingly under suspicion with respect to our race loyalty. She also pointed us in new directions as she envisioned an updated version of *The Black Woman*, which would include position papers from the Women's Caucus of Student Non-Violent Coordinating Committee (SNCC), the Women's Caucus of the Black Panthers, and the Third World Women's Alliance. There would also be writings from "the campus forces, the prison forces, tenants' groups, and most especially from the migrant workers and sharecroppers of the Deep South." Clearly, her vision of women's liberation was sensitive to class differences and suspicious of monolithic conceptions of womanhood. She was also aware of the perils of exclusion and warned against the marginalization of particular women who were as critical to an understanding of the female condition and the history of women's resistance to oppression globally as were middle-class Euro-American women.

In an interview with Louis Massiah, "How She Came By Her Name," Toni reveals the genesis of *The Black Woman* which began in 1968 while she was teaching at City College's Search for Education, Elevation and Knowledge (SEEK) Program. Her initial goal was to collect position papers from black women in civil rights organizations such as SNCC, Congress of Racial Equality (CORE), and the Black Panther Party, who were "taking brothers to task for their foolishness," but their response was, "No, this is in-house stuff. We are not interested in going public."[7] After discovering how difficult it was to convince publishers to publish books about black women, she abandoned the working papers idea, and decided that she would create an anthology that would prove that there was indeed a market for black women's work so that more of their writings would appear in print. Within the second month of its hitting the bookstores, *The Black Woman* went into a second edition! Her insistence that it cost less than a dollar and be able to fit in your pocket turned out to have been a stroke of marketing genius.

In the preface to *Deep Sightings*, which was edited by Toni Morrison, her former editor, and published after Bambara's untimely death, Morrison speculates about whether her sister-friend realized how brilliant at writing fiction she was. I continue to wonder whether Bambara fully realized how profoundly she had impacted young black feminists-in-the making through the example of her unconventional life and utter clarity about the evils of white supremacy, misogyny, capitalism, stereotypical gender roles, as well as sexism within African American communities. In the *New York Times* obituary, Bambara is heralded as "a major contributor to the emerging genre of black women's literature, along with the writers Toni Morrison and Alice Walker." Her friend and film collaborator, Louis Massiah, captured her transgressive spirit with the eloquent observation, "She made revolution irresistible." Her vision of radical black struggle was deeply feminist and critical of its patriarchal, heterosexist paradigms:

> we are just as jammed in the rigid confines of those basically oppressive socially contrived roles. For if a woman is tough, she's a rough mamma, a strident bitch, a ballbreaker, a castrator. And if a man is at all sensitive, tender, spiritual, he's a faggot. And there is a dangerous trend observable in some quarters to program Sapphire out of her "evil" ways into a cover-up, shut-up, lay-back-and-be-cool obedience role . . . She is being encouraged—in the name of the revolution no less—to cultivate "virtues" that if listed would sound like the personality traits of slaves . . . Perhaps we need to let go of all notions of manhood and femininity and concentrate on Blackhood.[8]

The creative, political, and critical work of Toni Cade Bambara certainly made feminist revolution irresistible to many young black women over the past four decades. Her bold, unwavering commitment to liberation struggle, and her hard-hitting, incisive prose inspired a new generation of warrior women. We speak her name and honor her memory.

Beverly Guy-Sheftall [BGS]: Would you describe your early life and what caused you to start writing?

Toni Cade Bambara [TCB]: I can't remember a time when I was not writing. The original motive was to try to do things that we were not encouraged to do in the language arts programs in the schools, namely, to use writing as a tool to get in touch with the self. In the schools, for example, writing, one of the few crafts we're taught, seems to be for the purpose of teaching people how to plagiarize from the dictionary or the encyclopedia and how to create as much distance from our own voice as possible. That was called education. I'd call it alienation. You had to sift out a lot, distort a lot, and lie in order to jam the stuff of your emotional, linguistic, cultural experience into that form called English composition.

The original motive for writing at home was to give a play to those notions that wouldn't fit the English composition mold, to try and do justice to a point of view, to a sense of self. Later on, I discovered that there was a certain amount of applause that could be gotten if you turned up with the Frederick Douglass play for Negro History Week or the George Washington Carver play for the assembly program. That talent for bailing the English teachers out created stardom, and that became another motive.

As I got older, I began to appreciate the kinds of things you could tap and release and learn about self if you had a chance to get cozy with pencil and paper. And I discovered that paper is very patient. It will wait on you to come up with whatever it is, as opposed to sitting in class and having to raise your hand immediately in response to someone else's questions, someone else's concerns.

I don't know that I began getting really serious about writing until maybe five years ago. Prior to that, in spite of all good sense, I always thought writing was rather frivolous, that it was something you did because you didn't feel like doing any work. But in the last five or six years I've come to appreciate that it is a perfectly legitimate way to participate in struggle. That writing, sharing insights, keeping a vision alive, is of value and that is pretty much the motive for writing now. Although I can't really say I have a motive for writing now. I'm compelled. I don't think I could stop if I wanted to.

BGS: Do you remember the very first story you wrote and the circumstances surrounding it?

TCB: No, no. I was really little. I'm talking about kindergarten. Sometimes even now, a line will come out that will take me back to some utterance made in a story or poem I wrote or tried to write when I was in pink pajamas and bunny slippers. It's weird. I've been in training, you might say, for quite a while. Still am.

BGS: Were you conditioned by your family members to assume a traditional female role? I'm asking this because of the number of black female children in your fiction who do not conform to American society's notion of what is "proper" female behavior.

TCB: I think within my household not a great deal of distinction was made between pink and blue. We were expected to be self-sufficient, to be competent, and to be rather nonchalant about expertise in a number of areas. Within the various neighborhoods I've lived in, there was such a variety of expectations regarding womanhood or manhood that it was rather wide-open. In every neighborhood I lived in, for example, there were always big-mouthed women, there were always competent women, there were always beautiful women, independent as well as dependent women, so that there was a large repertoire from which to select. And it wasn't until I got older, I would say maybe in college, that I began to collide with the concepts and dynamics of "role appropriate behavior" and so forth. I had no particular notion about being groomed along one particular route as opposed to another as a girl-child. My self-definitions were strongly internal and improvisational.

BGS: Take the little girl in "Gorilla, My Love," a favorite story of mine. Would you say that she was like little girls you grew up with? Does she come out of your personal experience?

TCB: I would say that she's a highly selective fiction. There are certain kinds of spirits that I'm *very* appreciative of, people who are very tough, but very compassionate. You put me in any neighborhood, in any city, and I will tend to gravitate toward that type. The kid in "Gorilla" (the story as well as in that collection) is a kind of person who will survive, and she's triumphant in her survival. Mainly because she's so very human, she cares, her caring is not careless. She certainly is not autobiographical except that there are naturally aspects of my own personality that I very much like that are similar to hers. She's very much like people I like. However, I would be hard pressed to point out her source in real life.

BGS: Have women writers influenced you as much as male writers?

TCB: I have no clear ideas about literary influence. I would say that my mother was a great influence, since mother is usually the first map maker in life. She encouraged me to explore and express. And, too, the fact that people of my household were big on privacy helped. And I would say that people I ran into helped, and I ran into a great many people because we moved a lot and I was always a nosey kid running up and down the street, getting into everything. Particular kinds of women influenced the work. For example, in every neighborhood I lived in there were always two types of women that somehow pulled me and sort of got their wagons in a circle around me. I call them Miss Naomi and Miss Gladys, although I'm sure they came under various names. The Miss Naomi types were usually barmaids or life-women, nighttime people with lots of clothes in the closet and a very particular philosophy of life, who would give me advice like, "When you meet a man, have a birthday, demand a present that's hockable, and be careful." Stuff like that. Had no idea what they were talking about. Just as well. The Miss Naomis usually gave me a great deal of advice about beautification, how to take care of your health and not get too fat. The Miss Gladyses were usually the type that hung out the window in Apartment 1-A leaning on the pillow giving single-action advice on numbers or giving you advice about how to get your homework done or telling you to stay away from those cruising cars that moved through the neighborhood patrolling little girls. I would say that those two types of women, as well as the women who hung out in the beauty parlors (and the beauty parlors in those days were perhaps the only womanhood institutes we had)—it was there in the beauty parlors that young girls came of age and developed some sense of sexual standards and some sense of what it means to be a woman growing up—it was those women who had the most influence on the writing.

I think that most of my work tends to come off the street rather than from other books. Which is not to say I haven't learned a lot as an avid reader. I devour pulp and print. And of course I'm part of the tradition. That is to say, it is quite apparent to the reader that I appreciate Langston Hughes, Zora Hurston, and am a product of the sixties spirit. But I'd be hard pressed to discuss literary influences in any kind of intelligent way.

BSG: Did you grow up in New York primarily?

TCB: Primarily.

BGS: Let's move to some of your reactions to the literary scene. What would you consider to be some contemporary or past positive images of black women in literature, either by male or female or black or white writers?

TCB: I would define "positive" as usable, characters who can teach us valuable lessons of life, characters who are rounded and who give dimension to the type or stereotype that they are closest to. For example, Sula in the Morrison novel is interesting. She's a champion. She's an adventurer, and she gives up another dimension of the bitch stereotype. She makes us aware of how many people are locked up in that particular cage. Eva, who very much resembles the stereotypic matriarch, is more than that and she too helps us break open that old stereotype and force us to look for qualities, lessons, eclipsed by the stereotypic label. I regard them as positive, for they touch deep. In the contemporary poetry—that is, the poetry that came out of the

NeoBlack Arts Movement—there are female personae who are assertive and rounded and they also break open the bitch stereotype for us, so that we find under that label locked-up vibrancy—activists, combatants, the Harriet Tubman heirs, people who come from that championship tradition. That's what I would call positive and in fact there are very few works that are available to us now, say in the last decade, that are not like that. We have very little deadwood in the works that have come out of the sixties and are currently being produced. Very few flat, stupid, useless, and careless portraits.

BSG: Is there a particular black woman writer of fiction who you think best illuminates the black female experience, specifically the double oppression of race and sex?

TCB: No, and I think that's okay. I think if we were designing a course that attempted to project the profile of the contemporary black woman, particularly in respect to double or triple oppression, to someone who did not understand it, it would be necessary to pull out a lot of people because there are a lot of experiences. There is no *the* woman or *the* experience or *the* profile. I would assemble the works of writers like Zora Neale Hurston, Toni Morrison, Carolyn Rodgers, Lucille Clifton, Eloise Lofton, and a good many others and particularly young writers who are coming out of the workshops, in the Southeast particularly, and out of the Berkeley group.

BSG: Do you think the black woman writer has been treated fairly by the critical community, both black and white?

TCB: I have no idea. It's not something I have any comments on because it's not something I generally think about, that is to say, the black woman writer. We know for sure that any cultural product of black people has not been treated intelligently and usefully by white critics. That's one kind of answer. The fact that a good many black women writers do not get into anthologies that are put together by black men is another kind of answer. The fact that black women critics sometimes approach black women's writing as though they were highly particular and had no connection to the group traditions, that's another kind of issue.

I'm not so much concerned with whether black women writers are dealt with fairly but rather with what they're dealing with. And I think the great accomplishment of particularly the poets of the Neo-Black Arts Movement (sister poets) and perhaps to a lesser degree the dramatists, novelists, short story writers, have contributed a great deal toward not only commenting on, correcting, and countering the stereotypic images, but in blasting open a new road, if you will for younger writers who are coming now: dealing with women who have not been dealt with before, raising issues that have not been tackled before, grabbing hold of a vision that we have let slip and maybe never have laid out in print before. The production itself I find far more interesting than any critical response.

BGS: Near the end of her introduction to *Black-Eyed Susans,* a collection of short stories by and about black women, Mary Helen Washington asserts, with respect to the black woman writer, that "there still remains something of a sacred-cow attitude in regard to black women that prevents exploration of many aspects of their lives...There has been a desire," she goes on to say, "to protect and revere the black woman's image." She argues that we need books about black women who have nervous breakdowns, who are "overwhelmed by sex," who are not faithful, who abuse and neglect their children, and so forth. That is, we need stories about "real black women," stories which "interpret the entire range and spectrum of the experiences of black women." Would you agree with her assessment of the black woman writer with respect to these issues?

TCB: I don't approach literature from quite that direction. I think I understand what she's saying, but writing for me is still an act of language first and foremost. I don't know that I need to read a book about a nervous breakdown in order to understand nervous breakdowns or to protect my health. As an act of language, literature is a spirit informer—an energizer. A lot of energy is exchanged in the reading and writing of books and that gets into the debate of whether it is more important to offer a usable truth or to try to document the many truths or realisms that make up the black woman's experience.

I think I see her point and it's all very lovely but it doesn't concern me, and I'm not altogether sure it's valid or true. It is true that we're so defensive about our detractors, which I think is what one of her points is, that we are not approaching the complexity of ourselves in a fearless way. That is true, but I don't know that the nervous breakdown is what I would argue for. I would argue rather that there is an aspect of black spirit, of inherent black nature, that we have not addressed: the tension, the power that is still latent, still colonized, still frozen and untapped, in some 27 million black people. We do not know how to unleash, we do not even know how to speak of it in a courageous manner, *yet.* I think that is because we have been so long on the defensive and have invested a great deal of time and energy posturing and trying to prove that indeed we are as clean as they are. Since the sixties, however, a great many of us have been released from that posturing through having dialogues with each other which is a very radical and new dimension to the dialogue of cultural worker and community. It is in relation to potential that I might argue Mary Helen's general point. Namely, that we are not terribly fearless and courageous and thoroughgoing in dealing with the complexity of the black experience, the black spirit. As a matter of fact, music is probably the only mode we have used to speak of that complexity. But I would argue the point in relation to other aspects of self rather than to nervous breakdowns and the kinds of things that Mary Helen is talking about, which is not to say it has no usefulness, but it doesn't strike me as a priority at all.

BGS: Do you think that the black woman has an advantage or special perspective that may enable her to reveal aspects of the black experience or black spirit to which you refer?

TCB: No, I wouldn't say that black women or children or elders or men or any other sector of the community are any more in command of it or in touch with it than any other. I find it interesting in this period, the seventies, that we have begun to embrace within our community (and we can see parallels in the national as well as international community), an interest in holistic healing systems: astrology, voodoo, TM, etc. No, I don't think that any group within the community has any monopoly on that kind of wisdom, a grasp on that new way to prepare for the future.

BGS: Speaking of parallels, have your travels revealed to you how American black and other Third World women can link up in their struggles to liberate themselves from the various kinds of oppression they face as a result of their sexual identity?

TCB: Yes, I would say that two particular places I visited yielded up a lot of lessons along those lines. I was in Cuba in 1973 and had the occasion not only to meet with the Federation of Cuban Women but sisters in the factories, on the land, in the street, in the parks, in lines, or whatever, and the fact that they were able to resolve a great many class conflicts as well as color conflicts and organize a mass organization says a great deal about the possibilities here. I was in Vietnam in the summer of 1975 as a guest of the Women's Union and again was very much struck by the women's ability to break through traditional roles, traditional expectations, reactionary agenda for women, and come together again in a mass organization that is programmatic and takes on a great deal of responsibility for the running of the nation.

We missed a moment in the early sixties. We missed two things. One, at a time when we were beginning to lay the foundations for a national black women's union and for a national strategy for organizing, we did not have enough heart nor a solid enough analysis that would equip us to respond in a positive and constructive way to the fear in the community from black men as well as others who said that women organizing as women is divisive. We did not respond to that in a courageous and principled way. We fell back. The other moment that we missed was that we had an opportunity to hook up with Puerto Rican women and Chicano women who shared not only a common condition but also I think a common vision about the future and we missed that moment because of the language trap. When people talked about multicultural or multiethnic organizing, a lot of us translated that to mean white folks and backed off. I think that was an error. We should have known what was meant by multicultural. Namely, people of color. Afro-American, Afro-Hispanic, Indo-Hispanic, Asian-Hispanic, and so forth. Not that those errors necessarily doom us. Errors may result in lessons learned. I think we have the opportunity again in this last quarter of the twentieth century to begin forging those critical ties with other communities. It will be done. That is a certainty.

BGS: Do you consider it a dilemma for the black woman today who considers herself both a feminist and a warrior in the race struggle?

TCB: A dilemma? Personally, no. I'm not aware of what the problem is for people who consider it a dilemma. I don't know what they're thinking because it's not as if you're a black *or* a woman. I don't find any basic contradiction or any tension between being a feminist, being a pan-Africanist, being a black nationalist, being an internationalist, being a socialist, and being a woman in North America. I'm not sensitive enough to people caught in the "contradiction" to be able to unravel the dilemma and adequately speak to the question at this particular point in time. My head is somewhere else.

BGS: Turning to your own writings, you said in your preface to *The Black Woman,* an anthology of readings by contemporary black women published in 1970, that among other evils this country "regards its women as its monsters." Have you seen over the past seven years or so any changes in this country's attitude toward women, especially the black ones?

TCB: The country at large, no. You look at "That's My Mama" and I think it's clear that television program really centers around the son and the activities in the barbershop. That's the most dynamic aspect of that drama. But because the mammy looms so large in the American mentality, is such a durable, persistent psychosexual obsession on the part of white people, male and female, that need demands the presence of the mama figure: on the one hand, a gracious, giving, enduring mammy, but also a Hattie McDaniel sass. Sass as a comic-menace element. The menace element is a white fiction that is meshed into our women, that has to do with their whole "momism" pathology. So they get their thing off in three ways through her: She's useful to keep the "boy" thing going; she's the mother's milk nurturer; plus the "hate mom" white thing can be projected onto her.

I don't know that I have seen any change, by and large, in white America. In terms of black America, there are authors still—I'm thinking of John A. Williams in particular, as well as many other writers who don't come to mind at the moment—who are still a little scary in terms of the assertive black woman, still look at Sapphire as a threat, and who do not come to grips with how that myth functions in American society. The bitch helps to justify, for example, hustlers and other collaborators. The presence of the bitch myth also helps those societal restraints that operate on black women, as well as the rest of the community. No, I haven't noticed a change among black male writers either. Ron Milner's women are a change, though.

BGS: If you were to do another anthology of readings by contemporary black women today, what kinds of pieces would you include?

TCB: The papers that I was most concerned with at that time that never got into the book, and those were position papers from the Women's Caucus of SNCC, of the Panthers, of a number of other organizations that eventually did produce papers for publication through Third World Women's Alliance. I was particularly concerned with the evolution of women's groups that had begun as consumer education or single-issue action groups, began studying together and engaging in community organizing and are now, some ten years later, the core network of what will soon become, we hope, a national black women's union. I would include in a new collection writings from the campus forces, the prison forces, tenant's groups, and most especially southern rural women's works, particularly from the migrant workers and sharecroppers of the Deep South.

NOTES

1. See *Sturdy Black Bridges: Visions of Black Women in Literature,* in Roseann P. Bell, Bettye J. Parker, and Beverly Guy-Sheftall, eds. (New York: Doubleday, 1979), 230–249.

2. In my essay, "Other Mothers of Women's Studies," in *The Politics of Women's Studies,* Florence Howe, ed. (New York: Feminist Press, 2000), 216–226.

3. Toni Cade Bambara. *The Black Woman: An Anthology* (New York: Signet, 1970), 10–11.

4. A body of scholarly literature is now available, which documents the feminist viewpoints of black nationalist women including Amy Jacques Garvey associated with the Universal Negro Improvement Association (UNIA), founded by her husband Marcus Garvey in Jamaica in 1914 with his first wife Amy Ashwood. See Amy Jacques Garvey's woman's page, "Our Women and What They Think," published in *Negro World,* UNIA's weekly newspaper; Ula Taylor's unpublished dissertation, "The Veiled Garvey: The Life and Times of Amy Jacques Garvey."

5. Toni Cade Bambara. *The Black Woman,* 11.

6. bell hooks. "Writer to Writer: Remembering Toni Cade Bambara," *Remembered Rapture: The Writer at Work* (New York: Henry Holt & Company, 1999), 230–232.

7. Toni Cade Bambara. *Deep Sightings and Rescue Missions: Fiction, Essays, and Conversations,* in Toni Morrison, ed. (New York: Pantheon Books, 1996), 229.

8. Toni Cade Bambara. *The Black Woman,* 102–103.

At the Edges of the World

PAULA J. GIDDINGS

I can't remember the year I first met her. Time doesn't seem so important when thinking about Toni Cade Bambara. But I do remember the scene when we had our first long talk together. It was soon after the publication of *The Black Woman,* and I wanted to interview her for a magazine article. Toni suggested we do it at her place in New York.

On the appointed day, I took a taxi and spent most of the ride reading my notes. I did not look up until the cab driver announced that we had arrived. I gazed at the meter, gave him the fare, and started to open the door—then stopped. I couldn't imagine where I was. Nothing seemed familiar. The block was mostly made up of abandoned, hollowed out, industrial-like buildings. There were discarded shards of metal and fractured pieces of appliances lying around. There wasn't a soul on the street. With the images of Vietnam still on my mind, it reminded me of a village, that had been abandoned after being attacked. The scene was made more ominous by the fact that it was dusk slipping into darkness. Even the hard-boiled, immigrant, seen-everything, cab driver asked me if he should wait until I got safely to wherever I was going. My pride told him no (gulp) I was fine. I got out and proceeded to climb up a small flight of stairs to her address. None too soon, it turned out, a pair of rogue dogs patrolling their territory had eyed me. I scurried to the top of the landing where Toni, with exquisite timing, opened the door. She smiled, showed me to the kitchen table, and went to the stove to fix us some tea. When her back was turned, I furtively looked around. It was a comfortable nest that was a shelter against, but did not betray, what was outside.

The thing about Toni Cade, I realized years later, was that she could face the fact that her condition placed her at the edges of the world. For many, such knowledge inspires the longing to live in surroundings—superficial as they may be—to dispel the notion, but Toni found a kind of freedom-of-mind around the rim. She did not waste time or energy swimming against the material tides that pushed her/us there.

* * *

Many who knew her sent Toni notices, publications, reviews, and gossip as if she was stationed at some far reaches of the earth where printed matter might not be available. After sending her a number of such items, Toni sent me a letter from Atlanta, "What uncanny timing," she wrote. "Am in the process of reviewing a bulk of Zora NH stuff in preparation for a script, and the Dandridge article triggered a lot of stuff I'd sloppily forgotten. Thanks so much." This was followed by a litany of other things people were talking about that she hadn't seen, and an embarrassed request to send these to her too. "...hate to sound like an invalid but it's been 100 degrees for five straight days plus the bus/train company is doing a cut back as part of its orchestrated efforts to do some fare hikes..." But the real issue was in the next sentence, "Not only am I on the other side of the cultural embargo with fading ties to NY/Chic? SF and the Big Wurld, but am also erratic in keeping up with stuff..."

When Toni did "fade" back to the "Big Wurld," it was always temporary, and her observations could be hilarious. After an absence of a number of years, she had returned to New York City when it was in the throes of gentrification. "I haven't really gotten over the Third Avenue El to tell the truth," she wrote. "And then coming back to Third Ave to discover a cheese boutique, glove boutique, belt boutique, cooking boutique damn! take you five days to pull one meal together and get one outfit on your back. Sidewalk cafes and boutiques. I do believe I saw a Chinese rest. sidewalk café near 82nd. (Maybe I made that up in my head where I'm working on a magnus opus film. "The Peking Walk" it's called in my left eyeball reel...")

Wherever Toni placed herself, a part of her always stayed very close, very in tune, to others. "Take good care of your energies, your spirit, Paula...Have a fine, hilarious, sexy, resplendent, healthy, prosperous, productive and lucid summer.

Be well,

(I'm sapped)

Toni"

Toni was "sapped" in the way war correspondents are sapped. She knew that you couldn't report on the "front" from a boutique on Third Avenue. The result was those wonderful books and scripts she wrote that were visionary, marrow-true—and written from a place where few of us could live.

14

How Do You Measure a Revolution? Lessons Learned from Toni Cade

FARAH JASMINE GRIFFIN

> Para la hija Cubana quien es muy negra, muy hermosa y muy
> generosa, quien yo encontre en la calle. (Muchas gracias para las flores)

In the spring of 2001, I joined a group of writers, critics, and musicians on a trip to Cuba. The trip was organized and coordinated by Charles Rowell, esteemed editor of *Callaloo*, the premier journal of black arts and letters. At the end of our weeklong sojourn in Havana, we all participated in an academic conference, a series of poetry readings, and a musical performance. When Charles called with the invitation, he asked that I present a paper for a session titled "La mujer negra: feminismo y teoria del feminismo" or "Black Women: Feminism and Feminist Theory." I immediately knew I wanted to use my brief time to talk about Toni Cade Bambara. What I didn't know was how profoundly reading Bambara would influence the way I saw, thought about, and interpreted Cuba.

I was teaching an advanced undergraduate seminar on Bambara, Gayl Jones, and Ntozake Shange, so Bambara was on my mind, and throughout the last two or three years I have been trying to think my way through her corpus and have often used conference papers to do so. I knew Bambara had gone to Cuba in 1973 and that the trip appears to have had a significant impact on her, so it seemed only fitting to turn to her work for this occasion. Because I also believe that much of the contours of black feminist theory emerge in works that are not immediately labeled "theory," it made perfect sense that Bambara would also have something to teach me about both my theorizing and my politics. Finally, she seemed particularly appropriate because she is one of the founding voices of contemporary black feminism; she was a writer who always tried to establish links between the African American liberation struggle and similar struggles worldwide.

Bambara actually made two trips to Cuba, one in 1973 and another in 1986. She also visited Vietnam in 1975. During her first trip to Cuba she met with women's organizations and women workers. She credits the trip with inspiring her to think further about the connections between writing and social activism, though students of her work will know that she seemed always to be thinking about and writing about and through these connections. Nonetheless she told writer/critic Mari Evans:

> I did not acknowledge to myself that I was a writer, that writing was my way of doing my work in the world until I returned from Cuba in the summer of 1973. There I learned what Langston Hughes and others most especially my colleagues in the Neo Black Arts Movement had been teaching for years—that writing was a legitimate way, an important way to participate in the empowerment of the community that names me.

In another interview, this one with filmmaker Louis Massiah, she notes:

> When I came back from Cuba in 1973 I began to think that writing could be a way to engage in struggle, it could be a weapon, a real instrument for transformation politics. Let me take myself a little more seriously and stop just having fun I thought.

While Bambara's early short stories show a woman with a strong political consciousness as well as a gift for the craft of writing, her second collection, *The Seabirds Are Still Alive* (1977), clearly reflects the experience of her travels to Cuba and to Vietnam as she begins to make connections between revolutionary movements around the world. While Bambara does not devote an entire story to Cuba, the nation does pop up in several of the stories in the collection and much later in her second novel, *Those Bones Are Not My Child*. She also co-authored a collective piece, "Some of Us Had a Different Trip," published in *Liberation* (May/June 1974). She did, however, set the title story in Vietnam.

Bambara visited Vietnam as a member of a delegation of women's rights activists and upon their return they had to present their findings to their constituency. Instead of a more traditional report, she decided to create a story in seven parts about a group of people on a passenger boat. In between reading parts, someone else played music and another read cards written by Vietnamese children. For Bambara the power of storytelling worked best to communicate her findings and her vision. "The Seabirds Are Still Alive" is that story.

In "The Seabirds Are Still Alive," Bambara shifts locations from the United States, where her writing had been set, to Southeast Asia. The story appears in the middle of a collection whose other stories are set in the United States during the height of the Civil Rights and Black Power Movements. They range from tales of a movement organizer's wife in the American South to a group of community activists in Harlem. That she situates the Vietnam story within this collection serves to remind us that at the same time African Americans participate in domestic struggles, the United States is engaged in a war overseas with a people whose situation shares much with that of black Americans. The story serves to situate black struggle in an international context.

As such, the story may be seen as part of a longstanding strain in African American thought. Since the eighteenth century and certainly throughout the nineteenth, black American thinkers have written about black movements in an international context. Recent critical works such as that by Paul Gilroy have explored this phenomenon as it pertains to what he terms the "Black Atlantic." For Gilroy and others the mobile black intellectual is male and he is a cosmopolitan subject from the United States or the Caribbean or West Africa who is greatly influenced by Western European culture. Bambara is clearly a part of this continuum; however, she is more influenced by African Diasporan thought. Women and questions of race as well as gender are central to her writing.

Bambara doesn't seek to deny difference or forge commonality where none exists. Instead she focuses very closely on specific contexts, highlights the causes of human suffering, and represents very specific local resistance against acts of injustice. The consequence of this in a collection of stories that juxtapose diverse subjugated people is that we see common sources of oppression. The vocabulary used to describe human rights violations in New York, Atlanta, and Mississippi is similar to that which she uses to describe them in Viet Nam. In doing this, Bambara defamiliarizes the familiar so that we can see it more clearly for what it is: Poverty, Greed, Disenfranchisement, Dispossession, Racism, Struggle, Resistance, and Hope. Hers is not a development or a progression from a concern for African Americans to a diasporic focus then to a sense of internationalism; instead Bambara's trajectory is that of an intellectual with an understanding of black Americans on a global stage as part of an international struggle for human rights. And, in all of her stories, Bambara tries to imagine a new world.

In *The Seabirds Are Still Alive*, Bambara paints portraits of a number of people on a refugee/fishing boat, yet the story centers on a little girl who is feeding the seagulls at the story's opening. Centers is perhaps the wrong word, because there seems to be no narrative center, no central character. Instead the narrative circles around the little girl, who circles around the edges of the story in much the same pattern as the flock of birds circle above the boat. As is the case in most of her writing, in this story, Bambara tries to imagine the possibilities for a new world, gives us a vision of that world, and then demonstrates the hard, life-threatening work involved in making that new vision become a reality.

At one point the story turns to a "young man with a hard brown face" who meditates on the political and cultural dimensions of the word "home." Because of the way we have been taught to read, we expect this stern young man to be the center and focus of the story. But to read and write as a black feminist is to be attentive to the margins, to keep our eyes on those who inhabit the periphery, even as we remain vigilant about the center. I want to quote this at length, not only because it allows me to indulge in the pleasures of Bambara's prose but also because it is central to the argument. The young man has been watching a little girl feed birds from the back of the ship—an act he calls "wanton waste" in the face of food shortages. A French woman asks him if he is making his home in the city. He "leaned over the rail to spit in answer to the Frenchwoman's question." He then thinks:

> Home. In '46 when the United States notified the families their island was needed for nuclear tests, he'd been a child peeping through chinks in the bamboo awning, peeping at shells along the seashore. He couldn't even walk yet, much less protest. And the islanders, bowed down by centuries of servitude to the Spanish, the French, the Japanese, the Americans, complied.
>
> The lovely atoll that was home devastated by two decades of atomic, then hydrogen blasts. For years, with no compensation money, they waited for an unseen needle on an unknown gauge to record the radiation level and announce it was safe to return home. They waited, complied, were rerouted, resettled at this camp or that island, the old songs gone, the dances forgotten, the elders and the ancient wisdoms put aside, the memory of home scattered in the wind.
>
> Home for him had been a memory of yellow melons and the elders with their tea. Home after that a wicker basket and his father's uncle's pallet in muddy tent cities. Meager rations in one country, hostility in the next.
>
> Then finding home among islanders who remembered home, a color, a sound, the shells, the leaping fish, the cool grottoes. And home among other people foreign but not foreign, people certain that humanity was their kin, the world their home. Home with people like that who shared their next to nothing things and their more than hoped for wealth of spirit. Home with people who watched other needles on other gauges that recorded the rising winds. It was a good time in history to be on the earth, to be on the boat going home. He leaned way over . . . . Then he straightened, back stiff with the conviction that he, like many others going home now, was totally unavailable for servitude. (75–77)

In this passage Bambara moves from a specific location, culture, and people to all those who suffer from similar forms of injustice. In the span of one generation, the young man experiences the condition of a landless people for whom "home" exists as myth and memory, in song and story. But he is able to find home among others who have experienced similar acts of displacement and dispossession and because of this, because of his sense that identities are never fixed, he can construct a new one that provides kinship with others who are committed to a new vision, a new world.

The passage provides a glance at Bambara's own conceptualization of a new world. Here we have her sense of the need to place the African American struggle in the context of the people the passage describes; for the dispossessed of South East Asia and the dispossessed of the United States to see the commonalities of their experience and their enemies. She uses a vocabulary familiar to African Americans, the loss of home, of language, of culture—and the creation of a new, dynamic culture of resistance in the New World. That is the African American experience as well. The vocabulary is one that resonates with her audience. Here we must remember that Bambara reads the story as part of a presentation following her trip. It is a report of the conditions and an effort to demonstrate to her audience the kinds of connections that can be made between their struggle and the one she documents.

The thread that runs through it all is the little girl feeding the birds from the back of the boat. Bambara will share the rambling thoughts of a variety of individuals who watch the little girl or encounter her as her mother drags her away so as readers we work our way to the front of the boat stopping here and there to learn of their stories, but all the while our trajectory as reader (or as listener) is that of the child's. By the end of the story we follow her as her mother escorts her off the boat and delivers her to a woman who awaits them. The mother embraces the daughter and then returns to the boat.

At this moment we learn that the little girl has been the victim of a torturous interrogation by the police. She revealed nothing of what she knew of the resistance. When she is released one of the guards gives her a package of food "wrapped in plantain leaves and elephant ears." It is from this package that she fed the birds expecting them to "drop down poisoned into the waters." But the soldier had given her "perfectly good food." This soldier she thinks, will be overwhelmed when he "experienced his natural self and knew once more right from wrong." For she has been taught by her elders that revolution "gave one a chance to amend past crimes, to change, to be human." This is the right for which her ancestors fought "to be free, to be human." She recalls "That was why the elders had taught her in the first crop season, that she herself mattered, that what she did or did not do would matter for the yet unborn." Her mother has delivered her to a woman who will train her for the Front for she has proven herself to be an "elder in her mind," a child committed to a broader vision of humanity.

This little girl joins Bambara's precocious, fierce, and independent little girls of Harlem in the collection's other stories. In Bambara's work, in her vision, in her politics, little girls matter. Hers is internationalism that places the most vulnerable, most disenfranchised—little girls of color—at the center as active agents and participants in the struggle for their people's freedom. Consequently their people must be able to work for a world free of sexism as well as for white supremacy and poverty.

When I decided I wanted to talk about Bambara and especially about this story in Cuba, I did so because of the generosity of its vision and because I wanted, as I imagined Bambara wanted, to express a sense of solidarity with the Cuban people and the goals of the Cuban revolution. I wanted to acknowledge the importance of her visit to Cuba to her art and her politics. I also thought it would allow me to share some insights about black feminist thought and writing. And, in many ways it did all of these things. But it also complicated my life and my trip in ways that I could not have imagined. What did it mean to take seriously a reading of Toni Cade Bambara? What does it mean to see the world in the way she teaches me to see it? Trying to address these questions profoundly influenced the way I walked the streets of Cuba, the lens through which I saw the landscape and her people. For Bambara's story created the following questions for me: "What would it mean to follow the little black and brown girls of Cuba and of the United States? What possibilities do our respective societies offer them? What does the future hold for them? What does the future look like through their eyes? How will they measure their true value?" Bambara's fiction insists that I measure the success of revolutionary movements here, in Cuba, and elsewhere by the status of black and brown girls.

The Cuba I visited in the spring of 2001 is not the Cuba Bambara visited in 1973; nor is it the Cuba of her second trip in 1986. It was a Cuba forty years into a U.S.-imposed embargo and everywhere I looked it looked as if little black and brown girls would grow up to bear the heaviest weight of this condition. Among the youngest they seem no different from their counterparts, little boys and girls every hue in the rainbow, dressed in their school uniforms, playing, walking, practicing instruments (there is music everywhere). But it is difficult not to note the number of extraordinarily beautiful young (I guess 14- to 15-year-old) Afro-Cubanas, some still in school uniforms with middle-aged, balding, white foreign men from Europe, Latin America, and the United States. Some are with black men (many of whom are from the Bahamas I later learn). Upon our arrival in Havana we are met by a crowd of taxi drivers, men who offer to be our guides, men who offer to carry our bags. As we walked to the taxi, my male friend is approached by a beautiful dark brown young pregnant woman who offers herself to him for $1.00. Soon she is joined by her competition, all black, all young, all beautiful. This scene is repeated throughout our stay: those who offer themselves and those who are attached to the old white men. It is a scene as common as the huge colorful murals with socialist slogans painting on them. It is a scene that breaks my heart, because I am falling in love with this nation and with its lovely, smart, and generous people, because I am a black woman who wants to believe that somewhere on earth black women are free.

Everyone I meet in an official capacity tells me there is no racism in Cuba; the Afro-Cubans I meet on the street during long late night walks speak differently. It's interesting, they whisper their support for the revolution, note that the revolution has done much to erase institutional and state-sanctioned racism, but insist that attitudes have not changed, that there is still a racial hierarchy, that while all Cubans are suffering economically, many of the poorest are black. Many white Cubans have family in the United States who supplement their income; the tourist industry especially the hotels tend to hire lighter skinned Cubans who therefore have greater access to the dollar. It seems the greatest opportunities in the tourist industry for black women is the sex trade. In 1974 Bambara and her fellow travelers wrote that "Certainly racism has not been wiped off the Cuban map. And yet certainly, too, racism is being dealt with actively." This is still true I think, but it is disheartening to see that here as everywhere I have ever been on the planet, there is a strong correlation between poverty and skin color. Furthermore, the aesthetic devaluation of blackness seems alive and well in Cuba even as the darkest women seem the most desired partners of foreign men. Perhaps they are also the most available. Perhaps it is more noticeable than a young white or light skinned prostitute with an older white man might be. In that case I might have mistaken them for husband and wife or father and daughter, their common skin color hiding the nature of their liaison. Yet, somehow I think not. In an article titled "Picking the Flowers of Revolution" (*New York Times Magazine*, February 1, 1998), Andrei Codrescu documented the range of relationships foreign men set up with young Afro-Cubanas ranging from marriage to one-night encounters all fueled by the economic needs of young women and families in dire poverty.

Race in Cuba is not the same as race in the United States; sexism in Cuba is not the same as sexism in the United States. Literacy rates and access to health care in Cuba benefit black Cubans just as much as others and in many ways should embarrass and shame the United States. Manning Marable notes:

> It was literally impossible for the new revolutionary government to erase hundreds of years of racial inequalities and injustices in the span of several months or years. The new anti-discrimination laws, land reform, and the mass literacy campaign all had the greatest impact upon black Cubans but the ideology of black inferiority and white privilege could not be shattered simply by government edicts. It would require a deeper cultural transformation, the radical restructuring of the hegemonic ideas about race, color and class that defined social reality for most Cubans.[1]

As if the U.S.-imposed embargo was not enough, since the fall of the Soviet Union and the Communist Governments in Eastern Europe, Cuba has experienced a profound economic crisis. Castro decriminalized the U.S. dollar and encouraged corporate investment from Europe. These changes have had tremendous impact on race in Cuba. Marable writes:

> Prostitution is once again flourishing in major cities, and it is now virtually impossible to enter or leave a major hotel or nightclub without encountering prostitutes. To an uncomfortable degree, the Cuban state is now promoting sex tourism, marketing the bodies of black and mulatto women especially for European guests. (102)

I left Cuba reluctantly. I left with a sense of exuberance and admiration for this exquisite experiment. I left with the desire to come back, a desire I am sure Bambara must have shared. I left wanting to know even more about the history and the culture of the place and with the sound of Cuban jazz in my ears and the site of the colorful murals, the grand boulevards, the warm people, and the beautiful little girls and young women. More than anything they dominate my mind's eye. Reading like the black feminist Bambara has taught me to be, I am haunted by the little girls who circle the city, eyes filled with a beautiful, heartbreaking longing.

NOTES

1. Manning Marable. "Race and Revolution in Cuba: African American Perspectives." *Dispatches from the Ebony Tower: Intellectuals Confront the African American Experience* (New York: Columbia University Press, 2000), 100.

15

Drive This Thing

KRISTIN HUNTER LATTANY

When we were living in Atlanta, a visiting faculty member at Emory left us in charge of her Porsche while she returned to England for a brief visit. My husband, John I. Lattany, and I were extremely conscientious about never touching her splendid vehicle—until Toni Cade Bambara saw it parked in our yard.

"You got a key to that?" she asked in her usual direct manner.

"Yes," John replied. "But we don't use it. We're keeping it for—." He mentioned the Englishwoman's name.

"Does it run?" was Toni's next question.

"It did when she brought it here," I said.

"You know what we're going to do?" Toni said, nudging my husband in the ribs with her elbow. "We're going to drive this thing! Ain't we?"

And drive it we did, all through one gloriously roaring night, down Peachtree to Martin Luther King and back and forth on Sweet Auburn, through all the black neighborhoods, top down, laughing and shouting, scarves flying in the wind, hands waving greetings to all the homefolks

The next day we realized that, while we were having fun and feeling liberated, we were also learning from Toni. She had taught another of her invaluable lessons to a pair of uptight, overresponsible guardians of the ruling class's laws and property. Don't conserve the master's resources—use them, if you are fortunate enough to get your hands on a tiny piece of them. Drive this thing—this property you are holding, this story you are writing, this class you are teaching, this lecture you are giving, this money you are earning, this organization to which you belong, this community of which you are a part. Point it in the right direction—the direction of truth and positive change—and drive it!

Drive it the way she drove children into an awareness of economic disparities by taking them on a visit to FAO Schwarz in "The Lesson." There, Sugar says, "You know, Miss Moore, I don't think all of us here put together eat in a year what that sailboat cost."

And Miss Moore, the children's self-appointed teacher, says, "Imagine for a minute what kind of society it is in which some people can spend on a toy what it would cost to feed a family of six or seven. What do you think?"

And Sugar replies, "I think that this is not much of a democracy if you ask me. Equal chance to pursue happiness means an equal crack at the dough, don't it?" (*Gorilla, My Love*, 95).

Drive this thing the way she drove readers to understand that neither age nor physical handicap can define a person or limit love in "My Man Bovanne."

"You know what you all can kiss," the narrator tells her grown children after they finish taking her to task for dressing like a young woman and dancing close with the blind man, Bovanne.

"You gots to take care of the older folks," she concludes. "Cause old folks is the nation" (*Gorilla, My Love*, 7, 9, 10).

"Old person" or "blind man" is not an identity, as Toni Cade Bambara informed Louis Massiah in the marvelous interview with him that is published in *Deep Sightings and Rescue Missions,* though she was speaking of the term "slave."

In that interview, Toni describes the engine that drove her work as follows: "...a story should be informed by the emancipatory impulse... as exemplified by those freedom narratives which we've been trained to call slave narratives ... as if 'slave' were an identity and not a status interrupted by the very act of fleeing, speaking, writing, and countering the happy-darky propaganda" (*Deep Sightings and Rescue Missions,* 250).

The emancipatory impulse, of course, was the reason Toni persuaded us to drive that Porsche (which, incidentally, the owner's boyfriend came to collect the next day). And if it was the engine of her work, the power train was community and the destination was political change ("First stop Mercy and the last Hallelujah" —Robert Hayden, "Middle Passage").

"When I came back from Cuba in 1973, I began to think that writing could be a way to engage in struggle ... a weapon, a real instrument for transformation politics" (*Deep Sightings,* 219). From then on, every word Toni wrote and most of her actions, both public and private, were aimed toward "transformation politics." Actually they had been aimed and driven hard in that direction long before 1973.

I remember a literary contest I had been asked to judge in which I enlisted Toni's help in evaluating a daunting pile of manuscripts. Terribly conscientious as usual, I had been working hard to judge the submitted stories by prevailing standards, weighing such factors as style, tone, characterization, narrative tension and energy, emotional effect, and so on. Ten manuscripts out of about five hundred were supposed to be chosen as winners by us and then by another judge. When this became a collaborative job, we decided to pick five stories apiece. Toni waded into her portion of the pile, began speed reading, and swiftly selected her five manuscripts. "That writer's black, and that one, and that one," she said, slamming down three manuscripts. "And these two are Native Americans."

Case closed.

My mouth remained open for a while, though.

Years later, I decided that Toni might have been right. Mulling over the rightful struggle for reparations, I have decided that instead of languishing while we wait for them, we have to take them whenever and wherever we can. Toni showed me that without lecturing. Instead, in effect, she pointed out the keys in my hand and said, "Drive this thing."

Political clarity was the destination. Failure to achieve it is the main reason Toni Cade Bambara takes Spike Lee to task in a review of his film, *School Daze*. Though she finds much to admire in Lee's spectacle, she points out that Lawrence Fishburne's character Dap "blows the opportunity to achieve political clarity three times: with Rachel, when she challenges him on the color question; with Da Fellas, when they suggest that one of the reasons they won't back him is his personality; and with the locals, when they let it be known that the debate between the Greeks and the campus revolutionaries has no explanatory power in the lives of most Blacks" (*Deep Sightings*, 197–98).

The engine that drove all of Toni's work was social change, to be achieved through political education for black people. Her destination was always clarity, for her work was always aimed at clearing up the confusion that the majority and its media have created in our heads. She knew that the descendants of slaves had no business being conscientious about protecting their former owners' material property. But, like the artist she was, having confidence that we had at least enough intelligence to figure out a few things, she pointed this out to us indirectly.

And if political clarity and transformation were the destinations, the vehicle was black people organized in conscious, cooperative community.

Toni's depiction of communities organized for mutual self-help and political action began long before that post-Cuba epiphany in 1973. In "The Johnson Girls," a story written before that date, a tightly knit community of women forms an attentive, helpful circle around Inez, a sister in trouble and in need of their advice. In *The Salt Eaters*, a number of community groups and a couple of disembodied spirits take time out from their righteous agendas to coalesce around the healing of Velma and lend it energy. In her magnificent, posthumously published novel, *Those Bones Are Not My Child*, community organizing goes on all around and through the main narrative of the small, divided nuclear family with its missing son. Sometimes all of those meetings get in the way of the story the reader wants to follow, but Toni remains true to her ideal—community activism is what counts, and to produce that, you must have organization.

And in the writing that emerged from her later, film-and-video-obsessed period-obsessed at least partially because she saw "video as an instrument for social change" (*Deep Sightings*, 228)—Toni Cade Bambara again emphasizes community and communal values. She notes that in *Daughters of the Dust*, a film she admired without reservation, "no one is background scenery for foregrounded egos. The camera work stresses the communal. Space is shared, and the space (capaciousness) is gorgeous" (*Deep Sightings*, 120).

There are no coincidences. Toni spoke, in that interview with Louis Massiah, of seeing *Borom Sarret*, an Ousmane Sembene film, which featured a barrier district between Europeans and Africans called the Cordon Sanitaire, in 1964. "Now," she said, "*Borom Sarret* really resonated with me because I was working on a story called "Sanitary Belt," as in "Cordon Sanitaire," about that hedgerow built as a barrier between European quarters and native quarters" (*Deep Sightings*, 226).

I never saw Sembene's film, but it must have resonated with me, too. (Toni would nod here, wisely understanding.) The same year she saw it, I wrote and published an angry article about the virtues of South Street, the lively black strip in South Philadelphia which was my neighborhood, and which was threatened by an expressway designed to separate the gentry from the folk. My article influenced the community organization to change its position from conciliation to "Stop the Expressway!"—and it was stopped.

Process Junior, a South Street barber who was part of the protest, tells me that ours was one of the only two community organizations in the country to succeed in stopping an expressway. To this day, I am happy to report, there is no "sanitary belt" separating the black community of South Street from the yuppie strongholds of center city Philadelphia.

Like her seabirds, Toni's texts seem alive. They haunt us, prod us, point us in the correct direction. Yesterday I was nearly driven mad by the noise of drumming throbbing through my neighborhood. Not African-style drumming—that, I might have tolerated—but the hard, brusque sounds that accompany military parades. I have unpleasant associations with the military, so this noise seemed especially unbearable.

Someone said, "Call the police on them." Once, I might have done just that. But I had just been reading *Deep Sightings and Rescue Missions*, and so I said, "No, let me go and talk to the people first, see what's up."

I went around the corner—how life changes when you go around the corner!—and found a drill team of five boys, ages three to fourteen, practicing in a backyard for this small black town's seventy-fifth anniversary parade. I talked to the sponsor of the drill team, a neighbor whom I had never met, though we have both lived here for sixteen years. He explained his aims, the substitution of positive activity for the drug and alcohol consumption that had claimed most of the town's young men. He said next time he would take them to the park to practice. And we parted friends.

Later, my husband went around the corner and talked to the drill team's sponsor, Squirrels, and to another neighbor whose sons are members of the drill team. This younger fellow runs other programs for local youth. My husband and I both pledged renewed assistance to the youth group, for which I was once a writing advisor, though I hadn't heard from the folks who run it since our arts program stopped. The neighborhood ended up feeling more like a street festival or a block party than a DMZ of mutual hostilities, which it would have become had I called police. I felt Toni beaming benignly on all of us.

Like her seabirds, then, Toni Cade Bambara is still alive. And this, I feel, is her directive to us about whatever opportunities may come our way. Know where you are coming from. Know where you are going. Get some folks to ride with you. And drive this thing!

Teaching Usable
Truths

From "The Children Who Get Cheated"

TONI CADE BAMBARA

The education of the nation's young is a crucial subject. And in recent years the public schools have been front-page news. Strikes, riots, disruptions and exposés have revealed deep-rooted problems, have caused seemingly unbridgeable polarizations.

Parents maintain that they are treated as outsiders. Students reject the traditional power relationship of decisions from above and obedience from below. Administrators explain that they are the victims of bad budgets. Books by disenchanted teachers revealing the inadequacies, absurdities and injustices of the system have become popular reading. Many of us, educators and laymen alike, tend to agree that the schools are indeed a mess, that the nation has betrayed its young.

And yet there still are communities across the nation that have kept the faith; that are confident that the professionals know what they are doing, that the morass is merely temporary, that all we need is more money, more time, more patience.

These communities perhaps have good reason to be confident in their schools. No matter how trying disruptive students or striking teachers may seem, they still are part of their schools. They are white-controlled and white-oriented. They are run by white administrators. They are staffed by white teachers. They are attended by white children learning a white self-concept in the interest of white America. And that should give them some confidence. For isn't the main purpose of an institution the perpetuation of its cultural heritage?

We of the Black community, on the other hand, have no such confidence in your schools. Our memory of being shortchanged by these

Courtesy of Karma Bambara. Excerpted from *Redbook*, January 1970.

schools is a long one. We have no reason to put our faith in good intentions, experimental solutions, professional know-how. In recent years we have witnessed the mutilation of too many projects to "upgrade" or "integrate" schools, by bureaucracy or white pressure or sheer incompetence and indifference.

We have been too painfully aware of the damage done to the spirit of our young attending overcrowded classes in dilapidated buildings, trying to learn from obsolete books about the great wars, the great men, the great games, the great lies, taught by a series of middle-class white teachers who come and go in turnstile nonchalance.

The Black community now is moving toward solutions to a problem—the miseducation of our children—that would have provoked bloody warfare in a lesser people. In several major cities throughout the country, the Black community has become increasingly adamant in pushing for community control, for we regard the current system of remote control by non-neighborhood whites as a manipulative attempt to keep Black parents invisible, mute and powerless. We have become more and more uncompromising in our demand to participate at the policy-making level in the educational affairs of our children.

More money, more supplies, more experienced staff, an updated curriculum, new buildings, better working conditions for teachers, more adequate counseling services for students—all these promised improvements might result in better schools than now exist. But when you boil it all down, the essential ingredient of education is two-way learning: mutual understanding, mutual respect, dialogue. So most teachers under the present system are, very simply, incompetent to teach our children.

They are incompetent because they have too little knowledge of, too little appreciation for and very little professional encouragement to learn about the Black child, his worth, his possibilities. It would be asking too much, perhaps, to expect a white person conditioned by the social mores and myths of this country to have any attitude other than outright racist or paternalistic in dealing with a Black person.

But that is, of course, what we must demand of teachers who come into contact with our children—that they have to think more clearly and more honestly than they're been trained to, to react more authentically to what they experience with the Black student rather than to what they think they know of the Black children, to adopt a nonwhite perspective. For what the drive for community control represents, actually, is a long-overdue reaction to the intellectual imperialism of white America, the white control and conditioning of Black minds.

16

Dear Toni

AUDRE LORDE

Dear Toni Instead of a Letter of
Congratulation Upon Your Book and
Your Daughter Whom You Say You Are
Raising To Be a Correct Little Sister

I can see your daughter walking down streets of love
in revelation;
but raising her up to be a correct little sister
is doing your mama's job all over again.
And who did you make on the edge of Harlem's winter
hard and black
while the inside was undetermined
swirls of color and need
shifting, remembering
were you making another self to rediscover
in a new house and a new name
in a new place next to a river of blood
or were you putting the past together
pooling everything learned
into a new and continuous woman
divorced
from the old shit we share
and shared and sharing need not share again?

I see your square delicate jawbone
the mark of a Taurus (or Leo) as well as the ease
with which you deal with your pretensions.

I dig your going and becoming
the lessons you teach your daughter
our history
for I am your sister corrected and
already raised up
our daughters will explore the old countries
as curious visitors to our season
using their own myths to keep themselves sharp.
I have known you over and over again
as I've lived throughout this city
taking it in storm and morning strolls
through Astor Place and under the Canal Street Bridge
The Washington Arch like a stone raised to despair
and Riverside Drive too close to the dangerous predawn
waters and 129th Street between Lenox and Seventh
burning my blood but not black enough
and threatening to become home.

I first saw you behind a caseworker's notebook
defying upper Madison Avenue and my roommate's concern
the ghost of Maine lobsterpots trailing behind you
and I followed you into east fourth street and out
through Bellevue's side entrance one night
into the respectable vineyards of Yeshivas intellectual gloom
and there I lost you between the books and the games
until I rose again out of Jackson Mississippi
to find you in an office down the hall from mine
calmly studying term papers like maps
marking off stations
on our trip through the heights of Convent Avenue
teaching english our children citycollege
softer and tougher and more direct
and putting your feet up on a desk you say Hi
I'm going to have a baby so now I can really indulge myself.
Through that slim appraisal of your world
I felt you
grinning and plucky and a little bit scared
perhaps of the madness past that had relieved you
through your brittle young will of iron
into the fire of whip steel.

I have a daughter also
who does not remind me of you
but she too has deep aquatic eyes that are burning and curious.
As she moves through taboos
whirling myths like gay hoops over her head
I know beyond fear and history
that our teaching means keeping trust
with less and less correctness
only with ourselves—
History may alter
old pretenses and victories
but not the pain my sister never the pain.

In my daughter's name
I bless your child with the mother she has
with a future of warriors and growing fire.
But with tenderness also,
for we are landscapes, Toni,
printed upon them as surely
as water etches feather on stone.
Our girls will grow into their own
Black Women
finding their own contradictions
that they will come to love
as I love you.
    [September 1971]

Toni's childhood portrait (*courtesy Karma Bambara*)

Toni in her New York apartment, circa 1963 (*courtesy Harry Keyishian*)

Toni with Gene Lewis prior to birth of their daughter, Karma, circa 1968 (*courtesy Karma Bambara*)

Ernest Gaines, Toni, and Sylvia Wynter, chair of African and African American Studies, Stanford University, speakers on Black writers panel, Stanford University, 1978 (*copyright © Susan J. Ross*)

Toni and her daughter Karma at home, 991 Simpson Street, Atlanta, 1980
(*copyright © Nikky Finney*)

Toni leading discussion in West End park after screenings of films on Black women writers hosted by the Atlanta African Film Society, 1982 (*copyright © Susan J. Ross*)

Toni and Pearl Cleage at Spelman College, Atlanta, 1982 (*copyright © Susan J. Ross*)

"Sistran" writers at Johnetta Coles' inauguration as President of Spelman College, 1988.

BACK ROW: Louise Meriwether, Pinkie Gordon Lane, Johnetta Coles, Paula Giddings.

MIDDLE ROW: Pearl Cleage Gwendolyn Brooks, Toni Cade Bambara.

FRONT ROW: Sonia Sanchez, Nikki Giovanni, Gwendolyn Brooks, Mari Evans.

(*copyright* © *Susan J. Ross*)

Toni with her mother Helen Cade Brehon and her daughter Karma in background, 50th birthday celebration, Hammonds House, Atlanta, 1989 (*copyright © Susan J. Ross*)

Toni with filmmaker Haile Gerima at Black Arts Festival, Atlanta, 1994
(*copyright © Susan J. Ross*)

Long-time friend Eleanor Traylor with Toni seated next to Amina Baraka,
Renaissance Hotel lobby, Black Arts Festival, Atlanta, 1994 (*copyright © Susan J. Ross*)

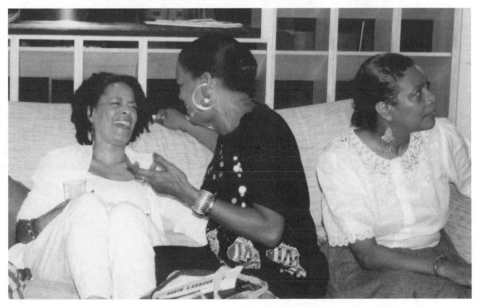

Sandra L. Swans, celebration guide, with "Bambara Memorial" program speakers (LEFT TO RIGHT): Eleanor Traylor, Amiri Baraka, Bernice Reagon, Sonia Sanchez, Toni Morrison, and Sarah C. Poindexter, Painted Bride Arts Center, Philadelphia, 1995 (*copyright © Susan J. Ross*)

Toni on W. E. B. Du Bois film set, Philadelphia, 1995, Carlton Jones, photographer for the W. E. B. Du Bois Film Project (*copyright © Scribe Video Center*)

Toni's brother Walter Cade, visual artist and musician, with Toni's daughter, Karma, and Toni's mother, Helen Cade Brehon, at the memorial celebration for Toni, Painted Bride Arts Center, Philadelphia, 1995 (*copyright © Susan J. Ross*)

17

We Drove Together: Remembering Toni Cade Bambara

NIKKI GIOVANNI

The funniest thing to me about Toni is that she was a true New Yorker: She could not drive. So I picked her up two days a week to take us to Rutgers in my 1960 VWBug, which cost $600 in those days. Ha! Never Again. And the drive gave us a chance to discuss and change the world. At least in our heads.

When I met Toni she lived in Harlem. Her apartment was what I had dreamed a New York apartment would be. She had a lot of room and rooms, but mostly she had a rooftop that was like a deck. You could actually eat lunch out there. My knowledge of New York was pretty much based on *My Sister Eileen* where Janet Leigh, and Rosalind Russell had a basement apartment somewhere on the east side. Toni's apartment was West-Side fabulous. I invited my mother to visit as soon as I was settled. I had found a home (apartment) on the West Side (84th and Amsterdam) that fortunately overlooked a schoolyard, which kept me from being fenced in. I called Toni because I had met her mother, and it seemed to me that the mothers should all meet to see that their children were doing all right. Toni invited Mommy and me to lunch with her mother, which was very kind of her. Now my mother could see that I had friends who were gainfully employed who also had mothers! It was perfect. Lunch was fantastic because Toni catered it. Maybe Toni could cook; that was not something I knew, but she sure could do the New York thing and have things done. It was great.

We talked occasionally. I had readings in Harlem, and she was an important author, too. I went to her readings, and she was involved with ninety million causes. I went to as many of those as I could.

I didn't at that point understand New York landlords, so when Toni started complaining that her landlord wanted her to move, I didn't see the problem. The more she tried to explain, the more complicated it became. It was years before I understood how dirty and underhanded New York landlords could be . . . especially when they got an offer on the building. Toni moved to the Village. I've got to tell you, the Village, the West Village, was my idea of Heaven. There were movie houses and cheese shops and wine shops and lots of poetry places and old bookstores and The Strand and the University Place Bookstore, and I just loved the Village. Plus, once again, she had a great apartment. I had recently moved to 94th and CPW [Central Park West] into a very nice apartment with brick walls and a fireplace, but Toni, well, Toni had a New York Apartment. I felt left behind.

It seemed that Rutgers University was building a new campus, Livingston College, which would be in New Brunswick, NJ. The head of the English Department asked Toni to pull together a few writers who might be interested in working there. I had a job working with Queens College, but Queens was difficult to get to because I never understood the bus or subway line. When Toni called I was more than ready. And when I saw the salary, it was a definite YES. Since I drove and she didn't, I asked if she would like me to pick her up. Those were the days when I was on time and I would come down 9th Avenue, swing over, get Toni, hit the Holland Tunnel, and get us to work on time. I was expecting then, though I hadn't realized it, and this was going to be a job that would carry me through my pregnancy.

We talked about my pregnancy and how I was feeling and all that, which I have to admit was pretty good. Actually, my first sick day; rather the first day I felt sick I was actually having the child. I thought I was having a girl because girls run in the family, so you can imagine my surprise when he was a boy. I wasn't out too long, because I come from people who had babies in the field and were back picking cotton. Toni had met Gene by then or had fallen in love with Gene or whichever way that went, but mostly her conversation was about Gene. When she started to talk about the names they were choosing for themselves, I realized she was expecting a baby. Karma was born and everything was wonderful. We shared what the kids were doing and how wonderful they were. I wrote a poem, "Dance Poem," because Toni and Jeanie Freeman and Barbara Crosby left me with Thomas and their kids to do their shopping one day. I have always liked children, but having a group was a bit more than I could figure out what to do with. On top of that, the Washington Market had featured rabbit, which I had purchased and fried. When my son Thomas asked what it was that we were eating, I said "Rabbit." He put his fork down and with indignity said: you mean we are eating Bugs Bunny! It took a lot to get that straightened out, but we finally did.

Ultimately, there were decisions to be made. Gene wanted to move to St. Croix; I wanted to know if I could have a writing career. So we drifted. Gwendolyn Brooks, Toni, and I read together, and Toni read from her book on the Atlanta child murders. The energy in that book should have taken her to a Pulitzer, but she was late finishing it. I saw her at Toni Morrison's birthday party at Princeton. She and Sonia Sanchez sat together, so I only got to say hello. Then I learned she was sick with cancer; then she died. I saw Karma at Sandy Govan's house, and I haven't seen her since. And we all miss the energy Toni Cade Bambara brought to everything she did. From *Gorilla, My Love* to *Those Bones Are Not My Child* Toni brought intelligence to her work. I remember this: when she was expecting Karma, she asked me: "Is it hard to drive?" "Why would you want to drive," I asked? "You live in New York and you don't even need a car." "I'm expecting a baby," she said. "I should know how to drive." We drove together, to Rutgers and through our careers. We all miss her.

Lessons in Boldness, 101

LINDA JANET HOLMES

When making course selections as an undergraduate student at Livingston College in the late 60s, the only criteria that mattered was relevancy. If there was a course catalogue, I never saw it. The student grapevine provided all the information I needed for selecting courses. Was the teacher black? Was the reading list radical? Did the professor accept "participating in protest" as a valid reason for missing class? Did the homework interfere with community organizing? Was the grading process collective?

Deciding on Toni Cade Bambara's class was easy; she met the activist definition of relevant. Talk about Toni's writing and literature classes swept through the black student community with the force of student sex gossip. Word spread about Toni's radical work in the academy not only at Livingston but also among the militant students on the other Rutgers campuses.

In the beginning, Livingston was little more than a few cement buildings facing a quad in the middle of an abandoned ROTC campus in Piscataway. There was no resemblance between this campus and its sister downtown campus, Rutgers University, draped in ivy and surrounded by green or the Douglass campus with bubbling brooks and a "sleepy hollow" in the student center for taking naps in between classes. Yet, when Livingston College opened its doors in 1969, many black students on the Rutgers and Douglass College campuses celebrated. We could take advantage of the new radical course offerings at Livingston, escaping the traditional course requirements of the ivory tower and still get credit toward graduation.

Much has been written about Toni as writer, but we know far less about her as teacher. Yet, a great deal of her time was spent in the classroom or in workshops at Rutgers and on campuses across the country. When teaching at Livingston, Toni often positioned herself on the side of the classroom rather than lecture from the front of the room. Her voice resonated in comfortable mellow ranges that registered like a swanky hypnotic jazz singer, making the challenge of the work before us less daunting. Mellowness scented the room like lavender in the classroom Toni created for us to recreate ourselves and imagine. Sometimes she shifted our attention from the day-to-day, luring us into collecting oral histories, writing creative stories, and engaging in community work which included assisting at community day care centers and publishing a community newspaper, all as a part of our take-home assignments.

About teachers, Toni wrote in "What I Think I'm Doing Anyhow:"

> Once I thought anyone with enthusiasm about information was a good teacher. Then, anyone with an analysis of this country who could help illuminate the condition, status, and process of the Family, who could help me decide how to put my wrath and my skill to the service of folks who sustain me. Later, anyone who could throw open the path and lead me back to the ancient wisdoms was teacher. In more recent times, any true dialectician (material/spiritual) who could increase my understanding of all, I say all, the forces afoot in the universe was teacher. I'm entering my forties with more simplistic criteria—anyone with a greater capacity for love than I is a valuable teacher.

In the classroom and in personal encounters, Toni offered long-term lessons along with day-to-day political tactics to encourage change. These ideas echoed the M'Dears, Miss Hazels, Miss Dorothys, and Mama Maes who frequent Toni's stories. Although I provide personal examples here to illustrate what I call "Lessons in Boldness, 101," Toni liked carrying lessons in her back pocket for anyone seeking a thread of truth to hang on to in her everyday conversations.

Be Loud

In the early 1980s, Toni agreed to facilitate a weekend writing workshop in the New York apartment of writer/early-childhood educator Gerri Wilson for a small group of black women, something Toni did countless times in her life. In that intimate circle-space, I read several of my poems for the first time. Focused on my new affiliation with New Hope Baptist Church, I wrote about the attentiveness of the preacher, the mighty voice and dance of the explosive minister of music, and my mystical Baptism experience. As I read, I was nervous about the subject—this was not a group of church-goers—and the quality of the writing.

To my surprise, Toni said little about the writing, but targeted the delivery instead. "Where is your voice?" Toni demanded, reminding me of an elementary school teacher rehearsing children for the annual end of the year play. "Speak loudly and read like you believe in your work," Toni demanded.

Claim Your Space and Tools

While centering work in community, Toni understood the importance of appropriate work space and work tools. Toni wrote in "Salvation Is the Issue:"

> I recall from teaching years of freshman English, particularly at Rutgers/Livingston, that students did remarkably better work once they found materials that suited them. Spiral notebooks felt like braces on the teeth to some. Legal pads reminded one too much of a probation officer. Soft black zippered loose-leafs the welfare's investigator's badge. Steno pads too confining. Red margins a straightjacket. Blue exam books, even for rough drafts, caused tremors. I'd accept assignments on the back of somebody else's stationery, on newsprint, on whatever. The issue was not economics—though all of us were broke—but affinity.

Once when I was failing to make progress on a writing assignment, Toni asked me where I did my writing. I replied, "Oh, anywhere." She paused as she often did to give me a chance to secure myself and float into a meditative focus for the followup. In this case, Toni did not suggest rewriting and rewriting. Her solution was a dedicated work space, a very large desk, to be used only for writing. That desk, built more than twenty years ago, is where I am writing now.

Make Community Your Training Ground

While recognizing space is needed for work, the spirit of community is the life force. As Tom Feelings, a radical visual artist, once said, when he hears the voices of community, he hears from the ancestors, and that sparks creativity. Toni urged us to anchor ourselves in communities in ways that allowed community voices and culture to influence our work. At Livingston, students reported on visits to the Schomburg, the Chad School, an independent black school in Newark, and visits to grandmother in rural communities on Easter breaks to tape-record life stories. We went back to the neighborhoods where we grew up to sit down with elders and kitchen storytellers.

Just as community flowed into the work, we needed to document bringing our work back to the community. When teaching at Livingston College, even creative writing exercises had community applications. When assigned to write children's stories, for example, students made plans to visit local libraries or day care centers to read their stories to an authenticating audience prior to submitting them as final pieces of work. Toni said, "Do not write term papers for me. Make sure they are useful for somebody else as well."

Take the Championship Position

In "What It Is I think I'm Doing Anyhow," Toni whoops it up for Muhammad Ali. His renowned resilience included an ability to find steady footing and keep dancing even when being hit hard with steady blows. What a metaphor for the black experience—knocked down, but not knocked out, stepped on but not weary—-the spirit required for the generations of protest and resistance championed by the black community. "How we got over" chatter frequently punctuates our conversations when families and friends gather in church, high five on the block, or gather at the Sunday dinner table where fried chicken and smothered biscuits kick off celebration of survival rituals.

The lessons continued years later. In 1995, when I visited Toni who was by then quite ill in a nursing home in Philadelphia, she told me how she kept busy by making carrot juice for the nursing home patients and workers. In the midst of our laughter, a physician barged into the room (without knocking) spouting ultimatums about length of stay, discharge rules, and hospital billing codes. In moments, I was in a heated argument with the doctor, taking an ardent stance on how quality of care, humanism, and equity also mattered even when making decisions about rationing health care. To my surprise, I glanced over at Toni and she was smiling, cheering me on for taking the champion position.

Always Organize

Belief in the power of organizing fueled Toni's optimism even when the burned-out fires of the 60s left pessimism and cynicism in their place. Even when others saw only the despair of the post-60s fervency, Toni could point to a tenant group, a women's organization, a prison group, a student movement, the release of a Julie Dash film, publication of an anthology of women of color as evidence of continued agitation for social change. All activism whether it be challenging homophobia in the church or being involved with a workplace union counted. Oftentimes, I lamented to Toni that I was no street organizer. Toni laughed and replied, "Organize where you are."

Take Care of Self

Toni valued style, beauty, care, and sustaining wholeness in her personal life and in her work. Healing rituals and therapeutic remedies included poultices, mud and dung pacts, bathing remedies, restorative salts, and herbs. Mid-wives, healers, and visionaries all frequented her writing long before the language of new-age alternatives became cliché. I recall spending the night with Toni on Simpson Street in Atlanta in the 70s. The next day Toni asked after early morning greetings, "Did you hear the Muslim in prayer chanting at sunrise?" We agreed that the chant penetrated our spirits, waking us gently from early morning dreams.

In the mid 1990s, just weeks before Toni died, we traveled together on an Amtrak train from New York to Philadelphia. Even though Toni was nauseous most of the time, she managed to sit down to a scrabble game and sell wolf tickets in the crowded Amtrak dining car. The couple who listened intently to her over-the-shoulder suggestions for Scrabble moves reminded me of the kind of folks who immediately become family even if they get off at the next train stop and are never seen again. In this black couple's company, for a brief moment, Toni was whole and well again.

The Last Lesson

A truly unforgettable lesson came earlier that morning while still in New York. Toni's daughter, Karma, had picked up the keys for the downtown apartment from her mother's friend, writer Toni Morrison, several weeks ago. In the early morning, Toni and I had a brief time alone in the apartment. Toni knew I rarely cooked, but I was the only one there to fix breakfast. Even though omelets aren't on my short list, who else was there to assign for cooking? So, there I was with asparagus, eggs, and salmon in hand trying to remember the fundamentals, like what were those previous lessons in boldness again? While stirring eggs, I wondered if I could look for missing ingredients by flying through the air with snakes in my hair, as Toni described Velma doing in *The Salt Eaters*? What incantations could I recall to make the meal a healing one? Where were the seven sisters of the Salt Eaters when I needed them? And, oh ancestors, reveal yourselves and do the grace thing now!

None of this worked. Filled with so much self-doubt, I tried chanting to myself that whatever I make for Toni will be fine; still the anxiousness mounted. Even with the late fall morning sun streaming through the sky light, I felt cold.

I said, "Toni, do you want the asparagus chopped into small medium or large size pieces?"

"Do I add the salmon now or let the asparagus cook a bit longer?"

"Toni, should I flip the omelets or wait a few more minutes?"

I was rapidly becoming one of *Salt Eaters'* "lost dead souls . . . doing the freakie dickie." As I fought back tears, I realized that Toni was cracking up with laughter, the kind she described in one of her essays as laughing so hard she had to lean against a wall to keep from falling down.

Only after what seemed to be an interminable amount of side cracking, Toni paused to say, "Do you ever enjoy sex?"

That worked. Suddenly I drifted into a childhood dream about cats being everywhere. When I told Toni that dream years ago, Toni interpreted the dream as representing sensuality. I entered that dreamspace. The omelet made it to the table.

19

A Timeless Truthteller

JAN CAREW

I vividly remember meeting Toni Cade Bambara in 1970 when I was teaching at Princeton University. I was one of the founders of their Afro-American Studies Program and I also was an exchange professor with Livingston College at Rutgers University. Toni Cade was a very handsome black woman, and what occurred to me after living for decades in Europe was why so many of the African American men whom I had entertained and showed around in different cities in Europe were more interested in European women than in women like Toni who were black, gifted, and beautiful. As I began to know black women like Toni better, I realized that one reason was that they put you under a certain kind of intense scrutiny, and you needed a sense of security to contend with that scrutiny. The truth was that you couldn't lie and you couldn't pretend that you were someone other than who you were. On the other hand, you could do this with many European women very easily and get away with it. I saw in Toni the kind of woman who was a very rare kind of intellectual; she knew who she was, where she came from, and she was confident about the talent she was bringing to the world.

Because of the Black Power movement, the antiwar movement, and the founding of institutions like Livingston College, there were new opportunities for a woman like Toni to give back to her people things that she was not able to give back previously in academic institutions like Rutgers. Livingston, a brand new college, provided a special environment in which we were all charting intellectual courses through a welter of uncertainties about race, class, and caste.

What made Livingston really fascinating was that there was a coterie of extraordinary black women. They ranged from brand new high school graduates to adult women, emerging from the tedium of being housewives and entering new intellectual arenas with a special kind of excitement, experience, dedication, understanding, compassion, and eagerness to learn. They possessed a fire that was genuine and unique, something that the men sometimes lacked. So Livingston at that time was a rare kind of intellectual arena. I don't know if we'll ever again have one like it. It will take half a century to dredge out, analyze, and bring into focus all of the factors, factions, tensions, and insights that this period bred.

At Livingston we saw women in leadership, yet we have yet to see much in print from that period about those women activists because that's the way that historiography is framed: women are left out. We, the scholars who came out of African American Studies, have to have new lenses to see that great men have mothers, aunts, grandmothers, great grandmothers, and that these women play a pivotal role in shaping the way these great men see the world. The mothers, aunts, and grandmothers also took charge at Livingston. Women like Toni have an exceptional independence that defiantly shakes the ground. When opportunities arise like the ones that came about at Livingston and Rutgers at that time, there surface great women like Cecilia Drewry and Toni Cade Bambara. At some institutions, these women might have been buried alive. At Rutgers, during this critical time of upheaval and change, these women found themselves in an environment where they could make the powerful statements that needed to be made. The role that women played at Livingston was particularly pivotal because it was a central role and not a peripheral one where women simply traipsed behind the men.

It's important to know that early on Toni was an internationalist. We did have some meeting of the minds there because I saw some of the Manichean aspects of the Black Power movement as flawed. There were those like Toni who were prescient enough to understand that there were elements of an intellectual motive energy inside the movement that needed a cool level-headed long-term analysis. Toni was one of the people who intuitively understood this. Of course, we had the Black Muslim factions, the cultural nationalist factions that were almost fanatical in their adherence to their own narrow ideological beliefs. There were also those who never understood, as my grandmother often told me, that a vision without action is a hallucination, and we must constantly strive to match the two. At the same time, the movement always had a Third World perspective that widened our views to the extent that class, race, and multiple factors could intersect and impinge on our black liberation struggle. We had a Third World faction at Livingston, and we drew some of the brightest and the best of the students into some new ways of thinking. We convinced them that this struggle must last beyond our immediate campus concerns. We did the same thing at Princeton at the Third World Center, which is there today, as we did at Rutgers. What has to be remembered is that then to propose a course in Third World Literature was to be ready for attack. The dean called me on the phone and said, "Don't you think you could change the name?" I said, "No, not at all, it has an absolute validity."

Toni had the right kind of instincts to see how the immediate situation at Livingston was a nexus from which could spill all kinds of useful and enduring creative activity. All of the great African American intellectuals I knew personally in the twentieth century who believed in the cultural unity of the black world were internationalists, and they included W. E. B. Du Bois, Paul Robeson, Alphaeus Hunton Jr., Langston Hughes, Arna Bontemps, and Anta Diop. Some of them are totally forgotten, but their legacy remains.

I remember sitting in Toni Morrison's office at Random House when Toni Morrison was an editor there. Morrison was absolutely enthused telling me about Toni Cade's latest collection of stories. Later when reading the stories in *Gorilla, My Love,* I realized that Toni Cade had an inner ear for the language of our people—its cadences and lyricism, and through that language her characters spring to life. She used speech to define for us who we really are as a people, and that was an act of genius. It wasn't taught to her. It wasn't acquired by taking writing classes. The gift was simply there.

Now, I must jump over periods of time to the last occasion I had extended talks with Toni. She had come to Hampshire College to speak about the importance of film as an artistic and creative media. In her absolutely lucid and intellectually honest fashion, she pointed out that our enemies knew what an elemental and powerful medium film could be. She argued that was why everything possible was done to prevent us from entering this particular creative arena as equals. She discussed the complexity, expense, and overall difficulty of working in a medium so hedged by intricate financial systems with layers of bureaucratic and bottom-line hustlers in between.

Toni brought to film her passion, her understanding, and her academic ability to analyze complex subjects and events. She adheres to that old axiom that tells us if you can't analyze the world, then you can't change it. We had met at Hampshire before the MOVE disaster had taken place. When I heard of that brilliant documentary film about MOVE, *The Bombing of Osage Avenue,* and heard her voice in the narration of that movie, it literally tore the heart out of me. Toni entered so deeply into the psyche of the people who had suffered during that atrocious bombing and had a kind of Nazi final solution inflicted on them. All too few had raised their voices against this atrocity, but of the few who did, none were more eloquent than Toni Cade as she spoke the truth to power with fearlessness. When I have the courage to see the documentary again (I see it every now and then), I do so just to hear this incredible voice of hers speaking across the ages and echoing both anguish and hope. In that voice of hers is the legacy of an invincible spirit that has helped our ancestors to survive down the ages. *The Bombing of Osage Avenue* should be a standard model for teaching about film and its usage. That film illustrates the way in which cutting-room skills can bring into sharper focus image, word, passion, and insights. We need to teach this film so that students can learn why makers of these kinds of films aren't better known.

Toni understood the importance of community, but at the same time Toni knew that writing is a craft that requires absolute privacy. She knew that the writers who shut themselves away from the community around them end up as dreamers in ebony towers, which reminds me of the Antaeus legends. When Antaeus was lifted off from the earth, he became weaker and weaker until he was vanquished by his enemies. Toni understood that we have to work out ways of connecting to the earth. I believe that this was a legacy that she brought with her from her ancestral past.

We now see a new generation of writers that grew up with access to elite universities, but that fail to connect themselves to the lives of people in our communities and the living histories of the ancestors. The academic output of this new generation is tepid, groping, and equivocal, while Toni's works, impregnated as they are with the dreams of our people, live on. Buried inside of the heart of Toni's work is a living pulse that is destined to live. Look at how much writing was coming out of the period, and why do we remember her? We remember Toni because her work had the essence of life implanted in it in a way that was magical.

Of course, I am dealing only with the tip of the iceberg right now. Underneath were all kinds of experiences with the men in her life, with her child, with her day-to-day dealings with people, and with small and big betrayals. She had to have a sort of central faith, an inner life that enabled her to focus on the impossible goals that her creative imagination encompassed and brought close to her. She remained involved in the struggle for black liberation, and that focus literally carried her over the hurdles from decade to decade. This focus meant discussing night and day with people, going home with the discussion still raging in her head, constantly thrashing out the true and false, and readjusting her vision from day to day. At other times the real eye-opener was learning from her daughter, Karma, who could somehow bring her down to earth when the constant focus on the immediate struggle had the potential to carry her away.

I think Toni had an incredible love for children. She was a writer with a listening ear, and she always listened to children. Toni represented the finest and the best of what a Pan-African woman is. Toni was endowed with humility and grace, and at the same time, she had a special kind of pride and strength. The way that she listened had a quality similar to that of Malcolm X. When you talked to her, she gave you the impression that she was giving you her full and undivided attention. That's a rare quality indeed. All too often, people's eyes stray and their attention drifts.

Toni was both a fighter for black liberation and a peerless contestant in the battle for the integrity of self. She understood that sometimes she could be more dangerous to herself than to an external enemy. She also knew that people close to her as meat to a bone were sometimes eager to tear her down, especially when they thought she was becoming successful. But, Toni never ceased to be a peerless fighter. I think that, as Marcus Garvey said, to be a fighter means that first you must change your way of thinking and then you must peacefully shape the weapons with which to fight. Toni fought with intelligence and integrity. Had she lived, Toni would have adapted to the times because racism is not immutable; you alter the analysis and the tactics as the face of racism keeps changing.

In some African and Amerindian societies, the people selected one person who would be a truth teller who regardless of the dangers would always seek out the truth. Toni was a truth teller like Malcolm X and Martin Luther King. As a woman, she understood the importance of history and carried that history with her everywhere she went. Toni made monumental efforts to unearth the essences of truth that she then distilled and bequeathed to us all.

T.C.B. – Taking Care of Business

PEPSI CHARLES

Toni Cade Bambara was/is one of the gems in my life. I was blessed to know from the beginning, over 25 years ago, how truly fortunate I was to have Toni as one of my mentors. Of course, I knew who she was before I met her. I vividly recall the first time I ever saw her. Nikki Giovanni was hosting a bid whist book party, complete with Queen of Sheba (black) playing cards; this was about 1973. In walked this incredibly striking couple, both bald, both beautiful, with glowing brown skin. It was all I could do to keep my mouth from falling open. "Who are they," I managed to whisper to Nikki. "Oh," Nikki said, "That's Toni Cade and her man, Gene Lewis." Toni Cade was the editor of the very hot literary anthology, *The Black Woman*. Sometime soon after that I went down to Houston Street in the Village to a bar that Gene was tending to a reading of "The Johnson Girls," a short story from Toni's *Gorilla, My Love*. Toni was reading from the story with her girls, including, Audrene Ballard, Hattie Gossett, and Hattie Winston . . . They were having so much fun. The language was so fresh, the attitude so self-empowering; and were they ever having fun!

My first real interchange with Toni Cade came when I applied to teach in the English Department at Livingston College in 1974. John A. Williams, the noted novelist and journalist recommended me, a young poorly paid WBAI producer to Hattie Gossett, the poet, writer. I was interviewed for the position at Toni's house on E. 124th Street in Spanish Harlem. Between bites of fresh artichokes (one of Toni's favorite foods), Toni along with Barbara Masekela and Hattie made me forget that I was being interviewed. I felt that I was sharing information with sister friends about myself. It was one of the most thorough and pleasant job interviews I've ever had. When I was interviewed at Livingston by the senior faculty, it was already a done deal that I'd be on staff. I admired the sisters' personal power and administrative skills. Toni was the prime manifestation of the Queen Mother at Livingston College in the early 1970s. Rutgers University's Livingston College was founded in the late 1960s to serve minority and working-class students. Toni was there from the beginning, formulating policy, designing courses and criteria, and

Courtesy of Rose Charles.

defining the contents of the circle. And she served as Faculty Speaker. The faculty was nontraditional, eclectic; and, to say the least, there were a whole lot of talented People of Color in one place. While I was a member of the English Department, my colleagues included Barbara Masekela, A. B. Spellman, Hattie Gossett, Miguel Algerin, and the late Marc Crawford; later came Al Prettyman, Jayne Cortez, and Wesley Brown; and I had been preceded by Nikki Giovanni, Jan Douglass, and Sonia Sanchez. I must say, on some levels, you had to be there, you had to "feel" it, cause it was really all that!

I mean, I could look out my office window and see and hear the great reed player, James Spaulding, soloing *Misty* on flute while instructing his class; once I caught a ride into town with master pianist Kenny Barron; we talked about ideal venues for musicians. I often had lunch with A. B. Spellman; we'd ponder many things, from the difficulty of using the word "love" effectively in a poem, to the ongoing significance of John Coltrane. And, I had the opportunity to cohort with Hattie Gossett and Avery Brooks (then a Rutgers MFA graduate student), who were performing and serving as faculty advisors to students, black and white, straight and gay, who conceived and constructed "The Great Wake" production (dirge provided by the late reed player, Junius Hemphill) that was held and forewarned Livingston's changing to a more traditional, less innovative environment.

Without question, Toni's initial impetus, powerful presence, and long shadow allowed for those things and many more to happen. The first month I was there, black students took over the Dean's office. They put in a call to Toni to come and listen to their demands. I tagged along. Toni read their demands out loud and told them they had her support. Then she drafted an ad hoc letter of support on behalf of the black faulty that was immediately turned over to the Dean. This had the effect of neutralizing any punitive action on the part of the Dean, and the issues were resolved without any of the students being punished. I was only a few years older than the students; I was awed by her focus and effectiveness. I have been ever since. Toni's students adored her. She provided them with a key to education. The key was that knowledge, identity, and purpose produce action. Toni's classes were action oriented. You had "work" to learn, "work" to discuss, and most certainly "work" to do.

I treasured still having Toni in my life as a trusted sister friend and colleague after she left Livingston and moved to Atlanta. We talked infrequently, about once every other month, but usually for no less than two hours at a time. I almost always called her. And she always made me feel that I had her undivided attention. She gave me the privilege of deciding when the conversation ended. She served diligently as my mentor and chief resource on an advisory board panel for an NEH grant I received as a WBAI producer. At my invitation, she returned to Livingston to speak as part of the Paul Robeson Scholar Project Lecture Series, a project that I could not have pulled off if she hadn't paved the way. I always made sure before sitting down to a phone conversation that I had a few working pens and some paper. Toni was a consummate resource person. I constantly marveled at the depth of her knowledge and how she knew the particulars about every aspect of a concept on which she focused. She knew where to get and how to use specific information, which were the reliable sources, and she knew how to bring qualitative form to a focused vision.

An activist intellectual, Toni impressed on me that intelligence must be moved on. Yeah, you could consider, discuss, and debate, but finally you must act on what you know, "So, what's the plan?" That was her refrain once the problem or situation was laid out. I learned early on: Toni could and would move you from thought to action, from hostility to helping solve the problem. Don't ask her to help you with a plan unless you were ready to move on it. She did not dwell, nor did she let you dwell on it, but the inspiration she provided often camouflaged how much courage this stance could take. Ancient Chinese philosophy teaches that the social responsibility of the artist is to reunite people with their reality. Toni did that consistently, almost effortlessly, but knowingly, and purposefully.

The courage with which Toni participated in investigating, promulgating, and helping to end the Atlanta child murders, and the determination with which she documented the bombing of Osage Avenue in Philadelphia, bespoke her worldview. Toni humbly submitted that her gifts as a writer, storyteller, facilitator, teacher, and filmmaker were tools to be used to enhance the common good and our quest for self-determination.

Toni once helped me affirm myself in such a deep way that it validated a change in my lifestyle. It was an act of kindness and insight for which I shall forever be grateful. I moved to Plainfield, NJ, in 1977, after the birth of my son, Ebon Paul. During those early years, I was unplugging from the New York City artistic lifestyle. I had an image of what I wanted to be a part of Ebon's childhood. I wanted him to be able to walk to school, to go outside, have a backyard and a bike, neighborhood friends; and beyond that, just to have an enchanted childhood. The principal at Woodland Elementary School, Dorothy Henry, wouldn't hear of me just dropping him off. I had to be involved. So I became the class mother and joined the PTA, which, with me, then consisted of three or four regulars. Even in a black-run school there were still issues, like struggling to control and relate cultural identification to our children; showing parents how to have input; providing useful information and activities for parents and children; and struggling against 1980s' perceptions of black single mothers as welfare recipients, uneducated, dysfunctional, and so forth.

It was easy to use my production skills to accomplish some PTA goals. Yet, I felt isolated and unattached to my professional life as a radio artist/producer/writer and felt that the work I was now doing was not that significant. But I couldn't deny how good I felt producing Woodland's first Kwanzaa program with my best friend, or hooking up a pinewood derby for Ebon's cub scout troop, or starting a newsletter that was definitely Afrocentric, and to which everyone in the school, that is, students, teachers, principal, and parents made contributions. Nor could I deny that wanting for Ebon made me want to do for all the kids. It was a thrill that a number of my New York friends didn't understand. When are you going to do a book? When are you going back to WBAI? What's your next major project? These questions, though meant to support and inspire, often annoyed me, because they made me face the fact that I was becoming immersed in my own community and with activities I could undertake and be part of, that I was not paying a lot of attention to my more worldly pursuits. "Hey mom," Ebon would say, "we want to know if you can take us to . . . , or help us do . . ." Now, that never failed to touch my heart!

Among all my artist friends, Toni most understood and encouraged my transition to community activist, and she participated in the process. Once when I was going to visit her in Philadelphia, on a whim, I took a copy of our newsletter. The PTA, by then a strong organization with ongoing activities, had just taken six busloads of our children, fourth-, fifth-, and sixth-graders and their parents to see the Broadway production of *Sarafina*, which was a South African play/musical that celebrated the 1976 Soweto Uprising, in which South African students, at great cost, resisted apartheid. Our children were enthralled. They were so well mannered that someone from the audience came up to me and asked what "private school" did they attend. "Public school; they're regular community kids," I said proudly.

So, when Toni asked what was I up to, I just handed her the mimeographed newsletter, saying it was the latest thing I'd worked on. She flipped through and came to the section that the kids had written about seeing *Sarafina* on Broadway. She remarked, "They saw '*Sarafina*'!" And then, she read one of the pieces aloud, effecting the voice of the child who wrote it. It was so full of wonder, excitement, understanding, and hope. There it was . . . enchantment! What I wanted these kids to possess—-through highlighting a captured experience and presenting it from the child's point of view—-Toni showed me that they had it! It was a powerful moment of self-realization. I never doubted in quite the same way that what I was doing mattered, that it made a difference, or that I should take it as seriously as any other project. My friend and mentor acknowledged that my work was important.

It never occurred to me that I would live in this world without Toni. Even when she got sick, very sick, I couldn't bring myself to think she'd really leave. There were some significant signs. Once while we were talking on the phone, she said she couldn't work because of the pain. And once, the only time she ever ended one of our conversations, she was too uncomfortable to talk. I went to see her in the hospital in Philly, just before I left for South Africa; I was going to Africa for the first time. When we walked into her room, she was sitting up entertaining two friends; she was frail, but smiling. I had brought my healer friend, Lorraine Baucum with me. She laid hands on Toni, she massaged her, and Toni lay down and closed her eyes. I kissed her on the cheek and said "I love you, Toni." Her eyes stayed closed, but she smiled, and we left.

Toni passed on while I was in Johannesburg. It was excruciating, the joy and ecstasy of finally making it to South Africa, the pain of knowing I wouldn't see Toni again in this life. Toni would've been one of the first people I'd talk to about the experience of going home for the first time. She would've asked those curious questions, like what did it smell like, what colors do the women wear mostly, what did the children do. She would have, as she always did when I brought my excitement to share with her, expanded my understanding of the experience.

Toni was an elder member of my tribe, a fully evolved Aries sister, beyond petty judgments, always demanding justice, and so totally creative and free and fun. There are places in my heart, mind, and soul where a true friend meets me, and we share an intimacy that is singular in its experience. We marveled at and dissected the serendipitous and cosmic occurrences in our lives. We chronicled the rise, talent, and sometimes the fall of young, old, and passed-on divas ranting and raving, but mostly rejoicing. Our conversations had a musicality about them; always there was harmony, pitch, rhythm, and collaboration. Toni left me her record collection that ranges from Horace Silver, Theolonius Monk, Nina Simone, Charlie Parker's All-Stars, Marion Brown, and Jaco Pastorius to The African Mbira—Music of the Shona People of Rhodesia, Eloise Greenfield's *Honey I Love*, K. Curtis Lyle's *The Collected Poem for Blind Lemon Jefferson*, and Jayne Cortez's *Unsubmissive Blues*.

I laughed, cried, despaired, rejoiced, comprehended, schemed, and shared secrets with Toni in the spaces we created and connected. So, now, there are experiences, ongoing sagas that we discussed about our own lives and understandings that I don't discuss anymore, because they were things Toni and I shared alone. Such is the nature of missing a loved one. It was simply a joy and inspiration for me to be in Toni Cade Bambara's presence, and always, each time, it was a thrill.

The Feeling of Transport

RUDOLPH BYRD

I first met Toni Cade Bambara in the most unexpected way, and the sense of the unexpected along with its attending attributes of discovery, mystery, and transport were features of our friendship.

Fall 1980

"Good morning. May I speak with Mrs. Cade please?" I asked, anxious to complete the first of many calls early in the business day. I had a full schedule and wished to set certain things in motion before setting out for a luncheon at the British Consulate, my first appointment away from City Hall as the Mayor's Special Assistant for International Affairs.

"Who is calling please?" asked an adult female voice that was friendly but also wary.

I introduced myself and then said: "I am calling Mrs. Cade to invite her to attend a meeting of the Atlanta Sister City Committee for Montego Bay. Mrs. Cade serves on this committee. I would like to speak with her to determine if she is available to attend a meeting." There was a pause. I wondered if I were speaking with Mrs. Cade or someone else. Before placing the call I had puzzled over the familiarity of the family name "Cade," and wondered if the Mrs. Cade I was trying to reach was in any way connected to Toni Cade Bambara, the writer. This thought hovered at the levels below speech.

"My mother is not at home, but I can take a message for her," said the unidentified speaker. As a result of identifying myself and stating the purpose of my call, I sense a modulation in her voice. She seemed now more friendly than wary. My excitement began to grow because I thought just perhaps I was speaking to a writer I admired very much. I searched for a tactful way in which to satisfy my curiosity.

"You say you are Mrs. Cade's daughter. Could you also be, by chance, Toni Cade Bambara, the writer?" I carefully asked this question, summoning up the best telephone voice of the diplomat I imagined myself to be and, or so I thought at the time, was on the way to becoming. There was another pause, this one a little longer than the first. I said nothing to break it.

"Yes. This is Toni Cade Bambara, the writer. The very one." Delivered in a straightforward manner, the second statement was laced with both pride and mischief. Or so I thought. I had been seated, but my excitement forced me to stand.

"It is a great pleasure to meet you. I admire your fiction. *Gorilla, My Love* is one of my favorite collections of short stories. You have a fine ear for the speech of adolescents as well empathy for their condition. The stories also are very funny." In the rush of feeling after delivering these statements I wondered about how I sounded to her. Had I gushed? How is it possible to "meet" someone over the telephone? Poor phrasing, I thought, very poor phrasing. Along with being guilty of clumsy speech, did I also sound pedantic? Had I avoided using the dry, haughty voice of the Professor of English, the voice of instruction, a voice always in my head as I recently had left (fled?) the academy to experiment, for the moment, with other vocations? More than anything else, I wished to be sincere and complimentary.

"Thank you. Those stories are some of my best work. I wrote them a long time ago." The wariness evaporated completely. She spoke in a manner that was relaxed and open.

"And what are you working on now?" I asked, eager to know more and to extend the conversation in new directions.

"I'm always working on something, in fact, I was working on something when you called." I felt a distance growing between us, a desire on her part to return perhaps to her desk.

"Of course," I said. "I wouldn't wish to detain you any further. It was a pleasure to speak with you. Please tell Mrs. Cade I would appreciate hearing from her. My office number is . . . . " I returned quickly to the purpose of my call, wishing not to keep her any longer than necessary, but delighted to have made this connection.

"I will tell her you called. Thanks. Good-bye."

"Thank *you*. Good-bye." I heard her receiver land roughly in its cradle. Only then, did I resume my seat. I have just had a conversation with Toni Cade Bambara. What an excellent way to begin my day, I thought.

February 1988

"Rudolph do you have any ideas regarding visiting writers for the spring term?" asked the chair of my department. We were approaching the conclusion of our weekly departmental meeting in which we had been discussing, among other things, recommendations for writers who would give our visiting writers series greater visibility. Of course, I was determined to blacken the already white list and to complicate it further by nominating a black woman writer.

"Yes, I have given this matter a good deal of thought. The writer at the top of my list is Toni Cade Bambara. I believe she would work very well with our students. She could teach a course on the techniques of fiction writing as well as a course on contemporary African American writers. She is someone I met some years ago. Again, I believe our students would like her very much."

Well, I had said my piece, made my recommendation, and as the junior and only black professor among so many senior and white professors I wondered what the outcome would be. As a department, we were in many ways a collegial group. Generally, we were very supportive and respectful of each other. This was the first time, however, I had made a recommendation that would make a claim upon significant departmental resources. Would support translate not only into dollars but also into two short-term courses? Two short-term courses taught by a black woman writer? It seemed to me, the vote could go in many directions.

After some general discussion in which I was silent but very observant, I discovered that there was considerable support for my recommendation. Shortly before the meeting adjourned, the chair announced that the consensus was for Bambara, and that I should proceed to invite her while also consulting with him. Needless to say, I was very surprised but concealed it. Instead I said, "I am glad that there is support for Bambara. I will contact her immediately."

After the meeting I returned to my office in Laird Hall and took my seat at my desk. I didn't turn on the light but chose to sit quietly in the bright light of a February afternoon. I looked out over the center of campus, otherwise known as the bald spot, which during the winter term had been converted to a skating and hockey rink. Snow and ice had settled on the campus as early as November. The sun upon the snow intensified the brightness of the afternoon. Beautiful, I thought, but this is a postcard I would rather receive than send. As I took in the landscape, I wondered if Bambara would actually come to a place where there might be snow in May. I picked up my Rolodex and began calling colleagues and friends who might be helpful in locating the whereabouts of Bambara. Perhaps she was still in Atlanta.

To my surprise and delight it was not difficult to locate Bambara, but it helps to speak with those who are knowledgeable and well connected. Within one week of the departmental meeting in which we had chosen her for the spring writers' series, I was dialing her telephone number in Philadelphia.

"Good afternoon. May I speak with Toni Cade Bambara please?"

"Speaking."

Struck by a feeling of déjà vu, I introduced myself and then said: "I am calling to ask if you would be interested in accepting the invitation to be Writer in Residence at Carleton College for the spring term?" I did not expect her to remember me (later she told me she had no memory of that early morning call from City Hall), although this possibility was, stupidly and vainly, on my mind.

"Maybe," she replied. "It depends upon what you ask me to do and my own calendar." Fair enough I thought. I very much wanted her to accept the invitation and appreciated her willingness to come quickly to the essentials.

After outlining her duties, the teaching, the special attention to students in Creative Writing and English, the public reading, the period of her appointment, and salary she said the following: "I will accept your invitation on two conditions. Number one, I ain't attending no damn departmental meetings. Number two, I ain't reading and grading no damn blue books and other types of final exams. If you accept these conditions, we can proceed with the appointment."

I appreciated her frankness and this lapse into the vernacular elicited a chuckle, but I felt I had an obligation to press her further on the important matter of evaluating the work of students. After listening to my questions about this aspect of the courses, she said with both kindness and firmness: "Well, all of that is for me to worry about, and as I have done this before I do not expect that there will be any problems. Alright?" The charged meaning behind "Alright" came through loud and clear. The meaning beneath this informal expression of agreement was this: "I can handle this. It is not complicated. Shall we move on?" And we did, and before too long we settled very amicably all aspects of her appointment.

This first telephone conversation was followed by others in which we discussed housing, enrollment, and book orders for her courses entitled "Short Stories and Script Writing" and "Contemporary Black Women Writers." These short-term courses meant being in residence for five weeks as well as the week during final exams. There was a great deal to organize, coordinate, and confirm. Toni, as she gave me permission to call her, focused with me on the details, the first of many signs that we would get along just fine.

In the process of settling the details of her appointment, I appreciated even more her candor and the empathy just beneath it. She probed carefully and with sensitivity about various aspects of student life at Carleton, the culture of the English Department, and the political climate on campus. She would often playfully but seriously ask, "What are you bringing me into Brother Byrd?" I responded to all of her questions and held nothing back. While I would discover that Toni inspired strong reactions in people, what she inspired in me was a willingness to speak honestly about my circumstances at a liberal arts college located in the middle of cornfields and later, as the trust between us grew, about private aspects of my own life. She continued to press me for information about the students; this I found most reassuring. I characterized them as bright, serious, earnest, demanding, and possessing a certain sophistication that masqueraded as maturity; in short, some of the best students I have had the privilege to teach I opined. "Really," was the offhanded reply. "Well, we'll see," she said.

Late April 1988

I am driving to the St. Paul/Minneapolis International Airport in an over-sized, four-door sedan. I do not know how much luggage Toni is bringing so I have reserved a commodious vehicle. I wish to be on time, indeed, at the gate when Toni disembarks. I am making excellent time, and thankfully the roads are clear. There is neither snow nor ice, but it is not the April weather I associate with spring mornings in Atlanta: short-sleeve weather, azaleas and dogwoods in bloom. Such weather will not descend on Northfield until June. I realize again that I live in a place where the weather can kill, and if one should happen to succumb to exposure in January, then one could not be buried until June, so cold and hard is the ground. This, I suppose, explains the high number of crematoriums in the Twin Cities. An unusual aspect of an urban landscape I was still, at the time, exploring. I wave away such morbid thoughts and think about the stranger, friend, writer I am going to meet. Accelerating, I drive through a flat, undulating landscape that strangely possesses the characteristics of the ocean. I can see for miles in any direction.

I arrive at the gate well before the passengers disembark. As I wait for Toni, I wonder what she will be like? I also wonder if hosting her for five to six weeks will be the pleasure I hope it will be, or will it be a test of my patience and diplomatic skills. Or put another away, thankless race work. I remind myself of the fact that I do not really know her. Looking out onto the tarmac filled with arriving and departing planes, I remember my experiences with writers in graduate school. Some were so rude and selfish they had to be reigned in and reminded of their duties to their host. I shall never forget one writer, who shall remain nameless, who dismissed my mentor and advisor at Yale as an "Ivy structuralist" and who, at a public lecture, proceeded to deliver a harangue replete with the well-worn phrases of a very narrow black cultural nationalism. Would Toni behave in so outrageous a manner? I hoped that she would not. In the instant I expressed this desire, her plane appeared on the tarmac and moved slowly toward the gate.

As I was on the only black person in the waiting area, I would be easy to spot, but I was careful to stand in a position where I could not be missed. A black woman of medium height, light skin, and a rather large and somewhat crumpled afro was making her approach toward the entrance of the gate. My view of her was sometimes blocked by other passengers. As she moved forward, I could see that she was wearing a black leather ensemble. A black leather overcoat was folded over her arm. She carried no luggage except her purse, which was also made of black leather and hung, by a strap, from her shoulder. I was struck by her very confident gait which had a strange up-and-down motion, this the result of something like a deformity in her right leg. All of this I processed in a matter of seconds. As she approached the concourse I asked, "Toni Cade Bambara?" She replied: "Who else could it be?" I laughed and appreciated the sense of drama and elegance on display. "I am Rudolph Byrd," I said, "welcome to the Land of Ten Thousand Lakes." All the while I was thinking how her arrival in Northfield will be noticed by everyone, but then she would be noticed anywhere.

As soon as we were settled in the car, she lit a cigarette, inhaling deeply. I found her easy to be with and to talk to. Certainly, this was the result of her obvious authority, maturity, her complete comfort with herself. And also her skill at negotiating the unfamiliar and the unexpected.

When we arrived in Northfield forty-five minutes later, she remarked, "Now, this is a town. How many black folks live here?" "Not many," I replied, "less than twenty I would guess. That's excluding the student population." "I am not at all surprised," she chuckled.

I drove to her campus apartment, which was not far from my own. I was relieved and pleased that she approved of the accommodations. I left her to unpack and promised to return in the late afternoon for a tour of campus and dinner. "Who is coming with us to dinner?" she asked. "No one, it will be just the two of us." "Good" was her reply, "I am not ready to meet any strange folk just now." I understood the meaning, smiled, and excused myself; I agreed to meet her at her apartment at 5:00 P.M.

As Carleton College has a small campus, the tour did not take long. While Toni was curious, it was sufficient for us to stand in the bald spot, now green and moist, while I pointed to and named the various buildings that ringed it. "And in front of us," I said having identified each building in our circle, "is Laird Hall, the home of the English Department, your office and the classroom in which you will be teaching." "Well, Brother Byrd let's check it out," and she confidently and bravely entered the unknown.

As we proceeded down the cement path to Laird Hall, I continued to adjust my gait to accommodate hers. As we walked, I felt more and more

176 • Rudolph Byrd

comfortable with her. And also intrigued by her. She had this way of walking in a measured way, while also conveying energy and intensity through her speech and gestures. As she remarked about the campus and the architectural features of Laird Hall, I was drawn in by her beautiful voice that possessed the intonations of the Bronx as well as the Delta and was always and clearly the voice of a black woman. And her face? An intense field of beauty and intelligence, her gaze was all-encompassing. In this moment, my concerns about the bad behavior of visiting artists fell away. The students, I thought, will love her. As for my own feelings? I was already enchanted by her. This I did not expect so soon.

As we negotiated the stairs that led to the second floor of the offices of the English Department, she remarked on the beauty of the darkly stained wood of the railings and the exceptional height of the ceilings. I said nothing to contradict her. I showed her first the classroom in which she would be teaching. "This is fine," she said. I then showed Toni her office. "This works," she remarked "but I will be more in my apartment than here." "Of course," I said. I then showed her my office and the main office of the English Department.

Entering the main office, I showed her the location of the coffee machine, the refrigerator where goodies are sometimes to be found, and the cabinet containing supplies of paper and other writing materials. "I said you may help yourself to supplies as you need them." Without a word she walked to the storage cabinet. She selected several pens, pencils, boxes of paper clips, several reams of paper, and even more legal pads. Before I could catch myself, I blurted out, "What are you doing?" "I am doing what you said I could do, helping myself to writing supplies." "But . . ." and she interrupted me before I could complete my sentence and said, "I am a writer and I am short on supplies. You know you had no business telling me that I could help myself to writing supplies and then not expect me to do just that. I'm taking what I need." "Of course," I said and then began to loosen up a bit as a result of the conspiratorial smile, and the deep brown eyes that missed nothing. Not even my thinly veiled discomfiture. "Let me help you carry these things," I said. So much did she have in the way of supplies that we had to make a stop at her apartment before proceeding to dinner at the only Chinese restaurant in Northfield.

The following day was her first day of class. I arrived at my office about an hour before Toni's class was scheduled to begin. I sat at my desk with the door open just in case she needed something. A few of the students enrolled in the morning course on contemporary black women writers peeped in to say hello, all excitement and apprehension, and to ask, "Is she really here?" I assured them that she was.

From my desk I could see Toni approaching Laird Hall. A slender, graceful figure dressed in jeans and a loose-fitting sweater of a dark color. She was wearing black boots and her hair was covered by a colorful and becoming wrap. She was on time and she took her time. She also smoked as she walked.

Just as I heard her climb the stairs to the second floor I left my office to greet her in the hall. "Good morning. I hope you slept well." "I slept just fine, Brother Byrd. And how are you today?" She was in good humor and it showed. "Very well. Several students have stopped by my office. They are anxious to meet you. Would you like me to introduce you to members of your class?" "No," she replied without altering her stride. "Would you be interested in making a brief appearance at this afternoon's department meeting so that I could introduce you to our colleagues?" I entreated. By this time Toni was halfway down the hall and I was addressing her back. She turned her head without stopping and said "No" very firmly. What she implied was this: they are *your* colleagues, not my colleagues. I will not be troubled by such things, and you should remember that. She continued walking toward her classroom and before entering turned again and offered, "I'll stop by your office after class." "I will be here," I said.

In the interim I read and graded the remaining midterm essays from my seminar on twentieth-century African American literature. It was not long before I heard a knock at my door. I assumed it was Toni stopping by to visit as she had promised. It was not Toni; but a group of students enrolled in her morning course. Many of them I knew by name; the others I knew on sight, for at a small college one knows, after a while, all of the students. All of them were female and all of them were black. Collectively their mood was serious. As I invited them into my office I wondered about the purpose of their visit.

"What may I do for you?" I asked. A student I shall call June was the first and only one to speak. June was a serious and talented student, but it was her seriousness that had sometimes worried me. Beneath the seriousness was, I felt, a certain bitterness and disappointment that stained all of her interactions. I never learned the basis for such feelings as she gave off a very adult sense of privacy. This I respected. She had enrolled in two of my courses, and while she wrote excellent essays, she contributed very little to discussion except to correct the white students who had uttered, in her opinion, some idiocy or who had, much to their peril, strayed too far off the point. As I was committed to a full airing of views in class discussion, June's habit of policing the white students was a matter of some concern to me. Nevertheless, I respected her intelligence and her seriousness. It seemed that she was at the head of this impressive delegation.

"Professor Byrd, we have come by to thank you for what you have done," said June. "We would like to thank you for inviting Professor Bambara to Carleton. We love her course. We have never felt so affirmed by a professor. We think that she is wonderful." Before I could respond June closed the distance between us and embraced me for the first time in the manner of a younger sister. As she stepped away I could see that she was somewhat tearful. For a moment, I said nothing. Subsequently, I found my voice and said something to the effect that I was pleased that they were pleased or some such silliness. I could not match June's poise and eloquence, so moved was I by this demonstration of feeling. As I had surmised, June had spoken for the group and after she delivered this message they followed her with nods and smiles out of my office.

Moments after their departure, Toni entered in my office, for I had left the door open. She sat down in one of the more comfortable chairs.

"Well," I asked, "how did it go?" "Just fine Brother Byrd. I have a good group. They seem serious, and they can talk. As for the writing that is still an unknown." As she spoke she smiled and also surveyed the wall of books behind me. As I looked at her, I focused on her eyes. Again, I was struck by their deep brown color and expressiveness. I thought of Jean Toomer's description of a character called Fern whose face "flowed into her eyes..."

"A group of your students just left my office. They came by to say how much they adore you," I said. As do I, I thought.

Late May 1988

The time seemed to race ahead of us and suddenly we were in the week of finals. Toni had developed a loyal and large following since that first day of classes. As she moved across campus she was the bright flame at the center of a crowd of rapt students. The unsolicited reports of her teaching that I received throughout the term were glowing. Classes were now over and we were preparing for finals amidst that strange and wonderful calm that settles on a campus after the labors of an academic year. And Toni, sadly, would be leaving us soon. I stepped out of the melancholy this fact created and returned to the work of preparing my final examinations. Unexpectedly, there was a knock at my office door. I yelled a friendly "Enter" and Toni appeared in the door's frame.

"Brother Byrd, what's happening?" which coming from Toni was both a question and an announcement. Characteristically, she emanated light, energy, and movement. In her presence, I felt transported without leaving the ground.

"Not a whole lot. Just preparing my exams. I am very glad to see you," I said.

"I've come by to invite you to my final exam. It will be held on Friday evening at 6:00 P.M. in the lobby of the performing arts center. It will be interesting I expect. Come and hang out for a bit." She spoke warmly.

"The *lobby* of the performing arts center? That's an unusual location for an exam. Yes, of course, I will be there. I am curious to know how all of this will turn out."

"I expect you are," she said her voice laced with mischief "See you Friday."

Two days later as I entered the lobby of the performing arts center I was greeted by a blues, much loud but cheerful talk, and a throng of students engaged in assembling what I later discovered were their final examinations. What was going on here, I wondered.

As I was to learn, Toni had asked her students in both courses to revisit the major themes of the readings through painting, collage, music, recitation, and enactments. The range, creativity, and beauty of the students' work were impressive. And even more interesting, she had structured her final exam, if that is the correct language for it, so that all of her students could participate in what was nothing less than an event. This, I thought, is most unexpected. Here I experienced the surprise of the supremely confident academic who has learned something important from an unexpected source. From this experience I acquired an insight into the basis of the unfortunate divide that generally separates professors of English from living writers.

I began looking for Toni and found her engaged in a critique of a collage inspired by a reading of *Sula*. The student who had made the collage was standing at full attention as Toni delivered a very thorough critique of this novel interpretation of Morrison's novel. Toni nodded and smiled in my direction and continued with her critique. I followed her as she negotiated a path through the many creations her inspired teaching had inspired. As I followed her, I thought, "I like this process. I will apply it in my own teaching." She carefully critiqued each "exam" and as she did so, I witnessed the depth of her impact on the students.

Some two hours later, she gathered the students around her and delivered an abbreviated lecture that addressed the core objectives of her courses and the manner of their translation in the many "exams." She then, to the palpable disappointment of all present, said her good-byes. The students and I detained her awhile longer with loud applause, whistles, and a standing ovation.

I drove Toni to the airport the following day. I marveled at her efficiency, for she had completed all of the work associated with courses as well as packed. Amazingly, she did not leave with more than she had brought with her, or so it appeared. I marveled not only at her efficiency but also at how much time had passed between us and joined us as friends since her arrival six weeks earlier. We had come full circle, and the circle contained many good and fine things.

As I drove, she talked about the students and emphasized the importance of my giving special attention to a certain number who needed, in her opinion, greater faculty support. I promised to follow through. "You had better," she said. We also talked of her novel on the missing and murdered children of Atlanta. She said that she had made significant progress in the writing of the novel during her time in Northfield. I complimented her again on the fine public reading on which occasion she had read from the novel.

We easily passed through the process of check in at the airport and walked together to her gate. We settled in our chairs at the gate and Toni began smoking what would be her last cigarette before her arrival in Philadelphia. We spoke of the summer ahead of us, what we would do and where, and then it was time for her to board the plane. And then there was silence between us.

In this silence, Toni put out her cigarette, but before gathering her belongings she rose to say good-bye. I followed her lead. She did not embrace me, as I expected, but instead placed her right hand on the left side of my bearded cheek and, looking into my eyes, said very softly "Thank you, Brother Byrd." I was very moved by this unexpected gesture, as well as her sense of balance in the presence of emotion. She then gathered up her belongings and boarded the plane.

I watched the plane back away from the gate. It moved slowly, ponderously in the direction of the runway. Finally positioned for take off, the plane accelerated and then achieved its ascent. As I watched the plane climb into the heavens, my mind was flooded with memories of Toni.

I continued to watch the plane, and then, seeing Toni's face in the sky, I felt again the familiar feeling of transport without leaving ground.

22

Teaching Toni Cade Bambara Teaching: Learning with the Children in Toni Cade Bambara's "The Lesson"

ABENA P. A. BUSIA

> I don't know if she knew the heart cling of her fiction. Its pedagogy, its use, she knew very well, but I have often wondered if she knew how brilliant at it she was. There was no division in her mind between optimism and ruthless vigilance, between aesthetic obligation and the aesthetics of obligation. There was no doubt whatsoever that the work she did had work to do. She always knew what her work was for. Any hint that art was over there and politics was over here would break her up into tears of laughter or elicit a look so withering it made silence the only intelligent response.—Toni Morrison[1]

> "Children are responsible, competent, efficient, and principled."
> —Toni Cade Bambara[2]

The Work She Did Had Work To Do

Toni Cade's young people live in an ethical universe. The issues they face are complex, and so are the answers, but they are there; rather, they are there to be sought. What matters to her is the process of their unveiling, the recognition of complex mutabilities, that the world of seeming certainties needs always to be reassessed, sometimes with painful difficulty. Yet, at the same time that assessment never diminishes the underlying principle of a moral universe that must govern the life of a community. Thus, everything can and does become a lesson.

My observations on teaching Toni Cade Bambara come primarily from observing the impact of teaching her stories, in particular, the short story, "The Lesson," in master classes on Curriculum Transformation for Multicultural or African American Studies for faculty, from K–12 teachers to college professors. The constant concern in these classes has always been the necessity of revitalizing the curriculum with integrity. This paper arises out of teaching Bambara's short story "The Lesson" in those workshops and realizing more profoundly through that exercise the significance of Toni Morrison's single resonant phrase, "the work she did had work to do."

In addition, the existence, in this story and many others, of adolescent narrators, those "tough and compassionate neighborhood kids," is one of the salient features of Toni Cade's work. They are always, as she points out, children of the neighborhood. They have a community to whom they belong, by whom they are taught to be responsible, and by and to whom therefore they learn to accept being held accountable.

In many respects these children are a tribute to Toni Cade's own childhood and to the community that continued to inspire and sustain her all her life. This is "the community" among whom she continued to live all her life, whether in Harlem, Philadelphia, Atlanta, or any of the other places she ever called home. This is the community for whom she worked, with everything she had and did. This is the community Toni Cade herself acknowledges as the community who gave her, her foundation and continued to teach her, and in many of her essays and interviews, she traces the roots and the routes of this learning process. Among the most clear-sighted exemplars of this tracing are to be found in the last two pieces in the collection *Deep Sightings and Rescue Missions*, the interview with Louis Massiah, "How She Came By Her Name," and "The Education of a Storyteller." Yet I would like to single out one paragraph from the title essay of that collection where Toni Cade gives a wonderful list of "Black folks thinking they had the capacity to rule themselves" with whom she became acquainted:

> Insubordinates, dissidents, iconoclasts, oppositionists, change agents, radicals and revolutionaries appealed to my temperament and my earliest training at home. They studied, they argued, they investigated. They had fire, they had analyses, they had standards. They had respect for children, the elders, and traditions of struggle. They imparted language for rendering the confusing intelligible, for naming the things that warped us, and for clarifying the complex and often contradictory nature of resistance.[3]

Such people as these believed their real work was in creating value in the neighborhoods, and they taught their daughter well. She did learn, and she created a cast of characters like herself who also learn, and learn well. And it is through watching them learn by sharing their journey that we learn with them. And the radicalization of their vision that comes through their formal and informal acculturation processes guides us, her readers, to see the world through their eyes, and thus to see our world differently. Thus my subject here is Toni Cade Bambara as a teacher, through her texts; more specifically, as a teacher of teachers through her texts.

Storytellers as Cultural Workers

In an interview with Kay Bonetti in 1982, Bambara says of her character Minnie Ransom from *The Salt Eaters,* words that are as easily applicable to herself:

> She's a healer, and to that extent, she's like a poet because poets are community health workers. I mean, it is their job to call people to something higher than a fish sandwich and a job, and certainly poets in my own cultural traditions have been regarded as priests and therapists and healers.

She goes on to add, about herself:

> As a cultural worker who belongs to an oppressed people, my job is to make revolution irresistible, and one of the ways I attempt to do that is by celebrating those victories within Black community . . . and to critique reactionary behavior within the community; and to keep certain kinds of calls out there—the children, our responsibility to children, our responsibility to maintain certain continuity from the past.[4]

It is important to bear in mind that though most of her stories are "neighborhood" stories, for Toni Cade that sense of community extends to the wider family of all peoples of African descent, and to all peoples in struggle. Thus regardless of locales limited to the world of a child, at the heart of all her stories are questions that always have larger moral implications which must be related to a world larger than the geographic space in which the children are living.

Thus my reading of her work is based on accepting two factors: first, that Toni Cade Bambara's stories are infused with and based on a very clear sense of community and community responsibility. And that given her acceptance of the role of the artist within the community, it is clear as Morrison says "that she knew the work she did had work to do." The stories she therefore wrote, and the films she subsequently went on to make, speak to her acceptance of that responsibility, and it is this clear-sighted and conscious acceptability of this role that makes her work at one and the same time so resonant of a sense of cultural community and so accessible for deployment as pedagogical weapons that "make revolution irresistible." And there can be no question of her sensibilities concerning the interrelation between the

184 • Abena P. A. Busia

role of the artist and communal responsibility. As Toni Morrison, again in that same preface points out: in her story, "Ice," for example, we watch her "effortlessly transform a story about responsibility into the responsibility of storytelling." What seems the central emotional focus of that story, the opening line that "none of the grown-ups [could] look us kids in the face because of the puppies," does indeed not change, but grows into an awareness that her own future kids to whom she daydreams about telling the story, might notice there is a hole in her story, a hole she would fall right through in the telling; not the question of the responsibility to the dead puppies, but the responsibility to the living crazy old lady. We have only to consider the same process as it takes place in the closing words of "Blues Ain't No Mocking Bird" or "Basement" to recognize that the lesson to be learned goes beyond the lesson itself to our own responsibility about how we pass those lessons on, not only what we say, but how and when we say it. The children in Toni Cade's community take this responsibility, the responsibility of storytelling, seriously.

Representing Community

Toni Cade is also very clear about who her community is. Speaking specifically about her community of readers, she acknowledges those people who often stop her in the street to thank her for her presentation of people like themselves, barber shop workers and hair dressers, or those who come and challenge her, telling her when they think that she's misrepresented someone or got something wrong in one of her stories. She does not limit her audience to those people who can accost her in the streets; however, she does validate them as a specific critical audience because they represent the community, in her own words, that "names [her] mother, daughter, sister," which in the dedication is the community she serves. That is to say therefore her stories are very self-consciously offered to a community to reflect on, and to see themselves reflected in. Their validation does not mean so much an uncritical celebration of her, as an affirmation that in her stories she is seeking their health and reaching for their truths.

That ability to critique, and be criticized by one's community is as true of Toni Cade as it is of the characters she creates. Her young narrators give us a sense of a coherent world. Any incoherence in that world must be made right again, sometimes through the very act of talking about it. The sense of an ordered world is always given to us through double gesture, carefully, by giving us the vision of the child recognizing what is normative and good and healthy about their society, at that moment when they recognize its disruption. In the story "The War of The Wall," for instance, the first charge laid against the "painter lady" when she ignores the children trying to tell her she has no business making any claims on their wall is, "You don't even live around here." The wall belonged to the kids of Talbro Street, and she was not of them.

"The Wall," like "Blues Ain't No Mockingbird," has a number of things at its heart, but what the child narrator responds to first is the way in which the person being critiqued, in this case, the person painting the wall, is clearly an outsider because of her lack of courtesy. She compounds the error of ignoring the children by disrespecting the adults:

> Then the Morris twins crossed over the projects and hung back at the curb to watch. The twin with the red ribbons was hugging a jug of cloudy lemonade. The one in yellow ribbons was holding a plate of dinner away from her dress. Some good aromas were drifting out from under the tent of tinfoil, and pale green juice from the greens was leaking on the twin's socks. The painter lady paid no more attention to them and the gift of supper than she did to me or Lou or the fire hydrant. When she wanted to deepen a line, she just reached around behind her for the blue chalk. When she wanted scissors to cut the string or lay the blade flat to pry the tape loose, she just fumbled behind her amongst the stuff she had laid out on a sawhorse table. I figured the woman for a rude, no-nose fool. Next to my mother Mrs. Morris cooks up the tastiest-smelling food in the neighborhood.
>
> ...But the painter lady was acting like a mental case. She was up on the milk crate, over the step stool, up and down the ladder hanging off it to reach a far spot. She was scribbling all over the wall like a definite crazy person and not even looking where she was stepping.[5]

When she is finally forced to acknowledge the presence of the twins, she declines the food, saying she had brought her own. This is later found to be untrue, for she goes to the restaurant to buy food. But she finds nothing there she chooses to eat. She behaves with such discourtesy, even their mother, the owner, feels the need to reprimand her and remind her of where she is: "I don't care who your spiritual leader is, eat in the community, Sistuh, you eat pig by and by, one way or t'other."

However, this is not the only point. As always, there is a lesson to be learned, and the narrator is not left free to hold on to her prejudices, even if she does have a valid point. The story is in the end a debate about the role and place of public art, and this is a story in which there is a learning process taking place. The narrator has to learn to challenge her own assumptions and prejudices. So, although her resistance is set up because of the outsider-ly behavior, the rude behavior of the painter who does not acknowledge them, who will not eat their food, who won't eat pork, won't accept their food, and does not accede to any of the social graces that make the community a community, she too does in the end have something to offer–her painted wall. In the end, the narrator, like the community itself, also has to acknowledge the possibility of a new meaning for the wall other than the ones she had previously assigned it. The painted wall suggests a space for the new information, another way of life, and new visions.

We see a similar kind of move made in the story, "Blues Ain't No Mockingbird," in which the young narrator has to process exactly what's going on, what is the nature, if you like, of the resistance, what is the nature of violation that Granny is resisting with the men with the cameras who feel they can come and stomp all over her fields, taking pictures of her life for the Council or whoever it is they're working for, only in this instance, the resistance to outsiders is affirmed, and their intrusion remains a violation.

The wonderful thing about "Blues Ain't No Mocking Bird" is the way the story is told. The technique is cinematographic. This story in fact makes textually palpable the transitions Toni Cade could make between print and visual media. The story unfolds as if the narrator were not so much a camera surveying the scene, but rather the principal spectator of the unfolding drama whose point of view structures and thus determines what we see and how we understand. We can tell from her descriptions exactly where she is positioned with respect to the other people in the scene, the buildings, and that landscape which they all inhabit. We begin with the closeup of the stomping feet of the girls masking crystal paperweight design, "like a spider web made by a spider with mental problems" in the ice. We move out to the twins swinging high in the air on the tire, and return to earth with a view of Granny on the back porch "making the cakes drunk" before we shift to Granny's point of view of the men in the station wagon intrusively roaming around in the meadow, walking with hubris into center frame. She is more than a camera, however well positioned and wide angled. Her point of view though literal is also moral and frames her telling of the tale.

The staging of the scenes continues throughout; however, what slowly dawns on us, as in the case of "The War of the Wall," is the moral universe that frames the action and separates the insiders from the outsiders. So although we get a story shaped by sufficient stage directions such as:

"Nice things here," said the man, buzzin his camera over the yard. The pecan barrels, the sled, me and Cathy, the flowers, the printed stones along the driveway, the trees, the twins, the toolshed.

"I don't know about the thing, the it, and the stuff," said Granny, still talkin with her eyebrows. "Just people here is what I tend to consider."

Camera man stopped buzzin. Cathy giggled into her collar.

It is the narrator's perception of Granny's behavior that ultimately underscores what is supposed to be right. As with the other stories, what unfolds is a sense of juxtaposed worlds in contestation, the men filming and taking pictures move like "they was invisible or we was blind, one" and are both intrusive, and un-self-conscious of that intrusion in their entitlement. Once again, the outsiders do not greet the people; and these filmmakers presume the people whose land they are trespassing on have no rights, that their private lives can just be picturesque backdrop for the county's food-stamps campaign, and that, like the man in the signifyin' story Granny tells, there need be no morality behind the circumstances under which they point and click their cameras. If Granny's monosyllabic answers and silences do not make the fallacy of these assumptions crystal clear to the children, Granddaddy Cain's actions certainly do:

Then Grandaddy's other hand flies up like a sudden and gentle bird, slaps down fast on top of the camera and lifts off half like it was a calabash cut for sharing... "You standin in the misses' flower bed," say Grandaddy. "This is our own place."

The Nature of Children

What Toni Cade Bambara manages to do so successfully with these children in her works is a number of things. In the first place, she is such a brilliant and gifted writer. We acknowledge that part of her power as a writer is the ways in which she makes their voices come to life. She herself describes the children in her stories as "tough little compassionate kids," and that is at the heart of the stories that she tells. The kids are tough because they face the world with a certain kind of truth.

That quotation about tough little compassionate kids is quoted in an interview that Toni Cade Bambara gave to Kay Bonetti in February 1982. In that same article, Toni Cade speaks about the different kinds of philosophies, if you like, governing the institution of education in the United States. She says a number of things which I will quote at length because they undergird her own writing and resistance, and make clear the principles behind the kinds of children she presents in her works.

I see four kinds of models in education. One that starts with the premise that children are Public Enemy Number 1, that they are an absolute menace to life and limb, and they must be defused and made obedient and robotized, and so we get schools that appeal to shame and guilt where the model seems to be "You ought to be ashamed of yourself." And so the children come out obedient true believers, and can be delivered up to the first demigod that comes along because they're not encouraged and equipped to think critically or to voice opinions, to raise questions. Then you have the kind of school that starts with the premise that children are innocent, that is to say stupid, and immoral illiterates, and they must be protected from certain kinds of information, and so you lie to them . . . [In those schools] . . . You do get more illiterates. You get kids who don't know how to process information, who don't know how to think critically.

She then goes on to critique the so-called progressive or alternative schools. These schools, even though they start off with a good premise— that children should be free—existed in a kind of vacuum, for most of them never had any sense of social theory of what, in the end, they wished their children to be free to do, what to train children for. They lacked any vision of what a good society could be, and thus never thought through clearly enough what to train children for, or even how to train them. In those schools the teachers became permissive simply because they were afraid to take responsibility for setting standards. In the end those places of so much potential left the children with no compass for social behavior, let alone social action. But finally, there's a fourth model, which she says is a model that she thinks exists in other communities, but certainly exists as the pan-African free schools, and that:

> starts with the premise that children are responsible, competent, efficient, and principled. In which case, in those schools, kids are encouraged to raise questions. They're encouraged to take on responsibility, they're encouraged to critique everything they read, everything they see.

These are the children that people the stories that Toni Cade Bambara writes. Her children are responsible, competent, efficient, and principled; and if they are not acting that way, the purpose of the story is to show them that they should be.

The Lessons of "The Lesson"

"The Lesson" itself is a lesson about learning. It is a story that reveals Toni Cade Bambara's lifelong passion for learning from life, and life as a shared learning process. She taught us through her stories, and very often her stories are about learning. It is a feature of her delicacy of touch, her sensitivity to learning situations, which in many of the stories the narrative "I," the teller of the tale, is not the person of wisdom, but the person who has something to learn. The pedagogy is thus light, oblique, and experiential rather than didactic. We enter into the world of her characters; their visions become our visions, their prejudices ours, so what they have to learn or unlearn, we learn and unlearn with them, alongside them. This is the gift of a teacher. That ability to make us share experience without letting us feel that our learning is only as a result of their superior knowledge.

Bambara gives us life as a learning process, and by making us partners with her characters, she shows us how to grow, as teachers. This is in fact the pedagogical strategy of Miss Moore in "The Lesson," but initially Sylvia the narrator doesn't appreciate this.

> Back in the days when everyone was old and stupid or young and fool-
> ish and me and Sugar were the only ones just right, this lady moved
> on our block with nappy hair and proper speech and no makeup.
> And quite naturally we laughed at her, laughed the way we did at
> the junk man who went about his business like he was some big-time
> president and his sorry-ass horse his secretary . . . Miss Moore was
> her name. The only woman on the block with no first name. And
> she was black as hell, cept for her feet, which were fish-white and
> spooky. And she was always planning these boring-ass things for us
> to do, us being my cousin, mostly, who lived on the block cause we all
> moved North the same time and to the same apartment then spread
> out gradual to breathe. And our parents would yank our heads into
> some kinda shape and crisp our clothes so we'd be presentable for
> travel with Miss Moore, who always looked like she was going to
> church, though she never did . . . She'd been to college and said it was
> only right that she should take responsibility for the young ones'
> education, and she not even related by marriage or blood.[6]

Her wonderful voice is so strong, and full of such undocumented certainties. Yet she tells us a world in that opening paragraph, her world. Togetherness and discrimination are so finely structured in this paragraph, we hear not only the respect for Miss Moore but also the talking behind her back, and through Sylvia's voice, we also hear revealed the tension between the mothers who know that Miss Moore is a woman worthy of respect, and yet who feel that somehow her ways segregate her from them. And there are different kinds of lessons in this particular story. In the space of one minute we have codified for us intragroup class distinctions; gentle and not-so-gentle pathologies, social sensibilities, and niceties, and all the politically incorrect attitudes of that enclosed culture. Clearly Miss Moore's oddities are her dark skin, nappy hair, and unpainted face. That coupled with her college degree make her a character all too familiar to some of us. But what matters is not that she is educated, but in the end, how she educates: informally but firmly. And we as readers are shown this with wit, yet with serious intention.

In the course of this story the narrator, who thinks she knows everything and is happy and proud of it, then learns to critique a world very different from the one she knows—a world in which $300 can be spent on toys and paperweights and $1,195 for a sailboat of fiberglass—the world of opulence that is represented by the toy store FAO Schwarz. This is a story that negotiates not only who are these young children, and even who is Miss Moore, but also the larger question of who are they when their idea of themselves is disrupted by the vision they get of their world when they enter a children's store on Fifth Avenue in downtown New York. The point is therefore not only that larger context which the children must learn to negotiate, but it also comes in a story where there are so many other little lessons about personal responsibility, and not cheating taxi cabs, and about broadening the vision of your world.

The story "The Lesson" is centrally shaped in two significant ways: first through the observations of the narrator herself, and second through the shape that Miss Moore gives the lessons she gives to the children. In Miss Moore, Toni Cade Bambara has created a character whose objective it is to use life experiences as a way of teaching to think; it is this technique that shows us how to grow as teachers. However, the feature that gives dramatic tension to the story, and in the end shows the effectiveness of Miss Moore's strategies, is the creation of the narrator as a resistant learner.

Sylvia, that narrator, structures her narrative through a combination of witty observations, incredulous comprehension, and incomprehensible rage. These are the ways she registers not simply her resistance to Miss Moore and her lessons, but specifically to the lessons of this day in particular. On this day, her wit registers her resistance, her rage, her comprehension. For she does have an ability to learn, and this ability is subtly given to us at various points in the story; one will suffice. At the start of the expedition, as she and her friends gather, she says "so me and Sugar leaning on the mailbox being surly, which is a Miss Moore word." That small gesture of acknowledging "a Miss Moore word" enables us to know that she does indeed learn and grow, however reluctantly, through listening to Miss Moore.

To speak first of Miss Moore's framing of the lesson. When the children gather it is clear that Miss Moore has structured the day as a day in which they should learn to think about money:

> Miss Moore asking us do we know what money is, like we a bunch of retards. I mean real money, she say, like it's only poker chips or monopoly papers we lay on the grocer. So right away I'm tired of this and say so. And would much rather snatch Sugar and go to the Sunset and terrorize the West Indian kids and take their hair ribbons and their money too. And Miss Moore files that remark away for next week's lesson on brotherhood, I can tell. And finally I say we oughta get on the subway cause it's cooler and besides we might meet some cute boys. Sugar done swiped her mama's lipstick, so we ready.
>
> So we heading down the street and she's boring us silly about what things cost and what our parents make and how money ain't divided up right in this country. And then she gets to the part about we all poor and live in slums, which I don't feature. And I'm ready to speak on that, but she steps out in the street and hails two cabs just like that. (88–89)

But Miss Moore's idea isn't simply the overall picture of money and class, though that is central. She also wants to bring about the recognition of individual responsibilities and individual relationships to money. That she is a sensitive teacher or one who can spot a potential learner is shown through the fact that she selects Sylvia, of all students, to give responsibility to; it is the mouthy, recalcitrant Sylvia who is given the $5 and told to work out the 10% tip to pay for the taxi. And it is that same Sylvia who will have to add the existence of that $4 change, still in her pocket at the end of the day, to the reflections that day will bring.

Once they arrive at FAO Schwarz, Miss Moore makes the children look in the window. That is to say, she makes them establish where it is they are, and what it is they are about to do. Once the size of price tags in the window register, they have to take cognizance of the fact that they are about to enter a place where paper weights can cost as much as $480:

> My eyes tell me it's a chunk of glass cracked with something heavy, and different-color inks dripped into the splits, then the whole thing put into a oven or something. But for $480 it don't make sense. (90)

And this is before they see the fiberglass sail boat costing over $1,000. Significantly, when it is time to enter the store, Sylvia is unable to do so, and articulates being overcome by a sense of shame; a shame born of seeing herself and her companions being looked at through puzzled eyes, "like a glued-together jigsaw done all wrong."

Once inside, Miss Moore continues her lesson by "watchin like she waitin for a sign," and responding to their spoken and unspoken communications. She structures each moment of re-thinking of their world around the children's conversations. Before entering the store she had described in great detail the function of the microscope they had seen in the window, and asked them to think of what it does, as well as what it costs. By the time they get inside, the incongruity of the juxtaposition of the world in which they live, and the world they have entered, is being keenly felt. Sylvia's recognition of these inequities is recorded in the sense of almost inarticulate rage, which she registers as feeling like punching people, somebody in the mouth. She asks "Watcha bring us here for, Miss Moore?" and slouches around the store pretending to be very bored, but Miss Moore's point has hit its mark in her:

Me and Sugar at the back of the train watchin the tracks whizzin by large and then small then gettin gobbled up in the dark. I'm thinkin about this tricky toy I saw in the store. A clown that somersaults on a bar then does chin-ups just cause you yank lightly at his leg. Cost $35. I could see me askin my mother for a $35 birthday clown. "You wanna who that costs what?" she'd say, cocking her head to the side to get a better view of the hole in my head. Thirty-five dollars could buy new bunk beds for Junior and Gretchen's boy. Thirty-five dollars and the whole household could go visit Granddaddy Nelson in the country. Thirty-five dollars would pay for the rent and the piano bill too. Who are these people that spend that much for performing clowns and $1000 for toy sailboats? What kinda work do they do and how they live and how come we ain't in on it? (94)

Toni Cade Bambara even encodes the way she communicates that Miss Moore has recognized that this outing may have had a greater emotional impact on the children than her usual outings. That these outings are intended for pedagogical purposes is underscored by Sylvia's account of the habitual nature of the de-briefing session back in front of the mailbox where they had first started. But this time, there is a difference. Instead of the "draggy-ass lecture" she usually gives, she asks a simple question.

That question "Well, what did you think of F.A.O. Schwarz?" elicits several responses, which capture the multiple negotiations of the day. The first emphasizes the sense of alienation they felt when they arrived on Fifth Avenue in the first place, "white folks crazy." The next response, from the girl Mercedes, "I'd like to go there again when I get my birthday money," again, reminds us of the interclass distinctions among them that had been evident throughout the day in such gestures as the recognition that among them all, only Mercedes had a place in her home set apart for her to write. However solid or fantastical her assertion is, the others recognize their own inability even to dream that possibility and "shove her out the pack so she has to lean on the mailbox by herself." But finally, it is Sugar's response to Miss Moore, and Sylvia's response to Sugar through which we come to comprehend the magnitude of the turbulence in them all, represented by Sylvia's bad-girl behavior:

> Then Sugar surprises me by sayin, "You know, Miss Moore, I don't think all of us here put together eat in a year what that sailboat costs." And Miss Moore lights up like somebody goosed her. "And?" she say, urging Sugar on. Only I'm standin on her foot so she don't continue.
>
> "Imagine for a minute what kind of society it is in which some people can spend on a toy what it costs to feed a family of six or seven. What do you think?"
>
> "I think," say Sugar pushing me off her feet like she never done before, cause I whip her ass in a minute, "that this is not much of a democracy if you ask me. Equal chance to pursue happiness means an equal crack at the dough don't it?" Miss Moore is besides herself and I am disgusted with Sugar's treachery. So I stand on her foot one more time to see if she'll shove me. She shuts up, and Miss Moore looks at me, sorrowfully I'm thinkin. And somethin weird goin' on, I can feel it in my chest.
>
> "Anybody else learn anything today?" lookin dead at me. (95)

Sylvia turns away, with much to think about, as do we.

NOTES

1. Toni Morrison. "Preface" to *Deep Sightings and Rescue Missions* (New York: Vintage Books, 1999), ix.
2. Toni Cade Bambara. Transcribed by the author from an interview with Kay Bonetti conducted in Bambara's home in Atlanta, February 1982. Audio Prose Library.

194 • Abena P. A. Busia

3. Toni Cade Bambara. "Deep Sightings and Rescue Missions," in *Deep Sightings and Rescue Missions* (New York: Vintage Books, 1999), 174.

4. Bambara. Bonetti interview noted above.

5. Toni Cade Bambara. "The War of The Wall," in *Deep Sightings and Rescue Missions* (New York: Vintage Books, 1999), 59–62.

6. Toni Cade Bambara. "The Lesson," *Gorilla, My Love* (New York: Vintage Books, 1992), 87–96.

23

Toni Cade Bambara

Ruby Dee

Toni Cade Bambara
Bamba, Bamba, Bambara
Toni Cade Bambara
Even her name a heartbeat
Ancient woman
Voodoo priestess with pen
Magna cum laude in
The politics of essential
Considerations.
Woman-to-woman
Sistuh-to-sistuh to
Child to husband to lover to
Family to government systems
To world to universe discovered
And undiscovered.

Technical,
Mind going every whichaway
In scary, funny, foot-patting
Order.
Coming at deep from way
Down under deep
No stone unturned where
Love might be or where
Snakes hide.

Bamba, Bamba, Bambara
Toni Cade Bambara
Even her name a harmony
Soul dancer

Courtesy of John Wiley & Sons, Inc.

Gold medal acrobat on
World brain bars.

Black goddess of connections
Riding hard and fast
On a miracle mule to
The far corners and to
All the spaces in between
Shaping ether.
Touching everything everywhere
Matching moments for all
Sorts of history to establish
New rhythms
Sanctify some old ones and
To throw wide open the doors
On the supply places
Housing the stuff to live by.
Making "Uh-Humm" the heaviest
Word in the dictionary.
Doing the world's necessary
"Spade" work to a pick-ax beat
A "Lady Day" blues
And a laugh that rescues beauty and
Truth from the tight spaces
The nasties have crammed it to.

Bamba, Bamba, Bambara
Toni Cade Bambara
Nurturer.
Love epitomized.
Handle on hope.
Black woman.

Guerrilla
Filmmaking

"Why Black Cinema? (1987)"

Toni Cade Bambara

> *"A classical people demand a classical art." Playwright Lorraine
> Hansberry wrote that deathbed statement as her last communiqué
> to us. A classical people, a classical art: classical in the sense that
> the people, the work, are informed by our origins, our precedents,
> our prospects, and are centered in the understanding that all great
> art is derived from the folk. For while we may feel compelled by
> circumstance to fashion new forms, new idioms, new modes, new
> genres, they are bound to be compatible with, centered in, and
> informed by the very old truth-speaking traditions from the ancient
> mother culture: the fables, the parables, and in the jet-age of
> instruction, single sayings. As in mama say, "Don't let you mouth get
> you into what you backside can't stand." Or daddy say, "Never mind
> getting over: let's first get up." Or in elder say, "It's not how little
> we know that hurts; but that so much of what we know ain't so."*

Thus, we find in the Afro-American narrative prose tradition as well as in the newly emerging Black cinema, attentiveness to time-honored ways of storytelling, constant use of circles, people gather, with the emphasis on *"we."*

Classical in the sense that the people and the work are coherent. That is to say, that the insights and impulses that give rise to our expression are made appropriable, apprehendable, usable, sensible through metaphors and patterns that are familiar to us from everyday occurrence, rituals, ceremonies, tradition, spiritual practice. Such as call-and-response which we know from our sermons, from our chorus/soloist songs, from our dance/drummer dialogues, and the instrumental variants of improvisational jazz. And we notice that as a weaving device, blending together seemingly disparate elements, the handing down from generation to generation, in baton-relay form, our mouth to ear memory speak (an absolute signature in all of Haile Gerima's films where the whole structure is always "relay").

Reprinted from *City Arts Quarterly*. Permission granted by Kwame M. Kilpatrick, Mayor of Detroit.

Another very obvious feature of our classical form is repetition: Motifs in textile design, in masks, in scarification patterns, in everyday speech:

"Oh, the troubles of the world, girl; the troubles of the world." And obviously in blues-bar poetry where we repeat the first line—not because we think people are stupid or inattentive or "cain't get it," but it is simply "the way."

And classical, too, in the sense that "It matters." That is to say what we are doing matters. That it's sustaining; that the work makes a difference between feeling disabled and enabled, between feeling invisible and feeling indelible. It is the difference between feeling mute or being very much in voice.

And what enables us? Information. Afro-centric perspectives. Critical/engaged viewpoints. We find in works like Billy Woodberry's film Bless Their Little Hearts, *about an unemployed worker and his family, difficult situations unresolved. Some people have problems with this film because the characters aren't all "positive"—meaning they would prefer, I think, flat, dull/normal propagandizing images pleading "We, too, are clean," "We deserve the vote" figures running around. But we demand complexity because we are a complex people. We need to view, to see, complex relationships that are linked; where domestic conflict is linked to social conflict, has a context in the wider world where things are not masked.*

Why new Black cinema? A classical people demand a classical art.

TO BE ENTRAPPED IN OTHER PEOPLE'S FICTIONS PUTS US UNDER ARREST. To be entrapped, to be submissively so, without countering, without challenging, without raising the voice and offering alternative truths renders us available for servitude. In which case, our ways, our beliefs, our values, our style are repeatedly ransacked so that the power of our culture can be used—to sell liquor, soda, pieces of entertainment, and the real deal: to sell ideas.

The idea of inferiority.

The idea of hierarchy.

The idea of stasis: that nothing will ever change.

These ideas, or ideological imperatives, are the real products of the so-called entertainment industry.

Have you seen for example, the movie running around called The Little Shop of Horrors? *Indeed, that little movie, which features a monstrous grotesque, colored, blood-sucking, people eating, entertaining plant with the voice of the Four Tops, a beast that must be slain so that order can be restored and the American Dream can be pursued without distraction or hindrance, is not an isolated or accidental phenomenon. In a 48-hour*

*period last week, I spotted no fewer than four political cartoons based on
this image of a greenish-browning, gap-toothed, buckeyed, liver-lipped
grotesque form with thick ivy tendrils shaped like octopus tentacles having
a grip on Uncle Sam, the Statue of Liberty, or the dollar bill (eagle
prominent), squatting in a flower-pot variously labeled: Welfare System,
Crime in the Streets, and Teenage Pregnancy. All code terms designed
to trigger mad-dog fury against this not-at-all disguised symbol for you
know who. Code terms that we've been conditioned to respond to with
shame, self-blame, and over- identification. Why Black cinema?*

*We're living in a period in which, temporarily, we are operating
without a coherent articulated Black political agenda. A period in which
the momentum of the previous decade when we seemed to have been
investing energies wisely in attempting to form independent Black political
party formations—that momentum is sluggish. A period in which random
and systemic bigotry, resulting in violent attacks on Blacks, progressives,
and other down-pressed sectors of the American Society whose tongue had
been appropriated but who have now found their voice, have escalated
to an alarming degree as documented by Klan-Watch (random,
racist-motivated violent newsletter) and the National Committee for
Democratic Renewal (formerly the National Inter-Klan Network). And
the official response, include Black faces in high places, has been "there
is no connection" "These are not racially motivated." Violent attacks on
anti-Apartheid workers on the Univ. of Mass., Amherst campus have no
relation whatever to violent attacks on Black students at the Univ. Of
Indiana, Bloomington campus, and no relation to Tenacious Slack in
Ann Arbor, etc. We're living in a time when the voices of progressive
organizations are being systematically muted (not to mention less-than
progressive organizations like the NAACP.)*

*Maybe I missed a beat, but did we not witness a tremendous amount of
energy being invested in decrying the film* The Color Purple, *and then in
the next moment, jumping up in indignation when it didn't win an Oscar,
and then, on the Image Awards, ignoring enabling, usable, enlightening
work of independent producers in video and film in favor of nominations
going to Nell Carter (or Nell Carter's character) as the faithful servant on
TV, who ain't evah comin' home to us. Anymore than Link of* Mod Squad
is ever comin' home to us. Anymore than them kidnapped youngbloods on
Diff'rent Strokes *and* Webster *are ever comin' home to us. Because there is
nothing worthwhile in the Black community to claim their loyalties. Why
Black cinema?*

*Hollyweird, like any other organization or industry—and this goes for
the education industry, too—has a product to sell. The seeming product,*

the movie, can be any old miscellaneous thing. It can be cornball, spectacular, hip, spooky, sentimental, freakish. It can be probing, even socio-political (quasi-quasi). It can be anything, so long as:

1) *It advances individualism and other bourgeois concerns, values, and agendas as normal, natural, virtuous, if not heroic.*
2) *So long as 'conflict' is not depicted in the onset of race, class, etc., but is reduced to "personality differences."*
3) *If the movie does traffic in socio-political constructs, they are subsumed under the Puritanical Manichean ethic of "good guys/bad guys" or Freud.*
4) *If there is, perchance, any political or moral commitment on the part of the lead character, then it's presented as a psychological aberration.*
5) *And if this character is able to resolve conflicts, it is seen as the isolated triumph of this one person—usually a white boy—and not to be taken as a cue that the socio-political arrangements of this joint can ever ever change.*
6) *And even when films flirt with revolution (as* Under Fire, The Year of Living Dangerously, The Circle of Deceit*), such revolution is only a backdrop for the rites of passage of the "hero." All of this, of course, is in keeping with the Empire Novel tradition from Kipling (pro-empire apologist) to Conrad (so-called 'critic' of imperialism) where no matter how treacherous things are, how unfair, evil, or awful, there is no revolutionary alternative ever conceived.*

And so, even if the script is 'tough' and should happen to get to the shooting stage,

1) *Visual opulence and megatech flamboyance will always take precedence over the writer's or director's social or political intent.*
2) *The viewer will be continually signaled* NOT *to take this drama as a cue to start thinking or acting by use of the manipulative devices designed to keep us passive voyeurs. Hence, in Hollywood, the persistent use of doors, windows, and other theater-like proscenium devices to say, "hey, this is just entertainment."*
3) *And all of this would be alright . . . if the drive to orchestrate ideological consent to a particular version of reality was not also reinforced by suppression, the suppression of any other version*

*of what possible values, relationships, contests there are to
consider, connections we can make, or actions we can take.*
WHY BLACK CINEMA ?

*It is not only that we are hired at the rate of 1% in the media when we
are 17.843% of the total population and hired only in cities where we
make up at least 30% to 70% of the local population. But also the fact
that 50% to 70% of TV and motion pictures on the screen and the tube
throughout the world are products of this institution called Hollyweird
that would annex the global mind by annexing the global screen,
maintaining control over production, distribution, and exhibition. This
industry, so adept at throwing up new spectaculars, but always with the
same-ole same-ole messages: dusty plantation dramas that now come
to us in sophisticated disguise, but are still imitation of life.*

You remember Imitation of Life . . . *in which the maid has a
prize-winning pancake recipe and makes a fortune . . . but remains a maid.
Faithful to the end. Well, they made this film in 1930 and liked it so much
that they made it again in 1950. They really liked it because it had the
double plantation number of the 'tragic mulatto' and the 'faithful servant.'
So there she was: with her fortune, but still a maid to Claudette Colbert in
the '30s and to Lana Turner in the '50s, losing her daughter, but stuck
with Miss Anne.*

*We got the space age version of that a few seasons ago with Matthew
Starr, where the faithful servant character played by Lou Gossett, Jr. says
to massa at some point of extreme danger (the mansion wasn't burning
down, but there was a runaway android threatening the spacecraft) and
'somebody' had to get out there and risk 'somebody's' neck, so Lou
Gossett says, "It's too dangerous, Matthew, I'll go. After all, you were born
to rule the Galaxy." Because, of course, it is like the Force. In our Galactic
Westerns, the Force is inherited; see the Grandfather Clause.*

*To get back to those hot-shot rites of passage movies in which we, or
revolution, is the background, it is films like* Trader Horn, Tarzan, Konrak,
Silvia, Out of Africa, *and* Official Story *(the Argentinean film) which I
think are immoral. In* Trader Horn, *in fact, our images are painted on the
backdrop where the 'real action' and live actors proceed in front: a very
compelling metaphor for the urgent state of international relations. So
when we get a film like Bill Gunn's* Stop, *in which the 'to-be-foregrounded'
media couple from the states is to play out their drama against the
background of the Independence Movement of Puerto Rico, all I say is, it's
not gonna happen that way. And because Bill Gunn also had an alternative
version in mind, that film has been stopped. In the can, on the shelf, locked*

up, under arrest. Entrapped in another people's version of... First Amendment rights? Cross-cultural dialogue? See the U.S. stand on the New International Information Order. Or, see the National Security Council paper #46, dated March 17, 1978, stamped "Highly Confidential," discussing why and how an agency had better suppress the Afro-American voice and, in particular, keep it out of the international arena.

A classical people demand a classical art.

We may not know the exact moment when the new generation of Black filmmakers discovered a sense of like-mindedness or the possibility of community or a movement to build. For some, it may have happened in the '60s when as a result of numerous struggles, they finally got access to materials and equipment and could stretch out. For some, it occurred in 1970 when Pearl Bowser arranged the first Black Film Retrospective and many of us present and many at a distance but who heard were absolutely struck that "Hey, we have a whole tradition of filmmaking. There were others who came before and threw open the path." That was very usable information. It was enabling information. It put a bone in our back.

For others, it occurred in the '70s when bloods trained in film schools like Yale got out of there and hooked up with people who trained at City College in New York or NYU or were trained in community-based institutions or were self-trained in the streets, and hooked up and formed the Black Film Foundation. Or, on the West Coast, bloods who were at UCLA got out from under the shadow and the spell of Hollyweird to hook up with others, some of whom finally collected around Haile Gerima at Howard Univ. And others went on to make videos elsewhere, make films elsewhere, training others elsewhere, providing occasions for organizing film festivals, encouraging the production of newsletters and other forms of communication and critical publication.

We may not know the exact moment when there was a sense among these filmmakers that launching a movement, that moment when they recognized the necessity for institutionalizing and internationalizing. But by the 1980s, potentially powerful links had been forged between African filmmakers in the US, the UK, in Europe, and on the Continent.

Why celebrate Black cinema?

To return to the static (the maid who never changes, or any stereotype your mind can conjure), the stereotypes are pernicious, have a pernicious influence on spirit not simply because they are inaccurate, inadequate, and flat, but because they never change. They have no capacity for transformation. And if that message is pushed out there often enough, of course it erodes political will. The notion that "You can make all the pancakes you want; nothing will ever change."

In the face of this, the transformation drama is clearly the hallmark of Afro-American literature, of our culture, as it is and must be of any people under siege. It is an imperative for survival. And so we find it cropping up all the time in our work. We find the remark "People change" as an obligatory bedrock perception, and the action flowing from it a necessity, whatever the particulars of the story being told. We also find any number of filmmakers devoting their entire story-line to transformation, see Haile Gerima's Bush Mama (set in Los Angeles) and Menelik Shabazz' Burning An Illusion (from Britain). The compelling message: people can awaken, people can change, and in changing enable each other.

We can be concerned with something larger than ourselves. We CAN rise above our training. We can think better than we're taught. And we can transform a society. A CLASSICAL PEOPLE DEMAND A CLASSICAL ART.

24

Asserting My In(ter)dependence: The Evolution of NO!

AISHAH SHAHIDAH SIMMONS

Toni Cade Bambara was accessible to the people. She did not allow her fame to separate her from the community from which she came. Toni was interested in character, personality, principled behavior, and commitment to struggle, *not* to status. If you met her and didn't know that she was a BAAAAD ASS writer, filmmaker, cultural critic, organizer...she didn't announce it...She was just Toni—sistah, cultural worker, mother of Karma Bene Bambara, woman, friend...one of THE ULTIMATE BLACK WOMEN that I have had the pleasure of knowing in my lifetime. Ase. Ase. Ase.

I was fortunate...blessed to have Toni's presence in my life at such a critical time in my life. In February 1990, at the very ripe age of twenty, I confided to Toni my feelings of alienation and inadequacy at Swarthmore College. I also shared my frustration with the film department at Temple University—-where, at that time, students watched and critiqued camera techniques in films like *Birth of A Nation* and *Imitation of Life* without any social commentary. After hearing my frustration and disappointment, Toni told me to come to a place called Scribe Video Center to take her scriptwriting workshop. I told Toni I didn't have any money. Her response was "I didn't ask you if you had any money, I told you to come to Scribe Video Center and take my scriptwriting workshop." Toni's response forever changed my life.

What an awesome place Scribe Video Center was and still is. Twenty-five years strong and responsible for educating a generation of grassroots media artists who use the camera lens as their tool to make progressive revolutionary change irresistible. For over a decade, I've had the opportunity to take and proctor classes, to co-facilitate a community video project, and to hear lectures from a wide range of cultural workers, including Louis Massiah, Arthur Jafa, Gladwin Marumo, Michelle Parkerson, Ada Gay Griffin, Manthia Diawara, Yvonne Welbon, Ayoka Chenzira, BarbaraO, Marlon Riggs, Essex Hemphill, Maureen Blackwood, Isaac Julien, June Givanni, and Haile Gerima, as well as Toni Cade Bambara.

It was at Scribe Video Center that I learned about the Black American Independent Cinema Movement, which contrary to popular belief, did not begin with Spike Lee. It was through Toni that I learned the names of eighty-four Diasporic African women film- and videomakers. Were it not for Scribe Video Center, I don't know if I would be a documentary filmmaker. It was at Scribe that I learned the art and craft of storytelling. It was at Scribe, under Toni's tutelage, that I was empowered to create images that affirm my existence as a Black feminist lesbian, and rape and incest survivor.

My steps to becoming an independent video and filmmaker began in 1991. I began co-producing *Out of the Closet,* a monthly public television program for WYBE-TV35, which featured the voices from the lesbian, gay, and bisexual community in the Delaware Valley. During that time, I also enrolled in a Bambara scriptwriting workshop at Scribe. In that workshop, I developed the screenplay for my first independent video *Silence . . . Broken,* an eight-minute experimental short about an African American lesbian's refusal to be silent about racism, sexism, and homophobia. In February 1992, Toni took me to the world premier of *A Powerful Thang,* a narrative film by Zeinabu irene Davis.[1] Toni told me that when Zeinabu walked into the room, it was important that we give her a standing ovation, because any Black woman who completes a film that tells our stories deserves a standing ovation. Prior to the screening, I didn't know anything about her or her ground-breaking work. I just knew that thanks to Toni, I had the opportunity to witness Black women's independent film *herstory* in the making.

In the spring of 1993, I began co-producing my second television show for WYBE-TV35. Like *Out of the Closet, ON! Sistahs,* was also a monthly public television program. This show was co-produced by, for, and about African women throughout the Diaspora. In May 1993, my first independent video *Silence . . . Broken,* had its world premiere at the Philadelphia Festival of World Cinema, Festival of Independents. Toni came with a beautiful bouquet of flowers in hand to celebrate the first public screening of my work.

In the summer of 1994, Nadine M. Patterson, an independent filmmaker and cultural worker, and I called a meeting of Black women media artists to come together to discuss a need for a Black women's media artist collective in Philadelphia. Many of these women were former scriptwriting students of Toni. Some of them had either taken additional classes or proctored classes at Scribe Video Center. Shortly after the initial meeting, the Black women's collective ImageWeavers was created. ImageWeavers was inclusive of all women of the African Diaspora. Its membership was diverse in national origin, sexual orientation, and media arts experience. We came together because we understood that Black women's cultural production was (and still is) under-valued and unrecognized. Our mission was to bring to the screen perspectives that are overlooked and taken for granted.

In October 1994, my dear sistah-cultural-worker friend Tamara L. Xavier and I had our very first preproduction meeting about a documentary project I had envisioned titled *NO!*. This project would unveil the reality of rape, other forms of sexual violence, and healing in African American communities. When Tamara heard me talk about this project, she expressed an interest in "helping" me. We held our meeting on the infamous SEPTA/New Jersey Transit commuter train ride to New York on our way to a meeting at the home of life long friends, Rosemari Mealy and Sam Anderson. We were twenty-three and twenty-five years old, respectively. Tamara and I had been coworkers/colleagues at the American Friends Service Committee, our previous employers. On our way to New York, we talked about our visions for the future and began jotting down notes about NO! Tamara's "help-ing" me has evolved into her becoming a co-producer and the director of choreography of *NO!*

In December 1994, Wanda Moore, Tina Morton, Crystal Morales, Sherri Denise Porter, and I, among other women media artists, were fortunate to be able to take one of Toni's last scriptwriting workshops. This particular class was very special because all of the students were women, and this is where I wrote my choreopoem "A State of Rage," which has served as the road map for *NO!* In Toni's workshop I expressed tremendous frustration and difficulty with transforming my thoughts and my feelings in my head about *NO!* to images on paper. In class Toni challenged me to go home and "free style" my feeling about *NO!* She followed up with a voicemail message telling me not to come to class empty-handed. That evening I conceived "A State of Rage."

As she did with almost all of her scriptwriting students, Toni wrote me a letter/memorandum that read in part:

> Your piece can be useful in giving women permission to be enraged and outraged. An angry woman, like a laughing woman, is often perceived as a danger to the status quo. A laughing woman might be laughing because she sees the hoax, the ridiculousness of the set up, and may next use her humor to point a finger and bring the whole thing down. An angry woman may be angry because she has peeped the scene and will now use her rage to mobilize others to topple the regime. Both kinds of women are threats and are therefore called "mad," "out of control," "strident." We are taught (women especially) that anger and rage are unhealthy that we need to muffle

it; medicate it, deny it, flee it. You clearly don't think so. Good. Apathy, despair, and amnesia would be the unhealthy responses in the project's "universe," and anger the most use-full.

Rage is fuel. It can leave the person smoldering. It can consume the angry one. Or it can locomote the feeling toward foolishness or usefulness. It can be a tool with which to access the power of the unconscious. It can point a way as well as point a finger, your piece seems to say.

Rage can be red (cholera, flames) white (white hot heat, light), a laser, a pen light, a snarl, a growl, percussive and off-axis movements, etc.

We don't usually associate rage (scary, noisy, frightening), with meditation (contemplation, solitude, tranquil) thus you have an opportunity to harness seeming contraires to produce surprises.

You have a very powerful project here, and you've clarified to yourself the most important issues—where you are in relation to material, what your motive impulse is, what you hope to effect, what content elements are available as a vehicle. Do start laying in some images. If you are having trouble generating visual sequences, trust your voice and simply begin as you intended to narrate the whole piece; then go back and substitute what we will see for what we can hear. Hope this has been helpful.[2]

Indeed, Toni's affirmations combined with her suggestions about *NO!* played a pivotal role in my being true to myself and my vision while navigating my way through the treacherous journey of raising money to make my film. There have been many days after receiving numerous institutional grant rejections indicating that the rape and sexual assault of Black women and girls wasn't a funding priority that I read Toni's memorandum to remind me not to give up on this journey to make *NO!* a celluloid reality.

During this same time period, the membership of ImageWeavers grew significantly. The collective met on a regular basis in preparation for our first public event, which would feature the work of ten of its members. In a January 10, 1995, press release announcing the screening, Nadine Patterson said, "When mainstream media highlights Black film directors, it often stops short of acknowledging the existence of Black women directors." She continued, "Only feature length film work is considered worthy of criticism and publicity. Even with complaints about the myopic view of Black life which reach the screen (i.e., 'Gangsta' films), few comments are made about the powerful and nourishing works of Black women's independent cinema."

On January 27, 1995, ImageWeavers showcased their work at the Community Education Center's Feminist Film and Video Series in Philadelphia. The theme of this herstoric event was "Black Beauty Without Boundary." It featured:

- *I Just Stopped But Never Gave Up* (5 min), an audio piece by Miyoshi Smith
- BLK *Erotica* (7 min), a mixed-media presentation—photography and audio by Barbara Kigozi and Denise C. Jones
- *The Moorish Light* (7 min), a video work-in-progress by Mee Lin Yuk
- *Silence . . . Broken* (8 min), a video by Aishah Shahidah Simmons
- *Shot for Shot* (5 min), a film by Charlene Gilbert
- *Yo Mama* (4 min), a video by Sarah Poindexter
- *Color of My Soul* (5 min), a video by Debra Smith
- *Shizue* (19 min), a video by Nadine M. Patterson and Emiko Tonooka
- *Sangre de Toro* (12 min), a video by Nikki Harmon
- *The Dance in Aunt Ida Lee* (14 min), a video by Tina Morton

With compromised health, Toni Cade Bambara came out to this standing-room-only screening on a cold and icy January evening. Toni didn't return home immediately after the screening to rest. She was in an organizing mode and asked members of ImageWeavers if she could screen some of our work at the Smithsonian Institution's "100 Years of Black Film Conference." Needless to say we enthusiastically said "Yes!" The following is another letter from Toni that was sent to our group after she presented our work at the conference.

My dear Sistus, Thank you so very much for allowing me to screen some of your work last week . . . Nadine Patterson masterfully assembled clips from 5 projects (SILENCE, SHIZUE, IDA LEE, SANGRE DE TORO, MAMA'S GIRL) as I requested from both the makers and from Nadine. . . . My purpose was and still is to persuade a major institution to establish an archives called "First Works" and to purchase and house contemporary works from practitioners such as yourselves . . .

Although shown under horrendous conditions—-trickle-in audience defying the snowstorm and stomping their boots and making noise, plus lack of understanding between me and the projectionist as to what tape was to be shown when (I was to lecture as clips from Scribe's "Community Visions" screened silently behind me, then shut up while ImageWeavers' stuff played with sound, then do hard sell to the African American Dept of the Smithsonian's National Museum of American History and others who see the wisdom of establishing an archives of contemporary works)—the tape nonetheless, captured the attention of successful filmmakers like Camille Billops (THE KKK BOUTIQUE AINT JUST FOR REDNECKS) and critics like Ed Guerrero (FRAMING BLACKNESS: THE AFRICAN AMERICAN IMAGE IN FILM) and Manthia Diawara (BLACK CINEMA; AFRICAN CINEMA), as well as exhibitors such as Carl Erickson (who is currently doing in Roxbury what I hope we will duplicate all over the country, namely, reviving old movies houses and showing Black independent products). Panelists throughout the day made reference to ImageWeavers as an idea (a young Black collective) and as subject matter, remarking on the variety of genre and modality and expressing an interest in seeing the works in entirety. Several conferees—such as cultural critic Greg Tate of *The Village Voice*, and Leasa Farra-Frazer, editor of *Black Film Review*—who'd not been in attendance during the screening, nonetheless inquired about "them Philly sisters we keep hearing about."

So with your permission, I would like to approach the Afro Museum here and elsewhere and carry the tape around acting as an IW pro bono agent/promoter. And perhaps we can add to the tape as products reach completion. I am thinking most particularly of Poindexter's YO MAMA. Meanwhile, as soon as you folks come up with a logo I'd like to have generic biz cards made for you as my contribution (people drove me crazy asking for the address—I gave a c/o Scribe response)...I cannot say enough how very honored I am to know you and to watch you make history as both individual practitioners and as an exemplary model of collectivity.

Respectfully & Affectionately
Toni[3]

ImageWeavers later had several public screenings at the Painted Bride Art Center, at the University of Pennsylvania, and more importantly at community-based organizations with young African American girls. ImageWeavers also held workshops teaching African American girls the craft of storytelling and the art of using the camera lens to bring their images from paper to the screen.

Though ImageWeavers is no longer an official entity, the spirit of camaraderie, sistahship and support lives on among many of the women of the collective. We continue to work on each other's films and videos, providing one another with technical and emotional support. The individual work of the women of ImageWeavers has won awards; been featured on local and national public television; been acclaimed at local, national, and international film festivals; and showcased at galleries and community centers. Through use of dance, the written word, audio, the photographic image, and the moving image, the women of ImageWeavers[4] pay tribute and bear witness to the struggles, defeats, and triumphs of Diasporic African people with a particular emphasis on women.

In February 1997, Charlene Gilbert, former student of Toni, documentary filmmaker, author, professor, mother, and I decided to organize a *Deep Sightings And Rescue Missions* reading on March 25, 1997, Toni's birthday, at Themes and Books, a Black-owned independent bookstore in Philadelphia. We decided to ask people to read passages of their choice from the newly released book as well as from Toni's previous books. Tina Morton, former student of Toni, documentary filmmaker, and professor, videotaped the event. One of Toni's dear friends, Arlene Wooley, brought this large beautiful photograph of Toni, taken by Carlton Jones, which served as the backdrop to the reading. Toni's Spirit was there with us. Louis Massiah, Wanda Moore, Lorene Cary, Zakiyah Ali, Charlotte Pierce-Baker, Carole Metellus, on behalf of ImageWeavers, Patience Rage gave reflections about their relationship with Toni and read passages from *Deep Sightings And Rescue Missions* and *Gorilla, My Love*. Ryva, a spoken word artist and cultural arts producer, closed the evening with both a reflection and a reading of a poem she wrote in tribute to Toni. The bookstore was standing-room only, filled with a diverse group of predominantly Black womenfolk. I believe Themes and Books sold out of *Deep Sightings And Rescue Missions*.

Patience Rage, essayist, poet, and painter, who met Toni in the mid-1980s, gave a very moving tribute. Later she remembered that Toni was one of the first people who gave her permission to do things that people said she couldn't do. Toni's position was that if you're bad enough it to think it, you're bad enough to do it. This permission opened Patience to a world of possibilities. Subsequently, she founded Hot Flashes Productions, a nonprofit arts organization that highlights the creative genius of Black women. Patience also shared that Toni was a hard person to give to because she didn't want folks pitying her because of her illness. Even during this intensely vulnerable time in her life, Toni had a keen sense of humor. One day, Patience took Toni to Weaver's Way, a coop in Mt. Airy in Philadelphia. During Toni's shopping, she went over her budget. Patience, immediately said to Toni, "No problem, the bank isn't that far from here, I can take you to there." Patience said Toni's response was "Do you have a ski mask? If not, there's no reason to take me to the bank!"

Zakiyah Ali, culinary artist, nutritionist, and poet told me that she didn't know anything about Bambara when she first met her. At an ImageWeavers meeting she heard sistahs talk about this woman whom they loved so much and wanted to help beat cancer. Zakiyah offered to prepare food. ImageWeavers would buy organic food and Zakiyah would prepare and take it to Toni's home several days a week. Toni would laugh, eat, and share loads of stories with everyone. Even on her sick bed, she gave advice about writing and encouraged everyone to follow her own vision. Zakiyah revealed that she wanted to attend the United Nations' Fourth World Conference on Women in Beijing. In preparation for her trip, Zakiyah had to write checks to pay for bills, her passport and other travel documents. She didn't have enough money to cover the checks and was literally praying for a miracle. Several days later, Zakiyah received a beautiful card from Toni. Enclosed was a check with enough money to cover her bills plus give her some extra change in her pocket. When Zakiyah wanted to acknowledge and thank Toni for her generosity, Toni didn't want to discuss it. She put her fingers over her mouth and then said "Gurl, we're on our way to Beijing." When Zakiyah returned, Toni's health had severely declined. Zakiyah visited Toni and sat on the side of her bed for several hours looking over a stack of photographs, journals, and papers from the Conference.

At the December 17, 1995, celebration of Toni Cade Bambara's life and legacy program, Toni Morrison described the "Black Women Walk On Water" awards. These prestigious awards are given out, without solicitation or a committee process, to Black women. They come in the form of a check, which enables a Black woman to financially keep her head above water while forging ahead with her plan. When Zakiyah heard Morrison talk about the award, she knew she was a proud recipient.

Toni was always championing, encouraging, and teaching folks. I only knew her for five years. And yet, I continue to know her. I continue to engage her. I continue to encounter her legacy across this country and throughout the world.

In August 2005, eleven years after the first preproduction meeting, I completed *NO!*. I believe *NO!* is groundbreaking and revolutionary in that it asks the viewer, for ninety-two minutes, to look at and experience rape and sexual assault from the enslavement of African people through the present, through the voices, testimonies, *herstories*, scholarship, and activism of Black women. And living in a white supremacist world—not only a society but also a world—that is a tremendous challenge. Because, to paraphrase Toni Cade Bambara, none of us are aurally or visually trained at all to prioritize much less make central Black women's lives.

On December 9, 2005, the tenth anniversary of Toni's physical transition, I received the inaugural 2005 Leeway Foundation Transformation Award for my work using film/video to create social change. This monetary award gave me the breathing room I so desperately needed after literally scraping to survive while I, in concert with others,[5] completed *NO!*. There was a cosmic symmetry in my receiving a critically needed check on that particular day in 2005. While I am grateful that the Leeway Foundation financially recognized my work to create social change, I credit Toni Cade Bambara for giving me the road map, in 1990, to create cultural work that will make social change and revolution irresistible.

NOTES

1. Zeinabu irene Davis's award-winning and internationally acclaimed films include: *Trumpetistically Clora Bryant* (2006), *Compensation* (1999), *A Powerful Thang* (1991), and *Cycles* (1989).

2. Toni Cade Bambara's "RAPE project description" Memorandum, December 13, 1994.

3. Toni Cade Bambara's ImageWeavers Memorandum, February 10, 1995.

4. ImageWeavers Roll Call...Zakiyah Ali, Denise Brown, Charlene Gilbert, Meryl Hamilton, Nikki Harmon, Charlene Horne, Denise James, Denise C. Jones, Yvonne Marie Jones, Barbara Kigozi, Evelyne Laurent-Perrault, Valerie Linson, Gail Lloyd, Taniyiki Marie, Carole Metellus, Wanda Moore, Crystal Morales, Tina Morton, Lisa Nelson, Portia Thuli Nxumalo, Nadine Patterson, Sarah Poindexter, Sherri Denise Porter, Charita Powell, Naomi Richardson, Anula Shetty, Aishah Shahidah Simmons, (the late) Barbara Smith, Debra Smith, Karen Smith, Miyoshi Smith, Nadine Stanley, Carmella Vassor, Roxana Walker-Canton, Gwen Watson, Tamara Xavier, Mee Lin Yuk...

5. The women and men behind *NO!* are: Tamara L. Xavier; Gail M. Lloyd; Joan Brannon; Sharon Mullally; Wadia L. Gardiner; Salamishah Tillet; Amadee L. Braxton; Nikki Harmon; Kia Steave Dickerson; Scheherazade Tillet; Elsa Barkley Brown, Ph.D.; Kimberly D. Coleman, Ph.D.; Charlotte Pierce-Baker, Ph.D.; Aaronette M. White, Ph.D.; Janelle White, Ph.D.; Michael Simmons; Tina Morton; Traci McKindra; Tonya M. Evans-Walls; Giscard (JEE EYE ZEE) Xavier; Monica Dillon; and Women Make Movies, Inc.

Things That Toni Taught Me

Frances Negrón-Muntaner

I don't remember the first time that I met Toni Cade Bambara, but I will never forget the first time she gave me a lesson.

It happened sometime between 1989 and 1990. I was a twenty-three year old know-it-all from San Juan, Puerto Rico fresh out of making my first film, *AIDS in the Barrio* (1989). The Neighborhood Film/Video Project, founded by Linda Blackaby to support independent film in Philadelphia, was presenting a comprehensive twelve-month retrospective on Latin American cinema curated by Beatriz Vieira and titled "Latin American Visions." I was one of a handful of people who attended every screening. Another one was Toni.

One night, after watching *Quilombo* (1984)—a film by director Carlos Diegues about a maroon community in seventeenth century Brazil—I made a comment that I curiously now cannot remember but must have involved the infelicitous phrase "black slaves." Toni, who sat across from me in the outdoor section of the now defunct Eden cafeteria where we used to gather, responded by whispering something that I apparently did not hear as I carried on with my argument. Then, with the grace and wit that characterized her, Toni leaned over to me and softly repeated what she had said so this time I would not miss it: "Enslaved Africans."

The moment that I registered her words was nothing short of revolutionary. Toni's suggested re-phrasing was the equivalent of an intellectual spanking, taking place exactly at the time of conceptual recklessness to assure remembrance. For the difference between "black slaves" and "enslaved Africans" was so fundamental (not to say monumental) that it was evident that these were not just two ways of naming the same object, but completely different ways of inhabiting the world and acting in it. If Toni once defined her objective in writing as finding out "not only how a word gains its meaning, but how a word gains its power,"[1] this was a pristine example of that search happening past the page, on the skin of interethnic exchange. And it also demonstrated an important aspect of Toni's teaching philosophy: any time and any place could—and should—be the site of learning.

Once the retrospective ended I no longer saw Toni as frequently. Yet, in part inspired by the movies and our conversations about them, I started to conceive my first narrative film *Brincando el charco: Portrait of a Puerto Rican* (1994). As I began to think about how to write about the massive migration of Puerto Ricans to New York after World War II, I recalled those Eden nights in which Toni shared her experiences growing up in Harlem during the 1950s. With the usual warmth and love that Toni had for all working people, she filled me in about a significant part of my national history, one that, as a child raised in Puerto Rico, I only knew from books and films. Unbeknown to me at the time, in trading stories about black and *boricua* New York, we engaged in "rituals of loss and recovery,"[2] as Toni would later write about Julie Dash's feature debut, *Daughters of the Dust* (1991).

Remembering Toni's stories and compelling physical voice, it occurred to me that she would make an ideal narrator for the film's meditation on migration. Although I figured this out early on in the writing process, it took me a few months until I finally gathered the courage—let us not forget that Toni *could* be intimidating—to ask whether she wanted to collaborate with me. As it turned out, first she said no. Then she said no again. I was not sure why—if the issue was that she didn't like me personally or didn't trust me as a filmmaker. But in many ways, you couldn't blame her for either judgment: I *was* a crazy kid, with a lot more bravado than experience. Which is why I begged and begged until she said yes.

After several calls about location, schedule, and other practical matters, we shot the interview and, of course, it was unusable due to sound problems. Somewhat scared but knowing that I could not live without this footage, I asked for a make-up interview as I would have asked for a make-up test from a respected teacher. As I feared, however, she said no. And then I begged and begged again and she agreed. This time, we got it right and after the shoot she gave me the pages from which she worked from so I could use them as a point of reference during the editing process.

The text was simply titled "Puerto Rico." It would make a brilliant entry into the *Encyclopedia of Diasporic Memories,* a book that may unfortunately never be published, but that I will record here for those of us who have a need for such things. The first sentences were as simple as they were beautiful: "It was the year of the big snow, the winter of 47/48. I was in the 4th grade, living in that part of Harlem strivers called 'Washington Heights' and the rest of us called 'Harlem.'" In the barely three single-spaced pages that followed, Toni brought to life an entire world: She noted the Puerto Rican propensity to live within a network of extended family members—"babies, married couples, two if not three sets of elders"—the ill-preparedness of these new New Yorkers who did not have "any winter clothes," and their curious proclivity to form multiracial families. Toni also puzzled over their tendency to constantly be on the move, and identified with the immediate discrimination that they came to face: "One of the boys was in our class—for about a minute...We heard that he'd been put in a CRMD class, the assumption being—-if you have no English, you have no IQ. We were curious about him. Some of his relatives looked like Gypsies. Some of his relatives looked just like us. Who were these people?"

By learning about myself from Toni, I picked up on a second fundamental lesson that has never left me since: despite the deep mistrust that characterizes interethnic relationships in the U.S., it is possible for the "other" to narrate "you" without defacement. And this is not only possible, it is also essential, for as anthropologist Clifford Geertz reminds us, "To see ourselves as others see us can be eye-opening."[3] Which is probably why in the arguably thousands of times that *Brincando el charco* has been screened, no one (to my knowledge) has ever critically noticed, not to say objected to the fact that the main authorized voice recounting the Puerto Rican experience in New York is not a *boricua*.

In Toni's own filmmaking, one could appreciate many of the same qualities that made her writing and teaching so life-altering. On the one hand, Toni's films were always intended to be part of a broader dialogue in which objectivity is to be found not in a sovereign claim to truth, but in the process itself of engaging with others and creating a context of debate. On the other hand, in fulfilling her commitment to "write" movies, Toni articulated a strong desire to re-view the world anew, particularly for the benefit of the next generation. If as bell hooks says, "there is power in looking,"[4] Toni was always on the lookout regarding how spectators "saw." Seeing for Toni was never innocent. It was instead an interrogation, a generative tension between seeing and saying that founded an inherently social and interactive space.

Toni's innovative approach to film writing is particularly evident in John Akomfrah's still unsurpassed meditation on Malcolm X, *Seven Songs for Malcom X* (1993). In this film, Toni fulfilled the role of what in less imaginative movies would be dubbed a "narrator." Relying on her impressive performative abilities, she produced a point of entry for every viewer by creating the effect of simultaneously being in the action and sitting next to you at the theater. In valorizing the voice as a vessel, Toni is part of an African American literary tradition that privileges orality as a trope for bodily presence, subjective agency, and truth. At the same time, she complicates this pact through the skillful use of irony, double-entendre, and the eliciting of complicity—a seduction of the listener—who is neither an "other" nor the "same," but a potential accomplice in the road trip of cultural intervention.

Similar strategies are evident in Louis Massiah's *Du Bois in Four Voices* (1996). Here, Toni writes and narrates the film's opening and third section, which not coincidentally corresponds to the time in Du Bois's life when his focus was on pan-African coalition-building, solidarity among people of color, and support of anti-colonial struggles. It also narrates Du Bois's marginalization as a socialist, and the missed revolutionary potential of the depression years in the U.S. Witty, sharp and folksy, Toni's commentary had the same structure of a mystery, relying on foreshadowing as a way of building suspense and provoking the viewer to be attentive: for he or she has little recourse than put the pieces together herself.

Even the knowledge that life and art were a mystery, however, could not prepare me for the news that Toni, a woman who for many of us appeared as an indomitable force of nature, was ill with cancer. During this relatively short period, Toni asked me on several occasions to pick her up from chemo sessions in West Philadelphia. During the drive from the hospital to Toni's Germantown apartment, we often talked about what it took to be a writer, about our projects, and also about in what parts of the world we felt most at home. It was during these trips of the imagination that I got to know Toni the most and it was to be a cruel coincidence that these were to be the last road trips that we would ever take.

The day that Toni died was my father's fiftieth birthday. For as long as I could remember I always called him on this day, exchanging jokes about the inevitability of family and getting older. Yet, on this symbolic year, I completely forgot to make the call. When I finally realized my oversight, I did my best to explain to my father the extent of the loss that I had experienced the day before: I was mourning not only Toni the artist and the teacher, but also one of the few people who made me feel at home in Philadelphia, a place where I resided in for many years but never truly lived. As a small tribute, shortly after Toni's death, I finished a video called *Homeless Diaries*, which I dedicated to her. The video intertwined the voices of several homeless advocates in North Philadelphia as they organized for affordable housing. In listening to Puerto Rican women who had few reasons to call Philadelphia "home" but were nevertheless bent on securing one somewhere in the city, I realized that I needed to head back south, home, to the Caribbean. Through this move, I was finally able to release the "nommo," which for Toni meant "that harmonizing energy that connects body/mind/spirit/self/community with the universe."[5] And I was able to accomplish this, thanks in part to quite a few lessons that Toni taught me.

NOTES

Acknowledgments: Many thanks to Louis Massiah for providing me with a copy of *The Bombing of Osage Avenue* and to Cheryl Wall for asking me to write about Toni.

1. Gloria T. Hull. "What Is It I Think She's Doing Anyhow: A Reading of Toni Cade Bambara's *The Salt Eaters*," in Barbara Smith, ed. *Home Girls* (New York: Kitchen Table: Women of Color Press, 1983), 124–42,138.

2. Toni Cade Bambara. "Reading the Signs, Empowering the Eye Daughters of the Dust and the Black Independent Cinema Movement," in Manthia Diawara, ed., *Black American Cinema* (New York: Routledge, 1993), 118–44, 125.

3. Wlad Godzich. "The Further Possibility of Knowledge," in *Heterologies: Discourse on the Other* (Minneapolis: University of Minnesota Press, 1993), vii–xx, xiv.

4. bell hooks. *The Oppositional Gaze: Black Female Spectators,* Diawara noted above, 288.

5. Toni Cade Bambara. "Reading the Signs..."

VI

"Have to be whole
to see whole"

From "Deep Sightings and Rescue Missions"

Toni Cade Bambara

I spend a fitful night fashioning questions to raise with myself in the morning. What characterizes this moment? There's a drive on to supplant "mainstream" with "multicultural" in the national consciousness, and that drive has been sparked by the emancipatory impulse, blackness, which has been the enduring model for other down-pressed sectors in the U.S. and elsewhere. A repositioning of people of color (POCs) closer to the center of the national narrative results from, reflects, and effects a reframing of questions regarding identity, belonging, community. "Syncretism," "creolization," "hybridization" are crowding "assimilation," "alienation," "ambivalence" out of the forum of ideas. A revolution in thought is going on, I'm telling myself, drifting off. Modes of inquiry are being redevised, conceptual systems overturned, new knowledges emerging, while I thrash about in tangled sheets, too groggy to turn off the TV.

It drones on about Maxwell, the publishing baron who allegedly went over the side of his private yacht at two in the morning. All commentary reduced to the binary, as is typical of thought in the "West": suicide or homicide? I smirk in my sleep, sure that Maxwell used a proxy corpse and is alive and chortling in, say, Belo Horizonte, Brazil. Jim Jones, no doubt, is operating, courtesy of the CIA's answer to the Witness Protection Program.

Still half-asleep, I rummage around in dualisms which keep the country locked into delusional thinking. The Two-Worlds obsession, for example: Euro-Ams not the only book reviewers that run the caught-between-two-worlds number into the ground when discussing works by Maxine Hong Kingston, Leslie Marmon Silko, Rudolfo Anaya, and other POCs, or rather, when reducing complex narrative dramas by POCs to a formula that keeps the White World as a prominent/given/

eternal factor in the discussion. Two-Worlds functions in the cultural arena the way Two-Races or the Black-and-White routine functions in the sociopolitical arena. It's a bribe contract in which Amero-Africans assist in the invisibilization of Native Americans and Chicanos in return for the slot as the "indigenous," the former slaves who were there at the beginning of the great enterprise called America.

The limits of binary opposition were in evidence in a manuscript I'd been reading on the way to the dentist's office. Articles that called Black cinema "oppositional cinema" to Hollywood totally ignored practitioners operating in the independent circuit, and focused instead on Spike Lee, Matty Rich, John Singleton, Joe Vasquez, and Mario Van Peebles— filmmakers who take, rather than oppose, Hollywood as their model of filmmaking. The articles reminded me of the way the establishment press during the so-called Spanish-American War labeled the gung-ho, shoot-'em-up, Manifest-Destiny-without-limits proponents as imperialists, and the let's-move-in-in-the-name-of-hemispheric-hegemony proponents as anti-imperialists. Meanwhile, only the Black press was calling for a genuine help-liberate-then-cooperate-not-dominate anti-imperialism. All that is to say, there are at least three schools of Black filmmaking in the U.S.: that which produces within the existing protocol of the entertainment industry and may or may not include a critique (Fred Williamson, for example); that which uses enshrined genres and practices but disrupts them in order to release a suppressed voice (Spike Lee, for example, who freed up the B-boy voice in his presentations, not to be confused with interrogations, offering a critique of U.S. society but not rising above its retrograde mindset re women and homosexuals in order to produce a vision); and that which does not use H'wood as its point of departure, but is deliberate and self-conscious in its commitment to building a socially responsible cinema, fashioning cinematic equivalents for our sociopolitical/cultural specificity and offering transformation dramas (Julie Dash, Haile Germina, Larry Clark, and other insurgents of "La Rébellion," who, in the late sixties, drafted a declaration of independence in the overturning of the UCLA film school curriculum).

The limits of binary thinking are spooky enough, I'm thinking, as the birds begin, but what are the prospects for sound sense in the immediate future now that conglomerates have escalated their purchase on the national mind? Since the 1989 publication of the Chomsky-Herman tome and the fall 1991 issues of Media Fair, *which drew a scary enough picture of media control by white men of wealth, the noose has tightened. And today seventeen corporations own more than 50 percent of U.S. media—textbook companies, newspapers, magazines, TV stations, radio stations, publishing houses, film-production companies. And computerization makes it all the easier to expunge from available reference material those figures, movements, and lessons of the past that remind us that radicalism is also a part of the U.S. tradition. Without models, how does any citizen break out of the basic dualism that permeates social, educational, political, economic, cultural, and intimate life in this country? I refer to the demonic model abridged below:*

We are ordained	*You are damned*
We make history	*You make dinner*
We speak	*You listen*
We are rational	*You are superstitious, childlike (as in minor)*
We are autonomous and evolved	*You are shiftless, unhinged, underdeveloped, primitive, savage, dependent, criminal, a menace to public safety, are needy wards and clients but are not necessarily deserving*
We live center stage The true heroes (and sometimes heroines)	*You belong in the wings or behind the scrim providing the background music*
We are pure, noble, upright	*You are backward, fallen, tainted, shady, crafty, wily, dark, enigmatic, sly, treacherous, polluted, deviant, dangerous, and pathological*
We are truly human	*You are grotesques, beasts, pets, raisins, Venus flytraps, dolls, vixens, gorillas, chicks, kittens, utensils*
We were born to rule	*You were born to serve*
We own everything	*Even you are merely on loan to yourself through our largess*
We are the dicks	*You are the pussies*
We are entitled	*You are obliged*

I slap the alarm clock quiet and roll over, pondering my own journey out of the lockup. Pens crack under me, paper rustles. When in doubt, hew close to the autobiographical bone, I instruct myself. But my own breakout(s) from the lockup where Black/woman/cultural worker in the binary scheme is a shapeless drama with casts of thousands that won't adhere to any outline I devise. I opt instead for a faux family portrait to narrate what I can't essay.

26

Toni Cade Bambara: A Political Life of the Spirit

BETTINA APTHEKER

S eeking a greater fusion between the spiritual and the political, and meditating on the unfinished liberations of the 1960s, I am drawn yet again into the extraordinary work of Toni Cade Bambara. Her novel *The Salt Eaters,* produced at a particular historical juncture in the late 1970s, offers us a critical assessment of the 1960s civil rights movement on the one hand and a clairvoyant call for a different kind of revolutionary ethos on the other. It fuses the political and the spiritual into a liberatory movement in which each is simultaneously a component of the other, each holding the elements of redemption and transformation. For this reason *Salt Eaters* transcends the historical moment at which it was created; it becomes a transcendent text beyond the particularity of the black liberation movement. Bambara, looking at the horizon as she could see it in 1979, visions our work in the twenty-first century: how are we to ensure that our movements for social justice embrace spiritual practice, are themselves healing, bring us personally into wholeness?

In an interview with Louis Massiah two years before she died, Bambara explained the origins of *Salt Eaters.* She was trying to resolve the apparent dichotomy between spiritual and political movements. She tells us that the novel began as a series of journal entries which grew longer and longer until they got completely out of hand because:

> I was trying to figure out as a community worker why political folks were so distant from the spiritual community-clairvoyants, mediums, those kind of folks, whom I was always studying with. I wondered what would happen if we could bring them together ... Why is there that gap? Why don't we have a bridge language so that clairvoyants can talk to revolutionaries?[1]

At the center of *Salt Eaters* is a story of healing. Velma Henry is a key community organizer in the imaginary, Southern, all-black town of Claybourne, perhaps modeled after the very real all-black community of Eatonville, Florida, in which Zora Neale Hurston was raised. Velma is founder of Women for Action which has, in the words of one of her sister-comrades, taken on "entirely too much: drugs, prisons, alcohol, the schools, rape, battered women, abused children. And now Velma talked the group into tackling the nuclear power issue ..." (198).[2] Velma is also employed at the local Transchemical Corporation, suspected of myriad violations of environmental laws, even as her sister-comrades wonder "how she ever got clearance to do government work with her background is past my brain ... How'd she manage to juggle that contradiction working for De Enamee? Either she's lifting info or sabotaging the works ..." (198). We conclude that she's sabotaging the works.

Velma has suffered a nervous breakdown, and she has attempted suicide. She has been brought to the "Southwest Community Infirmary, Established 1871 by the Free Coloreds of Claybourne" (120), Bambara thereby inserting a bit of Reconstruction history, and to Minnie Ransom, faith healer of the district.

"Are you sure, sweetheart, that you want to be well?" (3). This is how the story begins. Minnie Ransom is talking to Velma Henry. Velma is seated on a stool inside the Infirmary. They are in a public space in which other medical personnel, staff workers, and elders are witness to the healing work. It is a brilliant question. It tells us that healing is fundamentally about the patient's will to heal. The healer is a channel, can direct the energy, ground the center, provide unconditional love; but without the unambivalent will of the patient, healing is not possible.

Minnie Ransom poses the question again, this time in the form of an observation: "As I said, folks come in here moaning and carrying on and say they want to be healed. But like the wisdom warns, 'Doan letcha mouf gitcha in what ya backbone caint stand'" (9). And yet again, Minnie Ransom speaks to Velma: "Just so you're sure sweetheart, and ready to be healed, cause wholeness is no trifling matter. A lot of weight when you're well" (10). And again, a hundred pages later: "You'll have to choose sweetheart. Choose your own cure ... There's nothing that stands between you and perfect health, sweetheart. Can you hold that thought?" (104).

"Have to be whole to see whole," Velma's godmother Mrs. Sophie Heywood counsels (92). And in those seven words Bambara gives us an extraordinary gift of understanding. Healing is a continual process, and must be continually reinforced in the course of the struggle itself. The problem for all of us is to see widely enough, to take in enough, to know at least with fair certainty that our actions are well directed. The problem for all of us is to manage to benefit the community as a whole, to see to it that our process is suffused with love, and that our motivation is compelled by compassion and not driven by egocentric investments in power and outcome. To sustain such wholeness in ourselves is very difficult because we work in a political context, which continually fragments and splinters.

As the story of *Salt Eaters* unfolds we come to understand that Velma has been brought to the brink of suicidal despair by the weight of the political struggle that has unbalanced her judgment and led to bouts of paranoia. She has also been brought to this brink by the pain of personal betrayal. With Bambara's vision we see how the issues are all intertwined: racism, poverty, violence against women, betrayal of women, environmental degradation, police violence, child abuse, nuclear devastation, chemical pollution, sexual harassment. No issue escapes the purview of her critical eye as she puts into eloquent play the theoretical insights of the black feminist movement of the 1970s, the "interlocking systems of domination," as the Boston-based Combahee River Collective put it in 1977. Velma has tried to take on every issue as her personal crusade. To the weight of these political struggles is added the weight of personal betrayal. Velma confronts her husband:

> We've known each other too long, Obie, been through too much, been too much to each other. Why lie about such simple shit. And you been lying for months now, complaining about *my* aloofness, *my* fatigue, *my* job, willing to totally mess with my sense of what's real in order to throw up this smoke screen. You are sleeping around, Obie, and not very discreetly . . ." (231–32)

With Velma's words also comes her loss of denial: "Velma noted how different things looked and felt now that it had been said. A subtle rearrangement of the world . . . And now there was not trust" (232). The loss of trust is cataclysmic for Velma, feeds into the paranoia. Obie's personal actions translate into a catastrophic political liability.

The precise historical moment of the novel, the disjuncture, the despair, the point of crisis is put into words midway through it in a conversation between Velma's sister-comrades who see her desperation:

> Malcolm gone, King gone, Fannie Lou gone, Angela quiet, the movement splintered, enclaves unconnected. Everybody off into the Maharaji this and the Right Reverend that. If it wasn't some far off religious nuttery, it's some other worldly stuff . . . who could effectively pull together the folks—the campus forces, the street forces, the prison forces, workers, women, the aged, the gay. (193)

Later Bambara returns us to the same point, spiraling more deeply into it through Velma's consciousness, in an incantation that was the emotional center of the story for me:

> She thought she knew [how to neutralize the serpent's bite]. At some point in her life she was sure Douglass, Tubman, the slave narratives, the songs, the fables, Delaney, Ida Wells, Blyden, Du Bois, Garvey, the singers, her parents, Malcolm, Coltrane, the poets, her comrades, her godmother, her neighbors, had taught her that. She thought she knew how to build immunity to the sting of the serpent that turned would-be cells could-be cadres into cargo cults. Thought she knew how to build resistance, make the journey to the center of the circle, stay poised and centered in the work and not fly off, stay centered in the best of her people's traditions and not be available to madness, not become intoxicated by the heady brew of degrees and careers and congratulations for nothing done, not become anesthetized by dazzling performance with somebody else's aesthetic, not go under. Thought the workers of the sixties had pulled the Family safely out of range of the serpent's fangs so that workers of the seventies could drain the poisons, repair damaged tissues, retrain the heartworks, realign the spine. Thought the vaccine offered by all the theorists and activists and clear thinkers and doers of the warrior clan could take. But amnesia had set in anyhow. Heart/brain/gut muscles atrophied anyhow. Time was running out anyhow..." (258)

Velma saw the serpent in herself and fled in terror. What was missing? And how to find it? And again the cataclysmic shattering of what she thought she had understood about the movement, about her own life, about where they were going and to what end. "You honestly think you can change anything in this country?" a former SNNC worker shouted at Velma in rampaging despair. And she had answered her: "'I try to live,' Velma said, surprised at her evenness, 'so it doesn't change me too much'" (261).

Minnie Ransom coaxes Velma toward healing. There's a continual laying on of hands, a flow of energy, a searching for the center of Velma's strength, a constant humming, a singing, and a channeling of Old Wife, Minnie Ransom's spirit guide, conveyor of the old wisdoms beyond words. "Minnie would spin and she would sing and it would be silk. But when she opened her mouth out came fire" (168).

Minnie Ransom says: "I can feel sweetheart, that you're not quite ready to dump the shit...got to give it all up, the pain, the hurt, the anger and make room for lovely things to rush in and fill you full. Nature abhors a so-called vacuum, don't you know?'" (16). "Release sweetheart. Give it all up. Forgive everyone everything. Free them. Free self... Release sweetheart. Let it go. Let the healing power flow" (18, 20).

Bambara sets this whole story within one afternoon, and tells it through the alternating consciousness of all of the people present at and surrounding Velma's healing at the Southwest Infirmary and in the town of Claybourne that day. In this way she shows us how one moment in time is also every moment in time, every consciousness, every action, thought, all the energies of everyone matter. About a third of the way through the process Velma turns toward healing:

"Health is my right," Velma finally said with some clarity, no longer reeling and rocking on the stool. Her eyes were opening and the healer's hands were patting her. "My right," she said again. (119)

And a picture of little sprouting leaves appears in the text, the first sign of a spring thaw, the first sign of healing.

A bolt of lightning followed by a roar of thunder heralds Velma's return. It was the kind of event, so dramatic, so unexpected, that everyone in the community would in the future mark their place at the moment it happened:

Velma would remember it as the moment she started back toward life, the moment when the healer's hands touched some vital spot and she was still trying to resist, still trying to think what good did wild do you, since there was always some low-life gruesome gang bang raping lawless careless pesty last straw nasty thing ready to pounce... (278)

It takes the force of nature called up by Old Wife, channeled through Minnie Ransom, combined with "the old timers... in deep concentration matching the prayer group in silence and patience..." (107) and "Pony Daniels of the circle [raising] his voice and [singing] about the time his dungeon shook and his chains fell off" (278), and everyone in the community affected by the power of the healing, "Velma's glow aglow and two yards wide of clear and unstreaked white and yellow... Velma, rising on steady legs..." (295).

Studying *Salt Eaters* again in the context of my own spiritual practice was like meeting an old friend with new purpose. When I first read it in the early 1980s, I had only a superficial understanding. I followed the plot, tried to track a linear course through the maze of alternating flashbacks and consciousness. I read it again in the mid-1980s after I had begun a meditation practice, and again in the early 1990s while Toni was with us co-teaching a class at the University of California, Santa Cruz, with the Nigerian novelist Buchi Emecheta. I was the "instructor of record" to satisfy the absurdities of academic protocol. By 1990, I was studying Tibetan Buddhism, had heard the Dalai Lama in a prolonged teaching, adored him, believed in the mysteries of energy transmission, and was trying to practice compassion. We had lunch with Emecheta. It was in the middle of the Persian Gulf War. "You Americans are barbarians," Buchi said, "the world sees you as barbarians." She was furious at the days of unrelenting bombings, the CNN live coverage, the images of children crouched in bomb shelters terrified and screaming. Yes, I thought, we are. Toni teaching our mostly white, middle-class students, patient, intense, eyes glowing, mind alight, every class a "teachable moment," as she would say, drawing the students out, stretching them into their "higher selves," searching for connection, meaning, hope. I used *Salt Eaters* in my own work, charting its main healing connections in *Tapestries of Life*, in my last chapter, "Toward A Gathering of Women." I gave Toni a copy of the book, and watched her smile until her eyes lit like beacons. I started teaching *Salt Eaters* in my seminar on "Women's Culture," summoning the history of the 1960s, focused on healing, drawing maps on the board to plot the labyrinth of meaning.

But it wasn't until I read it again now writing this essay, and while immersed in writing my own memoir that I saw how closely Velma Henry's story parallels my own from the 1960s: sexual violence, personal betrayal, political strife, an object of sexual prey, raped while in jail seven months pregnant with my first child, coping with Communist politics, seeing for the first time the betrayal of principles I thought were part of who we were on the Left, my structure fracturing. I had a nervous breakdown, and came very close, too close to suiciding. I was 23. My Communist, Jewish culture provided no models of healing. Communists abhorred therapists! In my state of paranoia at the time I thought that if I went to one they would turn me in to the FBI, COINTELPRO, the Berkeley police's Red Squad. I finally went to my doctor, a kind man who prescribed valium. I pieced myself back together, worked like a demon to free Angela, running too hard to think. Working to save Angela's life as if it were my own which it was: friends since childhood, her in one jail after another, through a year and a half of pretrial motions, and four months of trial until the day of acquittal. There was a way in which her stamina, her sheer will, her love, helped to sustain me, brought me through the worst of it.

232 of Bettina Aptheker

Principles of healing emerge from Bambara's work, not only in *Salt Eaters* but also in her short stories, and in her furious indictment of child molesters and child killers written in response to the serial killings of black children in Atlanta in 1979 and 1980.[2] These principles, as Bambara framed them, are, I think, summarized in the following way:

1) Healing requires unconditional love of one's self, one's people, and one's community. Healing requires unconditional love of children.
2) Healing requires appreciation for and abiding counsel in the interdependence of all the elements, animate and inanimate, spiritual and material, and the energies and life-forces that comprise our planet and beyond. Healing requires a reverence for all life.
3) Healing requires a political and personal practice of equality, respecting the dignity of all peoples, and absolute integrity and equality between women and men.
4) Healing is a collective process, a pooling of energies, a coming together of community.
5) Healing requires a letting go of old hurts and angers, and pain. Healing requires us to forgive.

These principles are inherent in Bambara's abiding love for the women and children and men of the black community. This love is apparent in her descriptions of Harlem in the 1940s, in Micheaux's Liberation Memorial Bookstore, "the home of proper propaganda," and the Speakers' Corner, and in how parts of a Harlem childhood turn up in her imagined Southern community of Claybourne, and its Academy. These principles of healing are also in many of her short stories, like the sweet love of sister and brother in "Raymond's Run,"[3] and in the voice of the child narrator's purposeful grief over the puppies who freeze to death in a story called "Ice," symbolic of so much else in our lives.[4] I find these principles also in Bambara's insistence that she "never thought of myself as a writer. I always thought of myself as a community person who writes..." so that she persistently finds herself as something of a "community scribe."[5] And yet, even as she saw herself in this way, Bambara was, as Toni Morrison put it, "a writer's writer, an editor's writer, a reader's writer... Her writing is woven, aware of its music, its overlapping waves of scenic action..."[6] I have always been amazed at Bambara's ability to draw me into a story in a few lines and sustain my absorption so completely that every other sense and sound is banished from my consciousness until I surface to my surroundings at its conclusion. Bambara strove mightily to embrace these principles of healing in her own life. In the interview with Massiah she tells us:

I was writing [*The Salt Eaters*] in 1981 [actually 1979] so I could kick cancer's ass in 1993. That book taught me how to get well. If I hadn't written it, I'm not quite sure I'd be sitting here. I was writing beyond myself... When I look at that book now, I realize that I'm not there yet. I don't understand it yet. It resonates, it chimes in my bones, but I don't understand it yet. It was very hard work. It is a breathless book.[7]

Even as she strove to put those principles of healing into practice in her own life, Bambara had inscribed them for us, true to her service to community.

As a community scribe, Bambara was a central figure in the black literary and artistic renaissance of the 1970s and 1980s. She was in the company of many black writers and artists searching out a spiritual path as it was harder and harder to gain political purchase amidst the rubble of the Reagan years and the Bush years. Alice Walker wrote *The Color Purple* in 1982; Gloria Naylor wrote *Mama Day* in 1988; both steeped in the healing traditions and fiercesome power of Southern black women's culture. Paule Marshall wrote *Praisesong for the Widow* in 1983, at the center of which was the story of Ibo Landing, a cautionary tale set during slavery about what the future held for African people in the New World. Julie Dash produced and directed the extraordinary film *Daughters of the Dust* in 1991, which Bambara heralded as: "women's perspective, women's validation of women, shared space rather than dominated space... the thematics of colonized terrain, family as liberated zone, women as a source of value, and history as interpreted by Black people..."[8] Toni Morrison was Bambara's first editor at Random House. Such is the community of superb artistry in which Toni Cade Bambara was both participant and mentor.

Themes of spiritual renewal mark the works of a multicultural range of women writers in the United States in the same period. I do not know to what extent Bambara knew their works, but she would have liked them, and they would have deepened her stretch into and from *Salt Eaters*. I am thinking of Leslie Marmon Silko's *Ceremony*, emergent from the spiritual life of indigenous peoples of the Southwest in which Tayo, like Bambara's Velma Henry, is on a healing journey brought back into wholeness by Spider Woman, the Creatrix when he reunites with the land. And Maxine Hong Kingston's *Woman Warrior*, hailing from such a different space, reconciling the paradoxes between Chinese and American cultures tracks a child's journey towards wholeness. Ana Castillo's *So Far from God* is, as one commentator put it, "a Chicana telenovela," an excursion through magic realism in which milagros (miracles) inform a sacred and sainted journey. Every political issue enumerated by Bambara in *Salt Eaters* finds itself spun into new and damning indictment in the New Mexico terrain of Castillo's imaginary town of Tome. Ursula LeGuin's *Always Coming Home* synthesizes Hopi, Taoist, and Euro-American spiritual traditions onto an imaginary landscape set in the Valley of the Na near what is today the Napa Valley in California. Through the oral history of Stone Telling, a woman elder, Le Guin invents a culture of compassion complete with language, recipes, songs, and poems.

In May 1998 a group of women and men undertook an Interfaith Pilgrimage of "The Middle Passage" to honor the ancestors kidnapped from their African homeland, and to re-dedicate themselves to the struggle against racism. They retraced the steps of slavery from Massachusetts through the South, and across the ocean to South Africa. The pilgrimage was organized in part by the Nipponzan Myohoji Buddhist Order. Kathleen Anderson, who participated in this pilgrimage, wrote an account of their ceremony at the Door of No Return, the prison on Gorée Island, Senegal, the departure point for thousands of slaves. It was Friday, February 22, 1999, and many people from this island community participated in the ceremony:

> Several traditional drummers led our procession around the small island, culminating at the seaside in front of the so-called "Door of No Return." Walking back with us through the slave house were the thousands of ancestral spirits we had collected as we came through the U.S. and the Caribbean, as well as those raised up as we drummed our way around the island. Reversing the exit of our ancestors and coming back through the Door of No Return ... Imagine Africans from the Diaspora and Africans from the motherland reentering the door ... Imagine the tears which flowed from our eyes, the rejoicing which ensued, the whoops and shouts, the rhythmic beat of the drums celebrating our return home.[9]

I like to think of Toni Cade Bambara on such a pilgrimage. How she would have rejoiced!

"i give thanks," wrote the pilgrim poet Akiba Onada-Sikwoia:

> My dearest Ancestors, i thank you for the great sacrifice you've made to the continuations of life ... i acknowledge you for your endurance ... i acknowledge you for your unfaltering commitment to survival and life ... i thank you for the thousands upon thousands of gifts you brought to humanity through your suffering ...[10]

We thank you Toni Cade Bambara.

NOTES

1. Toni Cade Bambara. *Deep Sightings and Rescue Missions: Fictions, Essays, and Conversations* (New York: Pantheon Books, 1996), 234–35.

2. Toni Cade Bambara. *The Salt Eaters* (1980; New York: Vintage, 1992), 98.

3. Toni Cade Bambara. *Gorilla, My Love* (New York: Vintage Books, 1972), 21–32.

4. Toni Cade Bambara. *Deep Sightings* supra note 1, 67–77.

5. Ibid., 218

6. Ibid., viii.

7. Ibid., 235.

8. Ibid., 94

9. *Turning Wheel*. Journal of the Buddhist Peace Fellowship (Berkeley, CA: Fall 1999), 21.

10. Ibid., 20.

27

Toni Cade Bambara to the Bone: Cultural Worker in the Black World and the South

MALAIKA ADERO

> My memory stammers: but my soul is a witness.
> —JAMES BALDWIN (THE EVIDENCE OF THINGS UNSEEN)

"Those bones are not *my child*," are the words of a fictional character, Zala Spencer, whose young son went missing for months on end. When she finally sees him—once lost, now found—he, her child, is beyond recognition. She didn't deny the positive identification made by the authorities—police and official search teams—nor the boy's own father. She rather didn't want to believe her eyes nor any other sense that told her that she'd next be challenged to break the armor of a stranger to touch again, the warm heart of her first born.

Those Bones Are Not My Child is the last novel written by Toni Cade Bambara. It is a story of personal crisis, but also of community, society, and political crisis. Inasmuch as a work of literature can be, *Those Bones,* is a sum total of what Toni's life and work was about: motherhood, activism, education, and art. The story was born in her investigation of the reign of terror called the case of Atlanta's Missing and Murdered Children.

The characters central to *Those Bones* are a couple named Marzala Rawls Spencer (Zala) and Spencer (Spence) and their three children, Sundiata (Sonny), Kente, and Kofi. The reader enters their world in the longest, hardest year of their lives. Their experience of loss and recovery is embroidered against the crazy quilt of converging and conflicting interest of the Atlanta child murders phenomenon. The overriding questions of this human tragedy, media spectacle, and political firestorm: were the missing and murdered the victims of racial and sexual violence? Was this the act of an organization or an individual's madness? The criminal justice system determined that the one man, Wayne B. Williams, himself African American, committed three of the murders and consequently closed the entire case. Williams remains incarcerated.

Those Bones is not about Wayne Williams, and its significance does not hinge on the facts of or on the outcome of the case against him. Bambara wanted to shift attention away from focusing on the guilt of one individual, and invite readers to consider the larger implications of widespread unwarranted attacks on the black community. The novel sheds light on the race, class, and gender dynamics that were behind and affected the case.

Bambara's fiction is this: twelve-year-old Sundiata (Sonny) doesn't promptly come home from school one day. His siblings Kofi and Kente, who were the last in the family to see him that day, did not know what to tell their parents. The disappearance of a child is every parent's nightmare and universal fodder for any storyteller. That bad dream came true in Atlanta in the early 1980s, as police report after police and news report described corpses found of black boys and girls lost. A pattern emerged in this series of crimes. Parents began to identify with one another's loss and one another's efforts to get answers from the police and other officials. A campaign was waged to find the missing and the murderers, and a media circus came to Toni Cade Bambara's adopted hometown.

If *Salt Eaters* with its mystic and traditional arts overtones is Bambara's postmodern novel, *Those Bones Are Not My Child* is her return to the more conventional storytelling of her classic *Gorilla, My Love* collection. Either way, Toni spins a believable yarn with textured and recognizable characters and scenarios. We meet the mother, Marzala Rawls Spencer, the central character of *Those Bones,* pacing the floor, looking for her child to come home from the last place he should have been: his junior high school.

Bambara lived and raised her own child, Karma Bene, in a working-/middle-class community in Atlanta—on Simpson Road on the west side of the city—where some of the victims lived and the alleged crimes took place. She knew firsthand the daily terror of waiting for her twelve-year-old daughter to come home from school.

One of the hallmarks of Bambara's personality was her full engagement with life and people around her. She was no different in Atlanta. Bambara, respected as a good neighbor, activist, writer, and cultural worker was fully engaged in the community's response to the murders. As she had in anyplace she had ever lived—or spent a few days for that matter—she documented events in the endless journals she kept; established networks for community organizing and training; and helped to make people aware that local events mirrored national trends of increasing economic, physical, cultural, and political attacks on the black community. She dug into the psyche of the place, and like an archaeologist, acknowledged as keys to truth and treasures things that the rest of us could not see or value. What was revealed to Toni ended up in her creative work. She set at least two major works of fiction in Atlanta: *The Salt Eaters* and *Those Bones.*

Black Atlanta was a rich source of material for the kinds of people and communities represented in Toni's work: regular folk who hold down jobs, practice their religion, raise families, walk picket lines, stay out of jail (and go to jail), keep a nice house (or a messy one), speak the Queen's English. Or not. She neither sanitized nor sacrificed truth for beauty, beauty for truth. Atlanta provided an interesting setting, partly because of its long history of African American achievement that boasted a thriving black middle class when the North was alleged to be the Promised Land and the South, the land of hard times. Auburn Avenue, downtown Atlanta, was known in the mid-twentieth century as the "richest Negro street in the world." Before the rise of the black middle class, it was the unofficial capital of the Confederacy, and more recently in the 1970s, the murder capital of the country.

Zala, the protagonist of *Those Bones*, is a responsible, loving black woman with abundant skills and ability. Her lifestyle is familiar and respectable. She is house proud, creative, and a good mother, negotiating the pressures and pleasures of life in America in the 1980s the way black southern women do. Yet, the day after her son disappears she "leaned in, close to [a] mirror furry with grime. She had worried the fuzz escaping from her braids into corkscrews. Smudged mascara from the day before ringed her eyes like raccoon's. She looked about to boil over. He [Sonny] would stroll in [she hoped against hope], take one look, and know she had no good side to get on." She was still panging with hope and guilt nearly a year later. Zala could have been a character in *The Salt Eaters*—healing and teaching—and could have been Toni herself.

As James Baldwin, another writer who braved the subject of the Atlanta case put it, "Under the best of circumstances, and in the most accommodating of places, it is impossible to keep an adolescent male child at home." Baldwin was a black writer of international renown who did not shrink in the wash of tough issues and questions, and had a reputation for being an eloquent interpreter of social phenomena, particularly where African Americans were concerned. Consequently, much was expected when he came to Atlanta to distill truth from circumstance. Maybe too much. As Baldwin said forthrightly in *The Evidence of Things Unseen,* "I have never in all my journeys, felt more of an interloper, a stranger, than I felt in Atlanta, in connection with this case, and I sometimes cursed the editor whose brainstorm this had been." Bambara, however, was well positioned to write this story because of the way she embedded herself into all the communities in which she lived. This, she had been doing for years in Atlanta, through her work with the Neighborhood Arts Center, writing groups and political activists.

The idea of Baldwin deciphering the great murder mystery surely sounded like a good one at first, and *Evidence* is, in this writer's opinion, a brilliant example of Baldwin's prowess as an essayist, but not the key to the mystery nor the light to curse the dark days of unanswered prayers for black Atlantans. Not even our literary and intellectual giant could do that in a place he knew so little about and where he spent so little time.

Bambara's *Those Bones* is more confident in its message, because its author was intimate with the subject and experientially linked to its plight. She held a mirror to Atlanta that was clear and sure enough for its people, particularly the mothers and fathers of those missing, to see themselves and maybe start to heal.

> It was morning. "Morning:" The sound of it fueled her fire. Twelve years old and out all night long. She pitched forward, her toes sliding out of the sandals and clutching at shag. She mouthed all the things she would say to him, all the things she'd been lashing together to flay him with since the day before when Kofi had shrugged and said "Went."

There is no good time for a loved one to be missing, but the climate of fear and suspicion in Atlanta in the early eighties was stranger than fiction. There were checkpoints and roadblocks randomly set up around the city. You'd turn a corner, heading to or from work, or the grocery store, or a friend's house, and you'd have to answer to the police. Every black person was on alert, hyper-aware, and sensitive to the children around them. We watched ourselves and one another as we accompanied young people, looking for behavior out of the ordinary when the entire scenario was out of the ordinary. Every time you picked up a newspaper and turned on the TV or radio, there was another report, another theory, another statistic racked up by the villains and scandals surrounding the so-called heroes.

When Zala Spencer walks into the Youth Division of Missing Persons and says, "I need to talk to somebody," the scope of the story widens and we see that the Atlanta Child Murders case is its backdrop. The reader is fully engaged with Zala, her estranged but functioning husband, Spence, and their children as the multidimensional characters that they are; their enemy is formidable and multifaceted.

Bambara shows readers what happens to mothers and fathers who find themselves face-against-the-glass of policymakers and power brokers. We see portraits of black and non-black Atlantans rendered as few others have done before or since. We see "The city too busy to hate," as Atlanta calls itself on a good day, through the eyes of a community whose voices had no outlet in the mainstream media.

When I first moved south to Atlanta in the early 1980s to pursue graduate studies in Atlanta University's School of Library and Information Studies, I secured an internship at the *Atlanta Constitution Journal* in the reference library. One of my tasks was to rip the paper for filing and cataloging articles in what was known as the "morgue." The irony was not lost on me as I noticed a dramatic increase in crime reports detailing the discovery of the dead bodies of black children, boys and girls. The state of the bodies was both bizarre and tragic. Sometimes they were naked, washed, arranged just so, floating in a river.

The media drove the event as they do with so many sensational crimes and occurrences. But the outcries of parents did too. Before long people around the nation and the world were taking notice. Toni was one of the first persons I knew to collect intelligence including newspaper clippings, flyers for rallies, even programs from memorials. Black people and the rights of children were "her business," she would say.

"The summer before" the season of terror, Bambara wrote,

> [Zala] and Spence used to meet in the park for brown-bag lunches between her classes at Georgia State. They'd reminisce about picnics at real parks—Mozley and Adams on the south side, Piedmont in the northeast, especially during arts festival time, lounging on blankets, listening to jazz while the kids darted back and forth from the African Village the Neighborhood Art Center set up every year, reporting how many of Zala's halters, macrame hangings, tapestries, and weavings had been sold. Then, later, [daughter] Kenti worn out and asleep in her lap, Kofi leaning against Spence the way old folks do claiming they're resting their eyes, Sonny would ask for Spence's whittle knife to turn a tree branch into a royal staff.

It is a cameo portrait of a family at once universal in its dynamics and uniquely African American.

As a young writer, one of the many lessons I learned from Toni was the importance of what she referred to as "the emancipatory impulse." The highest purpose of art and craft anywhere is to liberate. And, liberation is the theme that runs through the black experience and, as Toni says, "characterizes our storytelling trade in these [American] territories."

Bambara acknowledged freedom narratives as the best example of writing out of an "emancipatory impulse." She wrote, "we've been trained to call [them] slave narratives for reasons too obscene to mention, as if 'slave' were an identity and not a status interrupted by the very act of feeling, speaking, writing, and countering the happy-darky propaganda." *Those Bones,* as an exploration of political and cultural issues, as well as—light and dark—human emotion, is emancipatory fiction. The willingness of Bambara to show the flaws in leaders and followers certainly serves as a counterpoint to representations of Atlanta as "The Black Mecca" of the South and the "City too Busy to Hate."

Toni recognizes the emancipatory impulse in the *Those Bones* narrative. She describes both the escalating suspicion and the vigilance as the terror heightens. I remember we became acutely sensitive to the children around us, watching for relationships and behavior between adults and children which seemed odd or inappropriate. We listened more closely to our children, mindful of the impact the news—on TV and the street—had on them. I had young nieces and nephews who discussed among themselves the likelihood of being "snatched." They had decided that one of the three of them had the most to worry about because he was darker skinned than the others. We did our best to calm their fears and offer some reasonable explanation for what was going on in Atlanta, but we didn't know ourselves. Law enforcement responded by monitoring peoples' movements as best they could. Checkpoints were randomly set up to monitor drivers of cars, vans, and trucks; who and what they traveled with. Those of us who called the city home joked about the police state Atlanta became, but we weren't laughing.

The Atlanta of the murdered and missing children was not the Atlanta that Bambara came to when she moved there with her young daughter in 1974. When Toni and Karma settled into a house on Simpson Road, they were welcomed by a black working-class community. The neighborhood and the street were lively with people and traffic, but you didn't notice it once you climbed the steps up to her yard and southern-style front porch. There was no manicured lawn, but rather a surround of untamed shrubs and trees that added a veil of privacy.

Toni's house reflected her personality. It was spacious, warm, informal, and filled with many items of beauty and interest representing the black world, for example, hand-woven rugs, musical instruments, shawls. The upstairs—Toni and Karma's personal space—was linked to the downstairs by a staircase ample enough to read and leave books on when you were done with them. Toni's brother Walter's art works incorporating their family photographs hung in her hallway. The living and dining room and kitchen were the center of communal action where I spent many hours with Toni and friends talking, politics, art, life. The walls were bathed in lemon yellow; the upright piano was turquoise, while deep purples and reds were splashed about in the textiles on the floor, sofas, and chairs. It was filled with the warmth and color, art, crafts, black music, books—and awareness of the world beyond.

I had come to Atlanta from my hometown of Knoxville, Tennessee, the year before Toni did. We met at the spring writers conference held annually at my school, Clark College. I would become a student of hers when she co-taught a creative writing course with Dr. Richard Long. I knew something of her work already. Toni's anthology *The Black Woman* had been a bible for me and my circle of friends in Knoxville. The book was a banquet for starving souls like us, hungry for ideas about how to be women; how to be black women, human, and free—even as we were marginalized.

My friends and I were the young, gifted, and black who were also aspiring to be politically active. *Black Woman* was an outgrowth of political action. In an excerpt of an autobiographical essay titled "The Scattered Sopranos," Bambara describes it as a work that represented a wide range of thought by women of fascinating variety.

Toni could dazzle not only with her intellect but with her physical presence as well. She was no neutered intellectual revolutionary sans makeup and donning Birkenstocks, nor was she a lady who lunched in pumps and pearls, but she did love jewelry. She had a style that was out of a sensibility that was globally black. Her hair was dark, plentiful, and natural around an oval face and high cheekbones. Her eyes were dark, kohl-lined, and animated. She had a mole in the middle of her forehead suggesting a third eye, deep sight, and quick intelligence. You knew how aware of her surroundings she was by her quickness to respond in a deep fertile feminine speaking voice and a laugh that made you think of piano bars and cigarette holders. She punctuated her statements with a fan of tapered fingers and sideways glances. The first time I saw her, she wore sheer black stockings with strappy sandals over polished toenails. Her skirt was black and short. She was, as Amiri Baraka describes, "Harlem born, Harlem hip"; and I was relieved to see that a writer, a professor, an activist, a mom, and a black woman could be beautiful and relevant. My sisterfriends and I said, "yeah, now that is a role model for me"; our brother friends said, "If that's what revolution looks like, I'm down for the cause."

My home away from home in Knoxville was a bookstore called Black World Books and Things owned by a local activist named Zimbabwe Matovou. It was because of him that I recognized the names and read the work of Toni, Nikki Giovanni, Sonia Sanchez, Amiri Baraka, and other eloquent writer/activists of the black struggle and Black Arts Movement. I came to believe that you had to be a poet, preacher, prisoner—think Martin, Malcolm, Medgar—to be a revolutionary. Toni Bambara disabused me of that idea. No matter what aspirations we held for being activists or artists, she said in her writer's conference presentation, our first responsibility is to our people, most specifically our mothers and fathers who sent us to school to study and excel at our course work. As Toni put it in *Black Woman:*

Running off to mimeograph a fuck-whitey leaflet, leaving your mate to brood, is not revolutionary. Hopping a plane to rap to some else's "community" while your son struggles alone with the Junior Scholastic assignment on "The Dark Continent" is not revolutionary. Sitting around murdermouthing incorrect niggers while your father goes upside your mother's head is not revolutionary. Mapping out a building takeover when your term paper is overdue and your scholarship under review is not revolutionary. Talking about moving against the Mafia while your nephew takes off old ladies at the subway stop is not revolutionary. If your house ain't in order, you ain't in order.

I got to know Toni best in the Pamoja Writers Guild, an organization we created with a group of Atlanta-based writers including Nikky Finney, Joyce White, and Shay Youngblood, who gathered at Toni's home once a month for more than a half-dozen years. Pamoja—a Kiswahili word meaning together—was a sure place to find moral, creative, and technical support. People were encouraged to proceed in their efforts to become—no matter their chosen medium or form—storytellers. The oral traditions were honored along with the literary; visual as well as verbal literacy was promoted. What you had to say was as important as how you said it; process was as honorable as product. The members of Pamoja made potluck part of our process. A bowl of popcorn, a pan of quiche, a bunch of grapes would be shared along with wisdom and response to one another's work.

Her own work seemed so accomplished. She was masterful at constructing dialogue that rang true; language that painted a picture, made a sound, evoked a smell and an emotion. She wrote about all of the kinds of people such as Velma in *Salt Eaters* and Spence in *Those Bones* that we know in life but are rare in fiction. She shows us the good and the bad about them; the loving and fighting, struggling, and laughter. One of the most memorable passages of *Those Bones* is a discussion between Sonny and his Grandmother about her late husband. Sonny describes him as "kind of mean . . . I remember one time he made you get out of bed to get him a glass of water. He was right there in the kitchen . . ." His Grandmother counters, "What did you make of it, my life with a mean man and all? . . . You thought I was a fool?" She goes on to say, "He was mean, but I loved him anyway. Why set conditions? Most people know they ain't worth a damn. That don't mean they undeserving." Bambara had heightened sensory perception. She missed nothing.

Terror at Home: Naturalized Victimization in Those Bones Are Not My Child

REBECCA WANZO

> What would a child have to introduce as currency by which care of the state would be a right?[1]

In 2002, the purported "year of child abductions," the U.S. face of victimization was a blonde and blue-eyed girl named Elizabeth Smart.[2] From Salt Lake City, she was affluent, Mormon, and played a harp. Less seen was the face of seven-year-old Alexis Patterson.[3] Disappearing in Milwaukee a month before Smart was abducted, she was, unlike the white teenager, from a poorer neighborhood, African American, and never recovered. What made Smart a universal sign of the endangered child and Patterson's victimization invisible? A few news producers argued that the sensationalism of Smart's abduction at gunpoint from an expensive home simply overshadowed the everyday nature of a young black girl disappearing on her way to an inner-city school. For them, Patterson's disappearance was a distressing but predictable outcome of identity and location. While Smart's wealth and religion would seemingly make her a less typical victim, she was constructed as the face of victimization.

As I watch the news stories about missing white girls and note the scarcity of highly visible stories about African Americans who number among the abused, the murdered, and the disappeared, I have often thought of the words of a Toni Cade Bambara character contemplating the abduction of black children two decades before Patterson's disappearance in Toni Cade Bambara's *Those Bones Are Not My Child*: "Tragedies, after all, happened in castles, not in low income homes."[4] Both phenotypically and economically, Patterson's story cannot access a princess-in-a-tower narrative. In a discussion of events years before the Patterson case, Bambara's novel critiques the invisibility and devaluation of black victimization.

Those Bones Are Not My Child recounts the black community's real-life struggle to deal with the devaluation of their children between 1979 and 1981 during the Atlanta Child Murders. Twenty-nine murders of children and young adults were placed on the official "List" of victims, and the authorities eventually and controversially attributed the murders to twenty-three-year-old Wayne Williams. However, many people argued that there were victims who were not included on the list and that Williams could not have committed all of these crimes. Bambara's novel treats both the crimes and the state response as domestic terrorism against the black community. *Those Bones* illustrates the rhetorical obstacles that black Atlantans faced as they struggled to draw the attention of the authorities, media, and other U.S. citizens.

A melancholy story about the community's grief and activism, the novel recounts their inability to sustain a debate that resists local answers about a lone killer and doomed street thugs. Bambara narrates how the families and communities of the disappeared and dead refused to accept the media normalization of black suffering, defended against the demonization of their parenting and children, and persisted in representing the violence as systemic and not isolated. Resisting normalization of black suffering was key to their activism then, and the novel remains a vivid illustration of what rhetoric undergirds other national narratives about black bodies at risk and who can function as citizens worthy of protection in the nation state. Bambara's mapping of the rhetorical struggles of victims' parents and other activists during the Atlanta Child Murders is just as resonant a narrative in the early twenty-first century, as stories of inequitable coverage of black bodies and the massive state devaluation of African Americans in the wake of Hurricane Katrina circulate in media outlets. *Those Bones* examines how the terrorism many citizens experience at home is constructed as hysterical and self produced, at war with mass-produced rhetoric discrediting the continued resonance of history and social forces as sources for violence enacted on black bodies.

"Blacks Just Aren't News Anymore"

Bambara's novel is a panoramic view of five pivotal narratives that must be grasped to understand the scope of the Atlanta Child Murders story: the psychological toll on the family, media coverage, state response to the tragedy, black community mobilization, and larger national and international issues converging at the dawn of Ronald Reagan's presidency. Through focusing on the struggle of the fictional Marzala (Zala) Spencer and her husband Spence to recover their eldest child Sonny, Bambara illustrates the traumatic effects of having a missing child and the resulting communal terror, trauma compounded by media and state neglect of the murdered African Americans, impugnation of the parents and children, and simplistic narratives about the perpetrator and victims that ignore historical and sociological contexts framing the crimes. The Spencers illustrate the difficulties of having claims responded to when citizens possess outsider status as citizens making claims on the state. They must rely on the mass media to reach policymakers and the general public. However, as black outsiders, the Spencers and the black community found themselves hamstrung by what Joel Best would call an absence of "sociological imagination" on the part of the press. Because news stories typically "ignore the role of social forces," and try to sell stories that can be perceived as "everyone's problem," telling a story about poor and working-class black children who are more at risk for violence would produce "distance" between "the viewer" and "the story."[5] The viewer is not constructed as African American, and "Americans" are not constructed as seeing the suffering of black children as something that should concern every citizen.

Many members of the press and U.S. public may lack a sociological imagination, but there is ample evidence of a nationalist imagination. A nationalist imagination is one that constructs some issues as crimes against the state. Zala argues that "in a just order, crimes against children would be dealt with more seriously than crimes against the state" (660), and crimes against children *are* narrated as crimes against the state—individual bodies are a means for mapping national stories about family, innocence, and futurity. In spite of this, black children do not receive the same attention, in fact they—particularly the boys who are the majority of the victims—are often viewed as enemies of the state. The black Atlantans are aware of their status, and many of the activists treat the missing and murdered as attacks against black citizenship.

Resisting local violence and connecting it to state violence, the Spencers and many other community activists read the disappeared and murdered in the context of crimes perpetrated against people of color internationally. The disappearances and deaths are not only read in relationship to historical attacks on African Americans, such as the Ku Klux Klan and its relationship to the "New Right," bombings, police attacks, and murdered civil rights leaders. The crimes are also read in relationship to other pressing social justice issues. Forced sterilization, torture, disappearances, and murders of the oppressed in Central and South American countries, Cold War politics, sexual violence, and police attacks on black Britons. Many characters in the novel treat the inadequate response to the disappearances as yet another act of violence against black bodies. These crimes are human rights violations, and the novel straddles a line that its characters and real activists often straddle—the tension between demonstrating the specificity of harm to a particular population and demonstrating the interconnectedness of their struggles. The specificity cannot be lost, but the interconnectedness of the harms cannot be ignored.

Negotiating a balance between particular and interrelated harms is mapped in localized ways onto the story of the Spencers. Sonny serves to represent a victim of both particular and representative harms. He returns to his family after a year and is unable to tell them where he had been. The text implies that he has been victimized by sexual predators, and while he had been gone for a year, like many others he had never been on the "List," the official listing of victims allegedly harmed or murdered by Wayne Williams. The "List" was controversial because of the criteria for inclusion and the number of disappearances and murders that many thought should have been considered in relationship to the case. Bambara's counterstory to the murders critiques a limited reading of who merits inclusion. Sonny's victimization is treated simultaneously as a harm facing all children and specifically related to the Atlanta Child Murder story. Sonny and others—both murdered and recovered—are not on the "List," but their individual stories are still evidence of systemic harms facing all children, black children in particular, and the terror engulfing black citizens in Atlanta.

Black terror, however, was not read as American terror, and this resulted in media neglect. As James Baldwin remarks in his essays about the murders, given the nature of "the slaughter," the coverage was one more "violation"; the murders "did not rival the American reaction to the fact of the hostages in Iran."[6] Through a dialogue between Zala and newsman, Bambara suggests many believe that, "Blacks just aren't news anymore" (273). The newsman claims that "Black boys getting killed in the South just ain't news," because the focus is on "Iran" and "international terrorism" (274). In a passage that resonates as much in a post 9/11 era as it did in the 1980s, he argues:

> The problem is—and I don't mean to sound insensitive to your situation—but the Atlanta story lacks scope, if you will, as opposed to, say, Iranian women putting the veil back on to become revolutionaries, or terrorists skyjacking jumbo jets. (274)

Murdered black bodies lack scope because they do not translate as harms that could affect the majority of U.S. citizens. Zala tells the newsman that there is "terrorism right here in Atlanta," but the terror she experiences is not read as communal terror.

Within a nation of competing interests, the fiscal survival of a political cause and the localized merits of a cause being embraced depend on the ability of advocates to demonstrate the relevance to individual citizens' lives, appeal to their sense of justice, and distress the populace with a narrative of suffering. These appeals are the means by which patriotism has been ignited in times of international conflict, and the rhetoric for other causes often mimics a language of warfare in which some afflicted population struggles behind inadequately protected borders to defend itself from an unambiguously evil enemy. The rhetoric about a "war" on children became common parlance in the 1990s and at the dawn of the twenty-first century, the culmination of rising attention toward child protection in the 1970s, 1980s, and 1990s, and reform rhetoric focusing on domestic "warfare." The challenge facing the Spencers and other activists was in making their war an issue affecting America, to make their war a war on all of America. The delicate balance they negotiate is arguing that black bodies are more at risk *and* that the issues confronting the black community should be a concern for everyone because these harms are civil and human rights violations.

In the twenty-first century, it is common for legislators, mass media, and many citizens to treat stranger abduction and the murder of children as a major concern facing the United States—not as an anomalous happening.[7] However, all abductions are not embraced by the media and politicians as national symbols under which the nation should unite and organize. The media's eye for the marketable and sensational is certainly a key factor in coverage and attention. Marketability is shaped by the artificial representativeness produced by these abduction stories. While stereotypical stranger abductions represent only 3 percent of missing children a year,[8] these stories have been normalized to represent the most pressing issue facing contemporary U.S. families. A study of this normalization of the exceptional could approach this problem from a number of different avenues—class, the construction of others/outsiders in our midst, critiques of the prison system—but what the Atlanta Child Murders and later abductions of African Americans tell us is that black bodies are devalued in the at-risk marketplace. Visually white children and grieving white parents who are secondary survivors shape this discourse. Most white children who are abducted do not receive the attention of Elizabeth Smart; but a clearly racially marked child *never* becomes a representative symbol of child endangerment. African Americans are disproportionately affected by crime, but they are viewed as "bring[ing] it on themselves."[9] The media response must thus be understood in relationship to the idea that contemporary African American suffering in the United States is largely self-inflicted.

Bambara's insistence on placing the abduction story in a larger context of state violence reveals the fissures in *all* rhetoric about the disappeared and murdered in the United States. The privileging of some stories depends on the erasure or relative inattentiveness to widespread harms. While a high-profile abduction that inaugurated late-twentieth-century legislative attention toward abducted children was the abduction of a six-year-old white boy named Adam Walsh, abducted boys do not receive as much attention, and abducted men are not even constructed as a category of interest. At least 24,950 children were murdered between 1980 and 2000, and 77 percent of them were male.[10] While the names of girls from Walsh's age to college age have filled the media when they are assaulted,[11] boys are not similarly culturally constructed as vulnerable unless attacks on their bodies can be narrated in relationship to anxieties about homosexuality. Much of the violence occurred among juveniles, facilitating the ideological construction of boys—particularly black and brown—as something other than innocent victims. And of these thousands murdered during that twenty-year period, 52 percent were blacks, in comparison to 46 percent whites.[12]

Twenty-first-century media representations of abduction skew the statistical realities of abduction. National Incidence Study of Missing, Abducted, Runaway, and Throwaway Children (NISMART 2) study in 2002 reported that the stereotypical kidnappings that garner "the most media attention" actually "represent an extremely small portion of all missing children"(7). While there is controversy about how many stranger abductions occur each year, the largest figures suggest that 200–300 kidnappings transpire. Read in relationship to the Atlanta Child Murders, this is a chilling figure, as some investigators and community activists wanted to place as many as one hundred African American children and young adults in Atlanta on "The List" of the missing and murdered. Even utilizing the official number of twenty-nine, that represents a staggering percentage of the abducted from a single community. This number garnered national media attention, but over the next two decades, missing children of color did not continue to receive widespread media coverage. What must a child of color or her family do to become legible as victims?

Monstrous Parents and Doomed Street Thugs

Activists for blacks often have difficulty evoking blamelessness, as black bodies seem to be always already at fault in the white imagination. Most children are harmed by caregivers, but Bambara's autobiographical narrator in the prologue to *Those Bones* argues that it is ludicrous logic to claim that in a single summer in Atlanta "seven or eight deaths did not constitute 'an epidemic of murder'" (5). The focus of the police and media was on "Monstrous parents, street-hustling hoodlums," and the "gentle killer"(5). Media juxtapositions of STOP's proactive political solutions with stories of black-on-black crimes, of black grief with narratives about the killer's apparent concern for the victims were an attack on arguments that the responsibility for and effects of the violence were outside of Atlanta's black community.

Bambara notes systemic attempts to construct the families as blameworthy; the gesturing toward the systemic was an acknowledgment that there was some widespread problem occurring that could not be marked as idiosyncratic. The problem is labeled as bad parenting, as the omnipresent Moynihan Report informs the rhetoric about bad black mothers. If the systemic nature of the problem can be assigned to the children or parents, then they are less worthy of sympathy. The parents of murdered children could thus be guilty of "negligence," and the black children, culturally constructed as poorly behaved, could be read as bringing it on themselves. Thus the disappeared could not function as a sign of all children—or all people—at risk. Blaming the victims deflects a systemic reading of the crisis. As Zala suggests, "when the children go out like they've got a right to and some maniac grabs them, then it's the children's fault or the parents who should've been watching every minute" (200).

Parents were indicted: the men were configured as perpetually absent, and the mothers struggled to function as maternal signifiers in the American imaginary. All U.S. women's public identities remain overdetermined by a nineteenth-century cult of true womanhood which identifies good women as homemakers who provide the moral backbone of the family and nation. African American women often utilized this narrative in their activist history in the nineteenth and early twentieth centuries. Civil rights rhetoric about motherhood and threatened children illuminates how depicting the Atlanta mothers' "good" mothering was essential in proving the children's victimization. As Ruth Feldstein argues, the mother of Emmett Till—murdered in 1955 by Roy Bryant and J. W. Milam for allegedly whistling at Bryant's wife—had to be constructed as respectable to warrant protection from the state.[13] Constructing Mamie Bradley as a respectable mother was a means through which African Americans could assert the rights of full citizenship: and "the degree to which Till had been successfully mothered would corroborate his innocence and his 'Americanism' as well as the legitimacy of those who opposed his murder" (91).

From slavery to the civil rights era, "good mothers" were often the signs of blacks' full humanity and worthiness of protection as citizens. This genealogy haunts the efforts of the Atlanta activists. A history of finding it necessary to prove humanity through manipulating representation and producing sympathetic narratives prefaces their rhetorical and political strategizing. On her first visit to the police station, Zala wonders if "Lying out on the cold floor, she could infect them enough with her desperation to get them mobilized" (71). Her vulnerability could signify her womanhood, but she also had to negotiate the fact that the mothers were often constructed as "female hysterics" (93). To mobilize the authorities, the mothers presented feminine vulnerability while speaking to significant systemic and structural inequities.

Unimaginable and Unmade: The Psychological Costs of Terror

The argument that the abducted served as a systemic and structural sign of all black bodies at risk was a beleaguered rhetorical move because the activists had to contend with the idea that the idea that the targeting of African Americans was a hysterical "conspiracy theory." In her autobiographical prologue to the text, Bambara writes that the official line is that "the terror is over." "Every day" they say "the horror is past" (3). The statement ostensibly refers to the Atlanta Child Murders, but also gestures toward historically situating systemic black suffering in a contained past. Many activists read the assaults in relationship to historical attacks on the black body: the Ku Klux Klan (KKK), medical experimentation, sexual exploitation, and genocide. The authorities stated that the KKK was "under control," and other suggestions were construed as hysterical. The accusation of hysteria is one of the most dangerous obstacles to activists attempting to mobilize affect for subjected citizens. The accusation speaks to the heart of the "unreasonable" charge often directed toward people of color. Bambara produced a counterstory to reading black readings of the events as unreasonable; regardless of the cause of the deaths, be it Wayne Williams or some other group or individuals, the reality was that reading the assaults in relationship to history can be read as the act of a reasonable citizen. Not reading the murders in relationship to that history could also be considered a willful act of unreason.

Part of what Bambara traces in the text is the path to what many would read as unreason: Zala's disconnectedness from everyday activities as her entire world becomes the murders and narratives circulating around the case. Zala addresses the fact that those working to address the murders allow themselves "'to be manipulated by name calling—'paranoid,' 'agitator'" (660). The theme of "unreason" runs through Bambara's novels because she recognizes that constructing blacks as "mad" members of society has historically been a powerful weapon of the state. The community's "madness" is discursively constructed: the narratives that reject the idea that there is a single solution to the murders, that the "agitators" are "paranoid," and that the story is more complex than the authorities claim are constructed as unreason and far from the truth, and thus those who circulate the alternative stories are constructed as unreasonable. The "truth" is the official narrative, but the "truth" also functions as state agents' and ideologically shaped citizens' own messy affective response to blackness.

Bambara suggests that many African Americans are also seduced by this division between the reasonable and the "hysterical." Through a short character study of the wife of a prominent black judge, Ivy Weber, Bambara describes how some blacks understand themselves as having created "a world whose center still held" (401). Mrs. Weber believes that the hysterical mothers are worthy of sympathy because they had "apparently been in much pain," but she wants to remind them and all of the other activists that the "center is holding" and that it is only through the center that political work can get done. However, the "madness" exhibited by the characters in Bambara's text is where work often gets done. Both the "center" and the "hysteria" are politically constructed categories, and all kinds of citizens are vulnerable to dismissing the "hysterical" and "unreasonable" as outside of political discourse. Janice Haaken suggests that "the embodied emotional conditions associated with women, whatever their material or immediate cause, often acquire social symbolic loadings as they traverse the cultural landscape,"[14] but people of African descent also embody a variety of emotional conditions that are deeply symbolic in U.S. culture.

Part of that symbolic tradition constructs black boys as invulnerable to the kinds of violence that afflict white children. There are people who feel it is unlikely they would be abducted because "a poor kid's supposed to run" (103). Even a family member, Gerry, tells the Spencers that she unconsciously blames Sonny for what happened to him: "It's not a lack of sympathy, or a lack of knowledge . . . a part of me is always thinking that they must have called it down on themselves somehow" (561). This response is a common response to survivors of a trauma—a self-protective mechanism that blocks off the possibility that such a thing could happen to anyone. As Spence suggests, Sonny is constructed as different from "you and me, pure and safe" (561) after his abduction. Because Sonny was not like "you and me," he was responsible for his abduction, and paradoxically, because of his abduction, he would no longer be like "you and me" (561). While Gerry's response is common, it is a racially inflected denial—one that speaks to consumption of ideologies about black boys' invulnerability. Gerry knows "the degree to which propaganda can contaminate," but nonetheless finds herself responding to it.

Trauma scholarship often discusses the unspeakable and unimaginable nature of trauma—particularly in relationship to survivors of torture.[15] Bambara evokes that aspect of it when Gerry describes torture—part of domestic terrorism in the novel—as "'an un-image'" (560). While Gerry can picture the violence she and others had experienced as social protesters during the Civil Rights Movement or as political prisoners in other contexts, she suggests that people talk about the emotions raised by torture in relationship to the un-image, and not the torture itself. Because they are, as Elaine Scarry argues, "unmade" by torture, the part of themselves that exists in relationship to the torture is their affect. Their affect is illustrated through the "longings"—to use Spence's words—they have because of the experience.[16] Many of the desires expressed in the novel could be understood as universal in the face of torture—for an incident to never have happened, for aid and support, and for the family to recover. However, the racially inflected desire in response to the torture is the longing for black people not to be marked for harm, or invisible when articulating the trauma of it. One reality of torture is that many victims are marked for it through their identities—race, ethnicity, religion, gender, or sexuality. While many claims-makers might experience invisibility, certain populations are faced with the historical specificity of their erasure. Recalling that history when also dealing with the effects of torture adds to the trauma of torture for bodies marked for subjection.

"Tell the People, Sister": Testifying to Domestic Terror

Twenty-five years after the alleged "completion" of the Atlanta Child Murder case, Bambara's novel is remarkably resonant in the post-9/11 era. Bambara names the attacks on black bodies as terrorism, suggesting that it is possible to name a trauma (such as the abduction of black children) using the state labels (terrorism) even if the authorities resist placing some harms in a national context. In the penultimate chapter of the novel, Zala testifies in the tradition of both church witnessing and posttraumatic disclosure. Her witnessing is a call to arms for more political work, a resistance to singular solutions to the crimes, and an indictment of all community members who "allow" themselves to believe "the line that security means secrecy and silence" (660). Because so many of the activists were labeled as "paranoid," "agitators," and hysterics, many of the community were silenced. Zala closes her speech with the "reminder" that "coerced silence is terrorism" and a call for her listeners to continue to produce counternarratives that name the events in Atlanta as systemic terror against black bodies.

Zala's testimony is also self-implicating. She indicts herself for her understandable, but politically problematic retreat from politics after Sonny's return, when she only cared about her own family. She confesses, "All I wanted to do was close the door, because I did not care" (660). Zala's sociological imagination failed her in the face of personal concerns, and she had to remind herself that what happened to her son was part of systemic violence. Her testimony reminds her audience—and the readers of the novel—how

254 • Rebecca Wanzo

easy it is to take comfort in local concerns, and ignore the fact that the local is inextricably intertwined with widespread issues. One of the costs of domestic terror is that it can damage the politically productive routes of sympathy that can exist in affected communities—perhaps through emotional fatigue. Through the Spencers' extensive and exhausting story the readers experience this emotional fatigue, even as we are constantly reminded how important it is to keep personal pains from blocking recognition of interconnected, community concerns.

Amidst the discussions of terrorism and child protection in the United States, the white individuals and families evoked often do not resemble the diversity of the population of the country. There is terror at home, but it does not only look like Islamic terrorism. This form of terrorism also can look like state apparatuses that do not support and protect its citizens. There are terrorists who are agents of ideological struggles and violent histories, but those struggles and histories are not as singularly located as the state suggests. Zala's speech also proposes that we're all implicated in our desire for our own comfort and protection of local concerns. "We"—progressive citizens—cannot allow ourselves to be silenced by the narratives produced by others, by the rhetorical transformation of reasonable claims into hysterical ones. Toni Cade Bambara's prescient last novel reminds us, as do the rest of her work and her life, of the importance of making the terror of the dispossessed and ignored visible. She illustrates that what seems to be an obvious solution—storytelling—is valiant action in the face of terror, as the dangerous comforts of selective blindness, acquiescence, and silence linger around every corner.

NOTES

1. From Patricia Williams's *The Alchemy of Race and Rights* (Cambridge, MA: Harvard UP, 1991).

2. Fourteen-year-old Elizabeth Smart was abducted from her own bed on June 5, 2002. Smart was later found alive with Brian David Mitchell on March 12, 2003, because a woman recognized her from the media coverage. Mitchell, who worked as a handyman at the Smart home, had allegedly wanted Smart for a bride.

3. Alexis Patterson was reported missing on May 3, 2002. She was reportedly dropped off by her stepfather at school. At the time of the writing of this article, she remains missing.

4. Toni Cade Bambara. *Those Bones Are Not My Child* (New York: Vintage Books, 2000). Subsequent passages noted parenthetically.

5. From Joel Best's *Threatened Children: Rhetoric and Concern about Child Victims* (Chicago: Chicago UP, 1990).

6. James Baldwin. *The Evidence of Things Not Seen* (New York: Owl Books, 1995).

7. A major turning point in the U.S. history of child abduction was the abduction of Adam Walsh, and his parents' subsequent activism. His father, John Walsh, is host of the long running *America's Most Wanted*, and a frequent advocate for the missing.

8. Andrea J. Sedlak, David Finkelhor, Heather Hammer, and Dana J. Shultz. NISMART 2 (National Incidence Study of Missing, Abducted, Runaway, and Throwaway Children) National Estimates of Missing Children: An Overview. U.S. Department of Justice: Office of Juvenile Justice and Delinquence Prevention October 2002, 6.

9. The words of a survey respondent in Robert M. Entman and Andrew Rojecki *The Black Image in the White Mind: Media and Race in America* (Chicago: Chicago UP, 2001), 35. Their study of white respondents demonstrates an overwhelmingly negative perception of blacks in the white imagination. Blacks are inaccurately viewed by whites as committing the vast majority of crimes.

10. U.S. Department of Justice. Juvenile Justice Bulletin. September 2004 "Trends in the Murder of Juveniles: 1980–2000." www.ojp.usdoj.gov./ojjdp.

11. From nine-year-old Amber Hagerman, after whom the AMBER alert is named, to 18-year-old Natalee Holloway, who disappeared in 2005 while on vacation in Bermuda, the missing white daughter has a great deal of currency in media outlets.

12. Alaskan natives, Pacific Islanders, Asians, American Indians account for the the remaining 2 percent. Strangely, Latinos are not included in this data. OJP Juvenile Justice Bulletin noted above.

13. Feldstein, Ruth. *Motherhood in black and white: race and sex in American liberalism, 1930–1965*. Ithaca, NY: Cornell University Press, 2000.

14. See Janice Haaken's *Pillar of Salt: Gender, memory, and the perils of looking back*. Rutgers University Press, 1998, 174.

15. See Cathy Caruth, *Unclaimed Experience: Trauma, Narrative, and History* (Baltimore: Johns Hopkins UP, 1996).

16. Elaine Scarry. *The Body in Pain: The Making and Unmaking of the World* (New York: Oxford UP, 1985).

29

"something more powerful than skepticism"

Avery F. Gordon

The Gift

The purpose of this essay is to examine Toni Cade Bambara's utopian thought, particularly the remarkably rich vocabulary she gave us for describing and analyzing the sensuality of social movement and the day-to-day practice of instantiating an instinct for freedom. Indeed it is my view that Toni Cade Bambara was one of the great utopian thinkers of our time. Most people treat the utopian as an ideal future world which, at best provides a beacon of hope and, at worst, reflects an unrealistic fundamentalism bound to failure. But Bambara acted and wrote as if the utopian were a standpoint for comprehending and living in the here and now. Consequently, she gave us an extraordinary example of how to combine complex and acute social analysis with a vision of how some people have lived and do live today, which is a model for how all of us could live. Without ever abandoning a strong sense of the past and the future, she always asked us to keep focused on where we live now, insisting that history is only ever made in that conjuncture. Bambara always insisted that the spirit of making history must be tied to, indeed generated from, an uncompromising diagnosis of the deathly apparatuses of power. Indeed, what seems characteristic of Bambara's work is the way in which she patiently yet urgently calls her audiences and the people who inhabited her imagined worlds to see how the devastations and afflictions to which we are too routinely subjected require from us "something more powerful than skepticism."[1]

"No, I wouldn't identify myself as a utopian writer."

In 1982, shortly after the publication of *The Salt Eaters,* Kay Bonetti of the American Audio Prose Library interviewed Toni Cade Bambara in her home

The full version of this essay previously appeared in Avery F. Gordon, *Keeping Good Time: Reflections on Knowledge, Power, and People* (Boulder, CO: Paradigm Publishers 2004), 187–205.

in Atlanta. Bonetti asked Bambara: "Would you be comfortable being called something like a utopian writer? Being seen in that tradition?"[2] Bambara responded:

Oh, absolutely not! No, I don't identify with the utopian literature tradition. There are several features of that kind of literature. One, it takes a satiric stance about the current society. I'm not so much satiric. I'm critical but not satiric. For satire, you need a certain kind of sneering temperament, and that's a little removed from me. Another feature of the utopian literature is that it presents a vision based on the assumption that the reader and writer share a common set of values. I do not identify with the values of most utopian literature. I mean it does not speak to the world as I know it. It certainly does not speak to the international scheme of things. Another feature of utopian literature is that it doesn't look at process, it doesn't attempt to look at this new society as part of a historical continuum and I find that a little stupid. And finally its most characteristic feature is that it's very futuristic looking. I'm also future oriented, but it has to do with memory, with what I know is possible because it already happened. People need not be corrupted or perverted because I know in the past people were not. So my glance is both a back glance as well as a flash forward. No, I wouldn't identify myself as a utopian writer.

By the utopian literature tradition, Bambara is referring primarily to the distinct genre of European and American fiction, running from Thomas More to Ursula LeGuin, which creates and peoples a distinctly other world in which the putative problems and limitations of the writer's existing world are overcome. Bambara's critique of this literary tradition, however, is applicable to the range of projects—both in writing and in doings—to which the description utopian can and has been applied. It is especially relevant to the field of utopian studies broadly construed, which has played a major role in constructing what the utopian means and who and what counts as an instance of it.

Not to put too fine a point on it, the Western historiography of utopian thought and practice and the contemporary field known as utopian studies is a decidedly Eurocentric and racially exclusive construction.[3] It is a field dominated by a limited and often formal definition of the utopian, and it is a field in which the definition of failure and success borders on the perverse.

For example, this is a field that treats the brutal colonization of the Americas as a successful utopian enterprise, but deems the long history of what Peter Linebaugh and Marcus Rediker call the "many-headed hydra" of the "revolutionary" seventeenth-century Atlantic as all but irrelevant.[4] The many-headed hydra–hewers of wood and drawers of water, prostitutes, prisoners and other conscripts, indentured servants, slaves, maids, pirates, sailors, runaways, deserters, religious heretics—all those who dared to challenge the making of the modern capitalist world system are simply absent, buried under the weight of a triumphant modernity and the specter of Stalinism. Consequently, this is a field that includes the French Revolution, but not the thirty-year war waged by the Black and Red Seminoles against the United States. It is a field that includes Karl Marx, but not Christian Priber, a German socialist exile who joined the Cherokee Nation in 1736 and was captured by the British (later to die in a South Carolina prison) because he refused to declare loyalty to the French or British and was helping to unite the Southern Indian Nations in what was then Cherokee Territory. This is a field that includes the craftsman William Morris, but not the worker Harry Haywood. This is a field that includes Ernst Bloch's dreamy anticipations but not C. L. R. James's philosophy of happiness. This is a field that includes the feminist Frances Wright's failed and deeply flawed abolitionist experiment at Nashoba in Tennessee in the 1820s, but not one example of any instance of maroonage in the entire Americas. This is a field that includes Brook Farm and numerous white middle-class separatist communities, but not the multicultural Combahee River Collective or the many coalitional collectives like them. This is a field that includes Ursula K. LeGuin's off-world anthropology, but not Toni Cade Bambara's in-the-here-and-now community studies.[5]

It would take a book to elaborate persuasively how and why the utopian is constructed as it is, and that is not my intention here. But the characteristic meanings and reference points attached to utopian thought and practice in the West raises the question of why I would want to associate Toni Cade Bambara with a tradition she not only rejects for good reasons, not the least of which is that it can't recognize her at all, but also which she's clear she doesn't need.[6] Better to be done with it, you say. You may be right. The utopian as we primarily know it has missed the opportunity to chart a richer and more adequate history and theory of our real and imagined strivings for a livable social existence. This missed opportunity is a blind spot. However, there's always something living and breathing in the place blinded from view.

In the place blinded from view is the tradition of black struggle and radicalism as Toni Cade Bambara knows it, conjures it, invents it, and pushes it along, taking up her role as a politically engaged radical critic, "sid[ing] with the excluded and the repressed...develop[ing] insights gained in confrontation with injustice, nourish[ing] cultures of resistance, and help[ing] to define the means with which society can be rendered adequate to the full breadth of human potentialities."[7] *I do not identify with the values of most utopian literature. I mean it doesn't speak to the world as I know it.* In the world Bambara knows and imagines, process, memory, and struggle replace the fantasy of a common culture realized as a little nation, magically preestablished, and founded on good rules given from above. In her world, contradictions abound and complex individuals negotiate the dialectic of enclosure and breathless expansiveness. In her world, there's a rich living history, filled with legends of people who can fly and walk across the water and who can also organize meetings, institutions, and what's needed to survive and thrive in a permanently hostile environment.[8] Bambara's world is not a nation-state, although she's an avowed Black Nationalist; her world is centered on a community capable of mediating between what we shorthand as the local and the global. In her world, freedom is not a futuristic construct; it is grounded in our present existence as we relay individually and collectively between what's past and what's to come. In Bambara's world, freedom is grounded in what we are capable of, the possibilities of which we know from who we are—always, always better than we're told we can be—from what we remember about what's *already happened*, and from what we do when we act on these capabilities. There is a premium on truth in Bambara's world, on finding a better language than *mercantile* English for using the power of the word to harness rage to a joyous spirit of release and an outrageous permissiveness to be anything but merely a mercantile subject.[9] In Bambara's world, the instinct for freedom or what Fred Moten calls the freedom drive is the antithetical core of culture, where the seeds of opposition *grow into something much much more powerful than skepticism.*[10]

It is my argument that the world Toni Cade Bambara knows, peoples, and describes is a model or a standard for making utopian thought and practice more "usable," a favorite word of hers. My aim in making this argument is not to tie her back to a tradition with which she doesn't identify, but to identify a few elements of what the utopian tradition could mean if we looked at some of what's been in its blind field. That we need an adequate utopianism—precise in its diagnoses, inventive in its political-aesthetic form, expansive in its vision, courageous in its anticipations, reflexive in its prefigurations—I take not only as a given but also as one of Toni Cade Bambara's most consistent and challenging claims. In my view, it is not the need for utopianism that is questionable. Rather, it is with what words, ideas, traditions, sources of authority—in short with what practical spirit—such a utopianism is created and maintained that's at stake.

"You can hear the voices"

"You can hear the voices long after you turn the final page," writes Farah Griffin. "Toni Cade Bambara's extraordinary ordinary people—streetwise, sensitive, and complex—taunt, tease, and haunt: don't you want to be free? Yes, You, Freedom. What are you going to do to be free?[11]

Yes, You. The "don't you want to be free?" and the "what are you going to do to be free?" go hand in hand not only because it's a serious responsibility to want to be free but also because wanting it really—not just intellectually or abstractly or for somebody else, but You wanting it as if anything else would be unheard of—is already about what you are doing. On the call—Yes, You—and on the inextricability of wanting and doing, Bambara is adamant and uncompromising and also very understanding, that is, both knowledgeable and sympathetic. The taunting, teasing, and haunting question "Don't you want to be free?" presumes that somewhere you do want it, and if you don't, then why don't you, exactly. As teacherly as it sounds "What are you going to do to be free?" presumes you can be doing something, and if you don't know what that is, you best find out. What is involved in wanting and doing freedom? The heart of Bambara's contribution to utopian thought and practice is contained in the answer she gives: to want to be free, you have to live and act as if you are free to live, right now, right this minute, in the midst of all the life-threatening forces arrayed and ready at hand. *Then he straightened, back stiff with the conviction that he, like many others going home now, was totally unavailable for servitude.*[12] I'll try to explain what I think she means.

Face Up to What's Killing You

She was turning the bend now, forgetting to not look, and the mural the co-op had painted in eye-stinging colors stopped her. FACE UP TO WHAT'S KILLING YOU, it demanded. Below the statement a huge triangle that from a distance was just a triangle, but on approach, as one muttered "how deadly can a triangle be?" turned into bodies on bodies. At the top, fat, fanged beasts in smart clothes, like the ones beneath it laughing, drinking, eating, bombing, raping, shooting, lunging on the backs of, feeding off the backs of, the folks at the base, crushed almost flat but struggling to get up and getting up.[13]

Virginia, The Organizer's Wife, *passed it quickly,* because *she'd been leaving since the first day coming, the day her sister came home to cough herself to death and leave her there with nobody to look out for her 'cept some hinkty cousins in town and Miz Mama Mae, who shook her head sadly whenever the girl spoke of this place and these troubles and these people and one day soon leaving for some other place.*[14] On this day, having absent-mindedly crushed the vegetables in her untended garden, *Virginia had no energy for a smile or a wince. All her energy summoned up at rising was focused tightly on her two errands of the day,*[15] both of which are oriented to getting Graham her organizer husband out of jail and both of them out of town. Because at this point in the story, Virginia just wants out. Away from *the farms, the co-op sheds, the lone gas pump, a shoe left in the road, posters promising victory over the troubles.*[16] Away from an imprisonment she had come to measure *by how many times that same red-and-yellow jumper met her on the road, faded and fading some more.*[17] Away from land grabs and mining companies, corrupt governments, opportunistic preachers, tobacco sheds, and *the troubles.* Away from the men waiting patiently in her garden, ready to help, away from the choir women and their *Everything all right?,* away from the *discipline, consciousness and unity* taught at the co-op school, away from the bound-to-come weariness of always *creating something from nothing.* All she wanted was the *thing stitched up, trimmed, neat, finished. Wanted to be able to say she asked for 'nuthin from nobody and didn't nobody offer up nuthin.* No attachments. No responsibilities, *Pay the ball and unhook them both from this place.*[18] Virginia wanted only to get out of "this place," which became her "situation," knowing well enough that there was something rude about treating other people's home as "this place." This place, her situation, killing her with isolation, loneliness, the struggles *WE CANNOT LOSE,*[19] and the notion, trapping her like a vise, that home is what makes you stay and fight.

Virginia has no intention of staying. She has a plan, her own freedom plan, an honorable one with a long history. Running away. *And isn't that what she thought initially made her fall in love with Graham? It was his would-be-moving-on clothes that had pulled her to him. But then the pull had become too strong to push against once his staying-on became clear.*[20] So, baby at her breast, men in her garden waiting patiently, she's focused on her errands, clear in her mind that she is taking charge, facing up to what's killing her, and finally doing what's needed to be done to improve her situation. The first errand is visiting Reverend Michaels before the men come with the surveyors and the bulldozers to get the granite. Virginia just wants *to hear him say it—the land's been sold. The largest passel of land in the district, the church holdings where the co-op school stood, where two storage sheds of the co-op stood, where the graphic workshops stood, where four families had lived for generations working the land The church had sold the land. He'd say it, she'd hear it, and it'd be over with. She and Graham could go.*[21] And he does tell her, indirectly of course: "Wasn't me, he stammered."[22] Virginia hears what she thinks she has wanted to hear—the land's been sold. But she does not walk out smiling to herself, feeling free to go.

An anger or a force Virginia *had no time to understand* compels her, and she grabs a ruler and brings it down on the Reverend's chair and then on his arm, dropping him and the chair to the floor. He's stunned in *disbelief*... Seeing the scene *detached*, this unknown Virginia, the one who, at the coop school, *had never learned to speak her speak*, surprises herself, hears herself both laughing and shouting: *And what did the white folks pay you to turn Graham in and clear the way? Disturber of the peace. What peace? Racist trying to incite a riot, Ain't that how they said it? Outside agitator, as you said, And his roots put down here long before you ever came... Thirty pieces of silver, maybe?*[23]

The story comes both fast and slow to a close. Jake, Boone, and the kindly patient men are waiting for her, now that she's ready to go and see Graham. In the car, they are talking, excited and explaining, and Virginia hears them: *Mother Lee who's secretarying for the board has held up the papers for the sale. We came to tell you that... We're the delegation that's going to confront the board this evening... They never intended to dig the wells, that's clear... That was just to get into the district, get into our business, check out our strength. I was a fool... Well,... Can't you read? That's what our flyers been saying all along. Don't you read the stuff we put out... We ain't nowhere licked yet, though... Listen, we got it all figured out. We're going to bypass the robbers and deal directly with the tenant councils in the cities, and we're... And you tell him... just tell him to take his care.*

"Don't talk the woman to death," says Boone for the second time. Virginia is listening enough to speak to them for the first time—"There's still Mama Mae's farm," she says with a smile. But she's remembering the last time she saw Graham and what she's going to say to him now and *how to explain this new growth she was experiencing.* Not like the old *dread*, not like the baby; *more like the toenail smashed the day the work brigade had stacked the stones to keep the road from splitting apart. The way the new nail pushed up against the old turning blue, against the gauze and the tape, stubborn to establish itself.*[24] She's trying to get a *hold of it,* but she can't quite yet. The "it" is still a memory of trying to *come through the shell* but not quite having the words for her feelings, *only broken threads and...* This is what she remembers, *grabbing herself up and trying to get to that place that was beginning to seem more of a when than a where. And the when seemed to be inside her if she could only connect.*[25] And she does connect, remembering a *when,* getting the words, as wishes, into herself as what she *knew exactly* now to tell Graham: *the bail'd been paid, her strength was back, and she sure as hell was going to keep up the garden. How else to feed the people?*[26]

"Are you sure, sweetheart, that you want to be well?"

That's how the story ends. Virginia doesn't even say these words to Graham. She just remembers, connects, and gets ready to. We do not know if the community will successfully have saved their land and if the hook-up with the tenant councils in the city will succeed. We're certainly not led to believe that what Helen Quan calls the forces of savage developmentalism have been conquered or that corruption in churches has been eliminated or that poverty and its issue has disappeared. We do not know if Graham is released from jail, much less that prisons have been abolished. We do not know what Virginia will or won't do next. She's not a New Woman in the Promised Land whose future is secured. She's just a young woman who has found a strength already with her—that is, a memory—to transform the place she was stuck in and running away from into a home. At the end of the story, all that seems to happen is that Virginia goes to see the husband she loves in jail and decides to stay and keep up the garden. That's it.

It takes Velma all three hundred pages of *The Salt Eaters* just to answer the question which the healer Minnie Ranson asks on the first page, *Are you sure, sweetheart, that you want to be well?*[27] At the end of that story, Velma, a much more experienced fighter than Virginia, who has tried to kill herself, just barely says yes to Minnie Ransom's question.

The healer's hand touches a *vital spot* and finally Velma responds. But even then, *she was still trying to resist* . . . It's only later when Velma is able to make a story of it, able to retrieve it as a memory, that she would be able to *laugh remembering she'd thought* barely saying yes *was an ordeal. She didn't know the half of it. Of what awaited her in years to come.*[28] The what's-to-come, Sophie Heywood warns, will be a *trial*[29] because the what's-to-come involves what Velma doesn't understand yet, which is how a politically astute, hard-headed critical, organizationally competent, knows-her-history, tough fighter was healed by another woman who needs her own guide to conjure the spiritual power she can wield. But the what's-to-come doesn't arrive; only the ending as it is. Velma answers yes, lets go of Minnie's hands, gets up off the stool on which she's been sitting for three hundred pages, and *throws off the shawl that drops down on the stool a burst cocoon.*[30] At the end of *The Salt Eaters*, environmental racism and corporate pollution have not been eliminated, the bus driver Fred Holt's friend Porter is still dead from exposure to state-sponsored radioactivity, police brutality remains a hazard of an active protest life, the enraging and exhausting gendered division of

labor within grassroots movements lingers, intimacy in love is still a difficult achievement, and careerism and opportunism are as much a concern
as the need to overcome the split between "race, class and struggle" and
the "spirithood arts"[31]—this split being only one instance of the "demonic"
binary model of thought in which we're often paralyzed.[32]

In other words, nowhere in any of Toni Cade Bambara's writings is
there the usual utopian scenario. No one is ever transported to a perfect
world where all problems are solved, where the past is over, and where the
future is all sweet perfection neatly organized according to nicely-sounding-
on-paper rules. Bambara does not create pictures of perfection, only stories
of living with the degradations and contradictions of exploitation, racism,
authoritarianism—what she calls the psychopathological world of lies and
inhumanity—differently; stories of living better than all that.[33] These are not
American dream stories all "innocence and clean slates and the future."[34] In
Bambara's stories, a different type of anticipatory consciousness is expressed,
oriented toward the future, but not futuristic; that is to say, it doesn't treat
the future as either an off-world escape or a displacing fetish. This anticipatory consciousness involves dreaming, but it also involves risks. (USE
EXTREME CAUTION, *Those Bones* warns at the start.) Like the storytelling form in which Bambara always presents the dream of better living,
this anticipatory consciousness "confronts, pushes you up against the eva-
sions, self-deceptions, investments in opinions and interpretations, the clutter that blinds, [and] that disguises that underlying, all-encompassing design
within which the perceived world—in which society would have us stay
put—operates."[35] In this anticipatory consciousness, it is confronting the
clutter that blinds and binds, which allows you to get a certain distance
or detachment from where you're told to *stay put*. This anticipatory consciousness is intensely in the present tense, moving back and forth between
memories of what has come before and what is to come next, folding itself
into sensual stories of movement, social movement, individual movement.

The emerging place that is inside Virginia that is more of a *when* than
a *where*, Minnie Ransom's "Everything in time"[36] speak not only to the
importance of time in Bambara's conception but also to the supreme importance of Taking Your Time. Bambara has spoken eloquently of how she was
given permission by her mother, by her daughter, by her friends, and by herself to daydream, to imagine, to know her work and do it, to change, and to
take her time to learn how to *practice her freedom daily*.[37] Bambara passes
this permission on to her characters and readers as a right and as a necessity,
graciously, with a casualness her mother passed on to her, tenaciously,
with the knowledge that the historic denial of this permission is a form
of spirit murder. And so people—ordinary "folks who've been waiting in the

wings"[38]—take their time to do what they need to do to face up to what's killing them, and others wait, instantiating a type of self- and other-directed love that's free of any guilt over taking time. And that's because in Bambara's world, there isn't a finite block of time out there that we all have to compete for a piece of. In Bambara's world, permission replaces competition.[39] You have to take your time and take it in your own way. In Bambara's world, unlike the "motif of [our] expressive society, there is ... enough ... space, livelihood, validation for all."[40]

Minnie Ransom "can wait," although at moments it does strain her while Velma takes her time deciding whether she wants to get well or not. It takes Velma a long time to make that decision, remembering and forgetting her life and the history of the people who surround her. The older men and women wait patiently and kindly for Virginia as she learns that she has a time of her own, a *when* that enables her to find a different place to live right there where a moment ago she could only meet the *same red and yellow jumper on the road*. We, and everyone around them, must wait for Spence to negotiate the time lost between his return from Vietnam and the present as he confronts the possible sources of his son's disappearance and the surprise of the aching loneliness and grief it produces in him. We also must wait for Zala as she struggles with the haunting time—sharp, anxious, suspicious, late, late, late (He should have been here already!)—that has her bound to making every single moment a terrible struggle to make her rage and also her guilt into a power capable of getting her son back or at least getting an accurate explanation for his absence.[41]

The structure of all Bambara's novels and many of the short stories consists in a relay between the present and the past, between the trouble afflicting you right at the moment and what else is going on around you, between there being no time to waste at all and the necessity of taking your time. It's not simply that Bambara doesn't have a linear sense of time, as many have pointed out. It's that she describes the meeting of collective forms of time—ancestor time, what she calls Black Family time—and individual forms of time. This meeting of collective and individual produces that abolitionist time of acute patience and urgency, which Martin Luther King tried to explain to the white moderate in his "Letter from a Birmingham Jail." This abolitionist time cannot wait for the "right" time, nor for others to decide when those who are "harried by day and haunted by night" can have their time.[42] In abolitionist time, nothing is inevitable except the struggle to make "now the time to make real the promise of democracy," to make time one's "creative" "ally."[43] Abolitionist time is a type of revolutionary time. But rather than stop the world as if in an absolute break between now and then, it is a daily part of it, a way of being in the ongoing work of emancipation, a work whose success is not measured by legalistic pronouncements, a work which perforce must take place while you're still enslaved.

Urgency and patience forged in the crucible of a historic struggle. A struggle for what? For Virginia to find her *when*? For Velma to get up off the chair? Yes. Because what's at stake in taking your time to face up to what's killing you is nothing less than the revolution in selfhood or subjectivity that, for Bambara, is the root of being capable of living better than is expected of you. And living better than what is expected of you is revolutionary, it is about changing how life is lived in the here and now. And that takes time. Time, Bambara says, we have. "That of course," she wrote in *The Black Woman*,

> is an unpopular utterance these days. Instant coffee is the hallmark of current rhetoric. But we do have time. We better take the time to fashion revolutionary selves, revolutionary lives, revolutionary relationships. Mouths don't win the war . . . It is so much easier to be out there than right here. The revolution ain't out there. Yet. But it is here. Should be . . . Ain't no such animal as an instant guerrilla.[44]

"It's so much easier to be out there than right here."

It's so much easier to be out there than right here.[45] Bambara knows this very well; it is what her healers know, and it is what the truth and justice fighters who change, who find wholeness—integrity, honor, health, responsibility— where before there was disconnection find out.[46] And as Bambara states,

> One of the greatest afflictions in American society for both the teacher/student and the writer is the affliction of disconnectedness. The separation between the world of academia and the world of knowledge that exists beyond the campus gates, the seeming dichotomy between politics and ethics, the division between politics and art, [between materialism and metaphysics] etc. . . . In this society, forgetfulness is a virtue, amnesia is a virtue . . . And we carry this habit, this outlook, into our daily lives. This is extremely dangerous. So, I teach about the necessity of being connected, and about the necessity of resurrecting the truth about our experiences (and revising the texts) in this place called America.[47]

The truth of our experiences. "Are you sure, sweetheart, that you want to be well," Minnie Ransom, "fabled healer of the district," asks Velma Henry, fabled worn-out activist. "Are you sure, sweetheart? I'm just asking is all... Take away the miseries and you take away some folks' reason for living. Their conversation piece anyway."[48] Minnie Ransom must ask Velma this question fifty times, repeating it over and over again, trying to make Velma hear the... question: are you ready to be better? Do you want to eliminate your own misery or do you need it to live? These are profound, difficult, and delicate questions that get to the heart of any utopian enterprise. What do you really want? What is involved in achieving what you want? What's the cost of taking away the miseries? What's the cost of holding on to them?[49]

What Bambara wants is revolution. Revolution involves a "free society made up of whole individuals."[50] Such a revolution begins, Bambara states, "with the self, in the self." The self is, for her, "the basic revolutionary unit" and consequently it must be "purged of poison and lies that assault the ego and threaten the heart, that hazard" couples, families, movements, and communities.[51] "A new person is born when he finds a value to define an actional self and when he can assume autonomy for that self," she writes. Assuming the autonomy to create a new person, from the bottom up, out of the messy, complex, and willful people that we are and will remain, is to assume the power to make history. For, as Bambara states, making history involves refusing to act "like we were just symbolic personae in some historical melodrama."[52] And so Bambara focuses her creative energy—her power—on showing the damage caused by alienation from creative labor, alienation from economic and political power, alienation from history, alienation from truthful knowledge, and alienation from ourselves. And on showing the intimate, sensual, and embodied process which heals that damage, from the bottom up, from You to the world waiting for you to be ready. This healing is absolutely crucial, a necessary part of creating free individuals and a free society now, when we need it. There is no free society without free individuals, Bambara says—or as Mrs. Sophie Heywood "counseled": "Have to be whole to see whole."[53] And so, individuals will have to be healed—it can't wait until later, it can't be done in a minute, and most importantly, it can't be done alone.

"Dreamer? The dream is real, my friends. The failure to make it work is the unreality."

Always in Bambara's stories, the community must be present for this revolutionary act of healing, of liberation, to take place. The community must be present for three important reasons. First, the community must be present because you can't do it alone; it's too difficult. It is difficult because *it's so much easier to be out there than right here.* And *it's so much easier to be out there than right here* because people often hold on

> to sickness with a fiercesomeness . . . So used to being unwhole and unwell, one forgot what it was to walk upright and see clearly, breathe easily, think better than was taught, be better than one was programmed to believe . . . For people sometimes believed that it was safer to live with complaints, was necessary to cooperate with grief, was all right to become an accomplice in self-ambush . . . Took heart to flat out decide to be well and stride into the future sane and whole. And it took time.[54]

It's so much easier to be out there than right here where, given all the unrelenting taxations on you, you have a right to what's familiar, to what's safe, to what you've come to rely on to keep you as sane as you are. You have paid your dues, you fight the good fight, you deserve to feel you're special. It is so much easier to hold on to the familiar costs, the cooperations you've trusted in the past, than to let that go, let go of a pride hard-won and rarely given, let go of the fear that raises the defenses that are your known strength.

In a remarkable passage, remarkable for its seeming counter-intuition, Minnie Ransom says, "There's nothing that stands between you and perfect health, sweetheart. Can you hold that thought?"[55] You usually can't. The immediate reaction, full of charged resistance, is almost always, "Are you crazy? What's standing between me and perfect health is the obvious reality of the sick world that's made me ill in the first place." For Bambara, healing is the process by which you hold that counter-intuitive thought and overcome the resistance to a truth that doesn't so much set you free, as set you up to practice a freedom that improves upon use. But this resistance is fierce, rooted in a self-protectiveness that feels absolutely essential, and so you're going to need some help. Indeed, you cannot do it on your own. The magic—and there's no other word for it—of the healings which Bambara demonstrates is effected by the complex of power that comes from a concentrated meeting of healer, sick person, and the group.[56] It is not a strictly speaking individual or dyadic process. The group's love, patience, concentration, and belief in the power to heal is absolutely essential to be there, even if you're not entirely aware of its presence, as Velma is not. Without the group, the healer and the other individuals present in your circle have no power, nothing to draw on to help you out. And like any other analytic and creative production, you want to be healed by tools and methods capable of doing and not botching the job.

Therefore, the second reason the community needs to be present is because the community is where *the dream is real*, where the *only unreality is the failure to make it real.*[57] The heart of the two-parts-that-go-together dream, which is a "chorus," is that, one, "exploitation and misery are neither inevitable, nor necessary," and, two, it is possible to "rise above" one's training, "think better than" one's "been taught,"[58] and defiantly behave accordingly. This dream is not, in Bambara's hands, fantasmatic or elusive or something people only experience while they're asleep. This is not a dream of color-blindness, of homogeneous self-contained alien societies, of perfect and perfectly conscious individuals, or of genocidal settlement masquerading as democratic freedom. Bambara's dream of a world in which exploitation and misery are neither inevitable nor necessary, a world in which we are better than we're expected to be, sounds so simple, simplistic even. But, to me, it is a profound standpoint, a utopian standpoint, magical in its ability to suspend disbelief, passed down to her as the community's teaching and tradition.

The community means everything to Bambara, and thus it is the focal point of her imaginative attention, a place she speaks from and speaks to, inventing it as often as describing it. The community is what's needed for healing. The community is the source of the history and the memory and the now of what's possible because it's already happened there. The community possesses a special way of seeing, a second sight, in which *the dream is real and the only unreality is the failure to make it real.* Many individuals, Bambara writes,

> spent a great deal of time, energy, and imagination encouraging and equipping me to practice freedom in preparation for collective self-governance...I became acquainted with Black books that challenged, rather than mimicked, White or Negro versions of reality. I became acquainted with folks who demonstrated that their real work was creating value in the neighborhoods—bookstores, communal gardens, think tanks, arts and-crafts programs, community organizer training, photography workshops. Many of them had what I call second sight—the ability to make reasoned calls to the community to create protective spaces wherein people could theorize and practice towards future sovereignty, while at the same time watching out for the sharks, the next wave of repression, or the next smear campaign, and preparing for it.[59] ...

Toni Cade Bambara rejects those Western utopian traditions "wherein people cannot be a higher sovereign than the state."[60] Instead, in Bambara's vision, people in community are a higher sovereign than the state or the market or the media or the academy. It is the sovereignty of people conducting the "daily rituals of validation," based on a second sight, that creates a "liberated zone" right there where they are "penned up in concentration camp horror."[61] This liberated zone is inhabited by bold insurgents and quiet plodders, by champions—those who get up when they are down for the count[62]—and those who want to hide, by adept healers and those who need some healing, by patient teachers and impatient learners, by people doing more than their best and others doing less. In this liberated zone, democratic, antiracist community values, whether in culture or in politics or in housekeeping, are practiced as sovereign and for future sovereignty. In this liberated zone, the morning how do's, the borrowing, the helping out, the "that'll be enough now" matter—matter because they are valued as the values we want to live by. In this liberated zone, some women want to run away, and some men need to be told to stay put. In this liberated zone, some people just need to figure out how to get up off their chair, and others are busy with meetings and keeping more lists of things to do than they'll ever accomplish. In this liberated zone, there's an effort to resolve conflicts with respect and care, and there are breaks that cannot be repaired. In other words, in this liberated zone, there is the ongoing meeting of those who believe the dream is real, of those who might be persuaded, of those who don't care all that much, and of those who oppose you all the way. The community is not a panacea for all ills, but it is the place where Bambara locates the practice of freedom, the *second sight* that gives us the knowledge that we have the sovereignty, the authority, to free ourselves on our own terms.

And thus, Bambara also rejects those Western utopian traditions which are rooted in the assumption that the powers that oppress us are not only bigger than us, as the spatial reasoning has it, but also the source of who we are and what we are capable of. As Cedric Robinson succinctly put it, "We are not the subjects or the subject formations of the capitalist world-system. It is merely one condition of our existence."[63] To understand as embodied knowledge, that is to say, to live by what this statement means, is to hold to a reality principle that runs counter to everything we are taught by all rulers, most scholars, and many radicals. To be intimate with this thinking is to hold to a reality principle in which the dream is real, and the only unreality is the failure to make it work. The dream that is real is both deeply subjective, in Bambara's conception, and it is also a supremely material way of conceiving our relationship to the systems that attempt to control and dehumanize us.[64]

The dream is the art of making things and relationships of value without believing that the rulers can successfully and completely rule you. The dream is about being *unavailable for servitude, back/stiff with conviction.* The dream is neither cynical nor naive toward power; it is in-difference to it. To live in the reality of the dream, you not only need to be different but also need to be in—different. Indifferent to the lure and the pull of the sacrificial goods and promises ubiquitously on offer and also indifferent to the familiarity of being sick of it all. To be in-difference is to refuse to be intoxicated with the "ugly" and with the deathly, to stop loving that which you claim to despise.[65] To be in-difference is to practice freedom in preparation for collective self-governance. To be in-difference is to believe that we are better and more human than the reactive subjects of a variety of abusive arrangements of power and authority. To be in-difference is to see all the winning ways in which many people, and for as long as anybody can remember, resist the degradations imposed on them and to see what those great and small acts of resistance teach us about the *fragility* of power and the ease with which it can *fail* to achieve its ends. To be in-difference is to see as real, as reality, that many people not only resist but also build worlds that live by better and more just and equitable rules, rituals, and relationships. To be in-difference is to refuse to collaborate by lending energy to that which oppresses you. To be in-difference is to be ready, in a moment, to let go of what's merely seemed a superficial or temporary investment in the way things are. In short, to be in-difference is to find "the work of revolution irresistible."[66]

The Work: To Make Revolution Irresistible

Thus, we come to the third and final reason the community must be present in the healing process. Finally, the community must be present because without it, you've got no place to go when you're better. Being well, in the way Bambara means it, as an act of liberation, brings a responsibility with it. "'Do we want to be well?' The answer tends to be 'no!' To be whole—politically, psychically, spiritually, culturally, intellectually, aesthetically, physically, and economically *whole*—is of profound significance. It is significant because there is a correlative to this. There is a responsibility to self and to history that is developed once you are 'whole,' once you are well, once you acknowledge your powers."[67] There's a great force, Bambara is suggesting, that comes from refusing to *cooperate with grief,* from insisting on the capacity and the right to be better than and in a sick society. This is the power of in-difference, the capacity to let go of the ties that bind you to an identification with that which is killing you, to assume a freedom or an autonomy you can own because you are one of its most important sources, and to share it with others so that it is "usable," not simply a private possession. The power to be in-different is a world-making power, the power to create an alternative civilization in the here and now, right there in the same place where greed, abusive authority, and all sorts of biological and social determinisms reside. The power of in-difference is more powerful than skepticism for the simple reason that it attaches you, not to what you hold in contempt (as cynicism does), but to that liberated zone where the daily practice of freedom constitutes the grounds for sovereignty and for a labor of love that's anything but misguided. On the contrary, the something more powerful than skepticism is guided by vigilance in the pursuit of a freedom you've already begun to taste.

Freedom? Yes. You. Don't you want to be free? Freedom is what Bambara, the dreamer, the organizer, and the bad housekeeper, is after.[68] What she does mean by freedom? Freedom means facing up to what's killing you, healing the damage, and becoming in-different to the lure of sacrificial promises of moneyed or exclusive happiness and the familiarity of your own pain. It means facing up and out with analytic precision, creative determination, and sympathetic understanding for yourself and others, with tenderness, as Herbert Marcuse advised.[69] Freedom, Bambara insists, is a process. It is neither the end of history nor an elusive goal never achievable. It is not a better nation-state, however disguised as a cooperative. It is not an ideal set of rules detached from the people who make them or live by them. And it is certainly not the right to own the economic, social, political, or cultural capital in order to dominate others and trade their happiness in a monopolistic market. Freedom is the process by which you develop a practice for being *unavailable for servitude*. It is an uneven process, not very linear, always looping around catching folks at different moments—facing up, healing, becoming in-different, already in-different. The practice of freedom is difficult; it can be overwhelmed by despair and depression, but it is also joyous. Freedom is, in short, the process by which we do the work of making revolution irresistible, making it something we cannot live without. *Then he straightened, back stiff with the conviction that he, like many others going home now, was totally unavailable for servitude.* Being or becoming *totally unavailable for servitude*, as Bambara herself declared, was the work she took on as her own and for us. Making revolution irresistible. This is how we make the best history we can now, which is only ever when we have a chance.

NOTES

1. The phrase "something more powerful than skepticism" is from Toni Cade Bambara, *The Salt Eaters* (New York: Random House, 1980), 86.
2. Kay Bonetti. "Interview with Toni Cade Bambara" (Columbia, MO: American Audio Prose Library, 1982).

3. For example, a title and abstract survey of several years of the *Journal of Utopian Studies* yielded, with the exception of the few articles on Octavia Butler and Samuel Delany, no African American or Diasporic presence.

4. Peter Linebaugh and Marcus Rediker. *The Many-Headed Hydra. Sailors, Slaves, Commoners, and the Hidden History of the Revolutionary Atlantic* (Boston: Beacon Press, 2000). See, for example, Roland Schaer, Gregory Claeys, and Lyman Tower Sargent, eds. *Utopia: The Search for the Ideal Society in the Western World* (New York: Oxford, 2000).

5. See Frank E. Manuel and Fritzie P. Manuel. *Utopian Thought in the Western World*. (Cambridge, MA: Harvard University Press, 1979). There are very few exceptions to this rule. Francis Robert Shor's *Utopianism and Radicalism in a Reforming America 1888–1918* (Greenwood Press, Westport, CT, 1997) is the rare work that not only includes African American literary utopias but also takes a social movement perspective, locating "articulations of utopianism" and "radicalism" in "the shifting and contested political and cultural terrain where class, race, and gender come into play" (xv). The other important exception is Maria Guilia Fabi, who has written a series of articles contesting specious claims that African Americans produced no formal literary utopias or utopian texts so impoverished in their imaginations they needn't count. She finds it unbelievable that "an oppressed population could be reduced to such a state of abjection as to lose the power to imagine and give fictional reality to visions of a better future." See M. Guilia Fabi. "The Poetics and Politics of a Feasible Utopia: Edward A. Johnson's Light Ahead for the Negro (1904)," in Vita Fortunati and Paola Spinozzi, eds. *Vite di Utopia* (Ravenna: A. Longo Editore, 2000), 303; and "'Race Travel': Towards a Taxonomy of Turn-of-the Century African American Utopian Fiction," in Raffaella Baccolini, Vita Fortunati, and Nadia Minerva, eds. *Viaggi in utopia* (Ravenna: A. Longo Editore, 1996).

6. A significant number of individuals called utopian by scholars and commentators by their contemporaries or subsequently also do not call themselves by the name. They rejected the effort to repress and stigmatize their ideas and projects, which the attribution utopian too often signaled. Charles Fourier is perhaps the most well-known example. See Vincent Geoghegan. *Utopianism and Marxism* (New York: Methuen, 1987), 17.

7. Chuck Morse. "Capitalism, Marxism, and the Black Radical Tradition: An Interview with Cedric Robinson," *Perspectives on Anarchist Theory* 3, no. 1 (Spring 1999).

8. See Toni Cade Bambara. "The Education of a Storyteller," in Toni Morrison, ed. *Deep Sightings and Rescue Missions: Fiction, Essays, and Conversations* (New York: Pantheon, 1996), 255.

9. On English as a mercantile language, see Toni Cade Bambara, "How She Came By Her Name," in *Deep Sightings*, 235; and Zora Chandler. "Voices Beyond the Veil: An Interview with Toni Cade Bambara and Sonia Sanchez," in Joanne M. Braxton and Andrea Nicola McLaughlin, eds. *Wild Women in the Whirlwind: Afra-American Culture and the Contemporary Literary Renaissance* (New Brunswick, NJ: Rutgers University Press, 1990), 347–48.

10. On the instinct for freedom, see Avery F. Gordon. "Some thoughts on the Utopian" in *Keeping Good Time* (2004) and Fred Moten. *In the Break: The Aesthetics of the Black Radical Tradition* (Minneapolis: University of Minnesota Press, 2003). On culture as where the seeds of opposition grow, see Amilcar Cabral, "National

Liberation and Culture," in *Return to the Source* (New York: Monthly Review Press, 1973), 43.

11. Farah Jasmine Griffin. "Toni Cade Bambara: Free to Be Anywhere in the Universe," *Callaloo: A Journal of African-American and African Arts and Letters* 19, no. 2 (1996): 229.

12. Toni Cade Bambara. "The Seabirds Are Still Alive," in *The Seabirds Are Still Alive* (New York: Random House, 1977), 77.

13. Toni Cade Bambara. "The Organizer's Wife," in *Seabirds*, 16.

14. Ibid., 7.

15. Ibid., 4.

16. Ibid., 9.

17. Ibid., 9.

18. Ibid., 7.

19. Ibid., 17.

20. Ibid., 14.

21. Ibid., 15–16.

22. Ibid., 18.

23. Ibid., 18.

24. Ibid., 19–23.

25. Ibid., 21.

26. Ibid., 23.

27. Bambara, *Salt Eaters*, 3.

28. Ibid., 278.

29. Ibid., 294.

30. Ibid., 295.

31. Ibid., 93.

32. Toni Cade Bambara. "Deep Sightings and Rescue Missions," in *Deep Sightings,* 163.

33. On being rescued from the psychopaths, see Toni Cade Bambara, "What It Is I think I'm Doing Anyhow," in Janet Sternburg, ed. *The Writer on Her Work* (New York: Norton, 1980), 153; Claudia Tate. "Toni Cade Bambara," in Claudia Tate, ed. *Black Women Writers at Work* (New York: Continuum, 1983), 24; and Toni Cade Bambara, "Language and Writer," in *Deep Sightings*, 139.

34. Toni Morrison. "Five Years of Terror.' A Conversation with Miriam Horn," *U.S. News & World Report*, October 19, 1987, 75.

35. Toni Cade Bambara. "Salvation Is the Issue," in Mari Evans, ed. *Black Women Writers (1950–1980): A Critical Evaluation* (Garden City, NY: Doubleday, 1984), 42.

36. Toni Cade Bambara. *Salt Eaters*, 295.

37. On practicing freedom, see Toni Cade Bambara. *Deep Sightings*, 174; and Cheryl Clarke. "1995 like 1992 like 1989 will mark me forever," *Gay Community News*, 21, no. 3–4 (Winter–Spring 1996), 10.

38. Claudia Tate. "Toni Cade Bambara," 18.

39. On the ways in which "permission" is tied to fate and the question of love in the black radical tradition, see Avery Gordon. "Preface" to Cedric J. Robinson, *An Anthropology of Marxism* (Aldershot, England: Ashgate Publishing, 2001).

40. Adrienne Rich. "Credo of a Passionate Skeptic," *Los Angeles Times Book Review*, March 11, 2001, 10.

41. Zala and Spence are the main characters in Bambara's *Those Bones Are Not My Child*.

42. Martin Luther King, Jr. "Letter from a Birmingham Jail (1963)," in James Melvin Washington, ed. *Martin Luther King, Jr., I Have A Dream: Writings and Speeches that Changed the World*, (New York: HarperCollins, 1992), 88.

43. Ibid., 92.

44. Toni Cade Bambara. "On the Issue of Roles," in Toni Cade Bambara, ed., *The Black Woman: An Anthology* (New York: The New American Library, 1970), 110.

45. A correction inserted by Fred Moten here: "But the specific genius of her utopianism is that she is out there in here."

46. See Justine Tally. "Not About to Play it Safe: An Interview with Toni Cade Bambara," *Revista Canaria de Estudios Ingleses*, November 11, 1985, 145.

47. Zora Chandler. "Voices Beyond the Veil: An Interview with Toni Cade Bambara and Sonia Sanchez," in Joanne M. Braxton and Andrea NicolaMcLaughlin, eds., *Wild Women in the Whirlwind*, 351. The "between materialism and metaphysics" insert is from Toni Cade Bambara, "What Is It I Think I'm Doing Anyhow," in Janet Sternburg. *The Writer and Her Work*, 154.

48. Toni Cade Bambara. *Salt Eaters*, 3, 15–16.

49. Ibid., 22–23.

50. Toni Cade Bambara. *Black Woman*, 105.

51. Ibid., 109. Bambara utilizes a type of base/superstructure model here (and elsewhere) in which, though recursive, the individual is the basis on which couples, families, communities, and entire societies rest. She thinks from the bottom up, always, and at bottom for her is the person with all their humanity, that is to say, with their strengths and weaknesses.

52. Ibid., 109.

53. Ibid., 92.

54. Ibid., 107–108.

55. Ibid., 104.

56. See Claude Levi-Strauss. "The Sorcerer and His Magic," in *Structural Anthropology* (New York: Basic Books, 1963).

57. Toni Cade Bambara. *Salt Eaters*, 126.

58. Toni Cade Bambara. "What It Is I Think I'm Doing Anyhow," in Janet Sternburg, *The Writer on Her Work*, 154–55; and Bambara, *Deep Sightings*, 175.

59. Toni Cade Bambara. *Deep Sightings*, 173–34.

60. Kalumu ya Salaam. "Searching for the Mother Tongue: An Interview," *First World*, 2, no. 4 (1980), 48.

61. Toni Cade Bambara. *Deep Sightings*, 95.

62. On the champion and Muhammad Ali as the paradigm, see Toni Cade Bambara, "What It Is I Think I'm Doing Anyhow," in Janet Sternberg, *The Writer on Her Work*, 163.

63. Cedric J. Robinson. "Manichaeism and Multiculturalism," in Avery Gordon and Christopher Newfield, eds. *Mapping Multiculturalism* (Minneapolis: University of Minnesota Press, 1996), 122.

64. See, for example, the exchange regarding colonialism between Bambara and Salaam, "Searching for the Mother Tongue: An Interview," in this volume.

65. Toni Cade Bambara. "What It Is I Think I'm Doing Anyhow," in Janet Sternburg, *The Writer on Her Work*, 157.

66. Toni Cade Bambara. "Foreword," to Cherrié Moraga and Gloria Anzaldúa, eds. *This Bridge Called My Back: Writings by Radical Women of Color* (Watertown, New York: Kitchen Table Press, 1981), viii.

67. Zora Chandler. "Voices Beyond the Veil: An Interview with Toni Cade Bambara and Sonia Sanchez," in Joanne M. Braxton and Andrea Nicola McLaughlin, *Wild Women in the Worldwind*, 347–48.

68. See bell hooks. "writer to writer, remembering toni cade bambara," in *Remembered Rapture: The Writer at Work* (New York: Henry Holt & Co., 1999), 234.

69. Herbert Marcuse. *Essay on Liberation* (Boston: Beacon Press, 1969), 90.

30

Remembering and Honoring Toni Cade Bambara

SONIA SANCHEZ

how to respond to the genius
of our sister Toni Cade Bambara? How to
give praise to this brilliant. Hard. Sweet
talking Toni. Who knew everything.
Read everything. Saw everything?

I guess if we remember Willie Kgositsile's lines:

if you sing of workers you have praised her
if you sing of brotherhood and sisterhood you
have praised her
if you sing of liberation you have praised her
if you sing of peace you have praised her
you have praised her without knowing
her name
her name is Spear of the Nation...

I would also add:

her name is clustered on the hills
for she has sipped at the edge of rivers
her words have the scent of the earth
and the genius of the stars
i have stored in my blood the
memory of your voice Toni linking continents
making us abandon Catholic minds.
You spread yourself rainbowlike
across seas
Your voice greeting foreign trees
Your voice stalking the evening stars.

And a generation of people began to question their silence. Their poverty. Their scarcity. Because you had asked the most important question we can ask ourselves:

What are we pretending not to know today? The premise as you said, my sister, being that colored people on planet earth really know everything there is to know. And if one is not coming to grips with the knowledge, it must mean that one is either scared or pretending to be stupid.

You open your novel with the simple but profound question: Do we want to be well? And you said in an interview with Sister Zala Chandler that the answer tends to be "No! to be whole politically, psychically, spiritually, culturally, intellectually, aesthetically, physically, and economically whole—is of profound significance. It is significant because there is a correlative to this. There is a responsibility to self and to history that is developed once you are whole, once you are well, once you acknowledge your powers."

Amiri Baraka wrote that Jimmy Baldwin was God's black revolutionary mouth. So were you Toni. You made us laugh resistance laughter. You taught us how to improvise, change shapes, sometimes change skins. We learned that if we are to be, sometimes we must have been there already and have people wondering about us:

> You asking about them colored folk?
> They were just here. Ain't they still there
> in place in Harlem, in Washington in
> Chicago? i just seen em a second ago
> they wuz dancing at the Palladium,
> picking cotton, having a picnic in
> the park drinking walking they
> sanctified walk talking they
> fast talk brushing the nightmare
> of America off they foreheads.
> Look there they be. That's them laughing
> that loud laugh over there. No that
> ain't them. They gone again like the wind.
> Oh. They asking for them people from
> forever ago time sifting time through
> hands, announcing they are here intend
> to be here. Listen. Listen you can hear
> them breathing breaths not even invented
> yet. laughing their resistance. hee hee hee.
> You got to find me to get me.

Get on board children.
This Bambara liberation train
of the spirit, soul. This Bambara
train doing what Audre Lorde said:
forever moving history beyond nightmare
into structures for the future...

Get on board this liberation train called Bambara. Cmon lil children. And
Toni had many children. She taught us how to organize. Be. Their names
are Aishah, Mungu, Karma, Kevin, D Knowledge, Ras, Nora, Louis, Tony,
Morani. Gar.

This is how i lay down my Praise:

What seas came from her eyes!
What oceans connected us from her
Southern and Eastern bones!
What waterfall of Bambara words transformed
Our lives, our hands into miracle songs!

Contributors

Bettina Aptheker is Professor of Women's Studies at the University of California, Santa Cruz, and author of *The Morning Breaks: The Trial of Angela Davis, Tapestries of Life: Women's Work, Women's Consciousness and the Meaning of Daily Experience*, and *Intimate Politics: How I Grew Up Red, Fought for Free Speech and Became a Feminist Rebel.*

Malaika Adero is author of *Up South: Stories, Studies, and Letters of This Century's African American Migrations* and co-author of *Speak, So You Can Speak Again: The Life of Zora Neale Hurston.* Currently a senior editor at Atria Books, a division of Simon and Schuster, Adero is founder of Up South Inc., an organization dedicated to promoting writers and authors.

Amiri Baraka is an important figure in the Beat Movement in the 1950s and central shaper of the Black Arts Movement in the 1960s. He is the author of numerous important books in diverse genres: autobiography, criticism, drama, fiction, music history, political thought, as well as poetry. Baraka continues to commit his life and work to the African American community.

Valerie Boyd is author of the award-winning biography *Wrapped in Rainbows: The Life of Zora Neale Hurston,* and is professor of journalism at the University of Georgia and former arts editor at *The Atlanta Journal-Constitution.* Her book, *Spirits in the Dark: The Untold Story of Black Women in Hollywood,* will be published by Knopf in 2008.

Abena P. A. Busia is Professor of English at Rutgers University, and is co-director of the groundbreaking Women Writing Africa Project, a multivolume anthology published by the Feminist Press. Co-editor of *Women Writing Africa: West Africa and the Sahel,* as well as co-author of *Theorizing Black Feminisms,* she has also published a collection of poems, "Testimonies of Exile."

Rudolph P. Byrd is Professor of American Studies at Emory University, and is author and editor of six books including *Charles Johnson's Novels: Writing the American Palimpsest, Jean Toomer's Years with Gurdijeff: Portrait of an Artist, Generations in Black and White: Photographs by Carl Van Vechten,* and *Traps: African Men on Gender and Sexuality* (with Beverly Guy-Sheftall).

Jan Carew, born in Guyana and educated in America and Europe, is a widely published scholar and artist. His latest book, *Guyanese Wonderer,* is a collection of short stories published by Sarabande Books. Living with his wife Joy in Louisville, Kentucky, Carew, continues to write and paint.

Pepsi Charles (1948–2002) earned her reputation as writer and broadcaster in New York City, but during the last twenty-five years of her life, she was immersed as mother and community activist in serving young people in her hometown, Plainfield, New Jersey. She was a teacher, notably in the English Department at Livingston College, Rutgers University from 1973 to 1981.

Pearl Cleage, the Atlanta-based novelist and playwright, has achieved both critical acclaim and commercial success with books such as *What Looks Crazy on an Ordinary Day, I Wish I Had a Red Dress,* and *Baby Brother's Blues.*

Jayne Cortez, celebrated for her political, surrealistic, and innovative lyrical sounds, is author of several books of poems and has made numerous recordings of her work. Cortez, who lives in New York, has presented her work internationally at universities, museums, and festivals. Her poems have been translated into many languages.

Ruby Dee, the legendary stage and screen actor, is author of *My Last Good Nerve,* a book of poems. A veteran social activist, Dee, along with her late husband Ossie Davis, made major contributions to the civil rights struggle in the United States.

Nikky Finney is Professor of Creative Writing at the University of Kentucky, and has published a book of poems "On Wings Made Of Gauze"; *Rice,* an award-winning collection of stories, poems, and photographs; *Heartwood,* a collection of short stories, and *The World Is Round,* which won the 2004 Benjamin Franklin Award for Poetry.

Paula Giddings is author of the pioneering history of African American women, *When and Where I Enter,* as well as *In Search of Sisterhood.* Professor of African American Studies as Smith College, she is completing a biography of Ida B. Wells.

Nikki Giovanni is a poet, writer, commentator, activist, and educator. Since publishing her first volume, *Black Feeling, Black Talk*, (1968), she has published more than twenty-five books, including *Quilting the Black-Eyed Pea: Poems and Not Quite Poems* (2002). Her outspokenness in both her writing and in lectures continues to capture worldwide attention.

Avery Gordon is Professor of Sociology at the University of California, Santa Barbara. She is author of *Keeping Good Time: Reflections on Knowledge, Power and People* and *Ghostly Matters: Haunting and the Sociological Imagination* and the editor of *Mapping Multiculturalism and Body Politics,* among other works.

Farah Jasmine Griffin is Professor of English and Comparative Literature and African American Studies at Columbia University. She is the author of *Who Set You Flowin': The African American Migration Narrative, Beloved Sisters and Loving Friends*, and *If You Can't Be Free, Be A Mystery: In Search of Billie Holiday*.

Beverly Guy-Sheftall's books include *Gender Talk: The Struggle for Women's Equality in African American Communities, Words of Fire: An Anthology of African American Feminist Thought*, and *Sturdy Black Bridges: Visions of Black Women in Literature*. She is Anna Julia Cooper Professor of English and Women's Studies at Spelman College.

Kristin Lattany, born in the all-black community of Lawnside, New Jersey, studied at the University of Pennsylvania, where she later taught for twenty-three years. Her many books of fiction for children and adults include *God Bless the Child; The Soul Brothers and Sister Lou; The Landlord; Kinfolks*; and *Breaking Away*.

Audre Lorde's many books of poetry include *The First Cities; From a Land Where Other People Live; The Black Unicorn*; and *Undersong: Chosen Poems Old and New* as well as the memoir *Zami: A New Spelling of My Name* and the influential collection *Sister Outsider: Essays and Speeches*. She died in 1992.

Frances Negrón-Muntaner, an award-winning filmmaker, writer, and scholar, has written *Boricua Pop: Puerto Ricans and the Latinization of American Culture* and edited four books, including *None of the Above: Puerto Ricans in the Global Era*. Her films include *Brincando el charco: Portrait of a Puerto Rican* and *For the Record: Guam and World War II*.

Kalamu ya Salaam, a New Orlean-based poet, is author of several books, including *What Is Life*. Founder of NOMMO Literary Society and Runagate Multimedia, he is the leader of WordBand, a poetry performance ensemble that combines poetry with blues, jazz and other forms music.

Sonia Sanchez, who is among the most influential female authors to emerge from the Black Arts Movement, is a poet and playwright. Growing up in Harlem, Sanchez has taught at several universities, including Temple, where she worked from 1977 until her retirement in 1999. The author of several volumes of poetry, Sanchez is an important voice in social movements.

Aishah Shahidah Simmons, a native Philadelphian who spent eleven years making *No!*, is an award-winning African American feminist lesbian documentary filmmaker, international lecturer, and social change agent. She is the recipient of numerous grants, including awards from the Ford Foundation and the Leeway Foundation, as well as a 2006 award from the National Violence Resource Center, and a 2005 Artist-in-Residency at Spelman College.

Salamishah Tillet is Assistant Professor of English at the University of Pennsylvania. She received her Ph.D. in the History of American Civilization from Harvard University in 2007, her M.A.T. in English Education at Brown University in 1997, and her B.A. in English and African American Studies from the University of Pennsylvania in 1996. Professor Tillet's major fields of interest are African American and Black Atlantic literatures, cultural studies, and feminist theory.

Eleanor Traylor, chair of the English Department at Howard University, has published numerous and influential essays on authors such as Henry Dumas, Toni Morrison, and Larry Neal. She wrote the introduction to the second edition of *The Black Woman* (2005), which is fitting since Bambara once called Traylor "the best critic/seer we have."

Rebecca Wanzo is Assistant Professor of Women's Studies and African American and African Studies at Ohio State University. Her research and teaching fields include Critical Race Theory, Cultural Studies, and African American Literature and Culture. She is currently working on a book about African American women and sentimental political storytelling.

Anne Wicke studied American Literature in Paris and at Northwestern University. Author of a "Doctorat d'Etat" dissertation on Herman Melville, she has been Professor of American Literature and Translation at the University of Rouen since 1996. She has translated texts by Toni Cade Bambara, Toni Morrison, Susan Sontag, and Ralph Emerson, and is now translating the first collection of slave narratives into French.

Index